"Ramsey has written a narrative that captures the life of Jesus so vividly, at times you'll wonder if he sat down and spoke with all the people involved in the story."
Trillia Newbell, author of *United*

"This book throws open the curtains on Jesus and invites us to taste and see the *only* love that is better than life. This isn't a great book just for the season of Lent but for every season of life."
Scotty Smith, teacher in residence, West End Community Church, Nashville, Tennessee

"This book succeeds at capturing and displaying the drama of Jesus—incarnate, dead, and risen—with memorable force."
Robert W. Yarbrough, professor of New Testament at Covenant Theological Seminary

"Ramsey's solid biblical teaching and storytelling have deeply impacted my journey as a Christian working in Hollywood. This is a book I will give friends to help them understand what I believe."
Korey Scott Pollard, TV producer and assistant director of *Grey's Anatomy*, *House M.D.*, *CSI*, *Monk*, and *Nashville*

"There is a graceful simplicity to Ramsey's prose—and to his retelling of the old familiar story—that enables him to truly move his readers with the potency of the gospel. Here is a quiet voice that can shake stone."
N. D. Wilson, author of *Death by Living* and *Boys of Blur*

"I don't know anyone who can make the stories—and the Story—in Scripture feel as present, as alive, and as sweeping as Russ Ramsey. His prose, his grasp of history and theology, not to mention his love of Jesus, do more than merely draw me into his book—they make me want to read the Bible."
Andrew Peterson, singer and songwriter

"With a writer's imagination and skill, a theologian's backbone, and a disciple's devotion, Ramsey weds knowledge to emotional resonance and information to immanence in this moving account of Jesus' life."

Dan Doriani, professor of theology at Covenant Theological Seminary

"Many of us have wondered at some point, What would it be like to live when Jesus did? With purity to biblical truth and perceptive insight into how the human heart works, Russ Ramsey answers that question. He tells the story of Jesus dwelling among us—a story filled with political intrigue, baffling miracles, relational complexities, and heartbreaking suffering—by presenting old truths in engagingly fresh ways. Read this book! And then share it with others who need to witness Jesus anew."

Jani Ortlund, speaker at Renewal Ministries, author of *Fearlessly Feminine* and *His Loving Law, Our Lasting Legacy*

"It gives me great pleasure to endorse the life and writing of Russ Ramsey. We have been in the trenches together caring for the 'called out ones.' Russ gave us gospel immersion and fruits of deep care with *The Advent of the Lamb of God*. He continues this life-giving pattern of grace and service with this new, beautifully written book pointing to the Hero King Jesus."

Charlie Peacock, co-executive director at Art House America, TV producer, and record producer for Switchfoot and the Civil Wars

"Ramsey's ability to knit the accounts of the Gospels into a highly readable, easily accessible, and grace-saturated narrative is a blessing for all. Telling the story of Jesus in bite-sized readings that can easily accord with anticipation and celebration of the Easter season makes this book a special gift."

Bryan Chapell, president emeritus at Covenant Theological Seminary

RETELLING THE STORY SERIES

THE PASSION
OF THE
KING OF GLORY

RUSS RAMSEY

An imprint of InterVarsity Press
Downers Grove, Illinois

InterVarsity Press
P.O. Box 1400, Downers Grove, IL 60515-1426
ivpress.com
email@ivpress.com

InterVarsity Press® is the book-publishing division of InterVarsity Christian Fellowship/USA®, a movement of students and faculty active on campus at hundreds of universities, colleges, and schools of nursing in the United States of America, and a member movement of the International Fellowship of Evangelical Students. For information about local and regional activities, visit intervarsity.org.

Published in association with the literary agency of Wolgemuth & Associates.

Cover design and illustration: David Fassett
Interior design: Jeanna Wiggins

ISBN 978-0-8308-4399-2 (print)
ISBN 978-0-8308-8525-1 (digital)

Library of Congress Cataloging-in-Publication Data
A catalog record for this book is available from the Library of Congress.

P	20	19	18	17	16	15	14	13	12	11	10	9	8	7	6	5	4	3	2	1
Y	35	34	33	32	31	30	29	28	27	26	25	24	23	22	21	20	19	18		

FOR CHRIS, MARGARET, KATE, AND JANE.

You give so much more than you take.

This book is for you.

I pray you would come to know

Jesus better through my life

than my writing.

CONTENTS

THE BOOKS THAT COULD BE WRITTEN

J ESUS' DISCIPLE JOHN WAS A WRITER. When John sat down to
write, he clearly cared not only about the content he meant to
convey but also about the way he put it all together. John was an
artist. The story he set out to tell in his Gospel is the most ambitious story there is—how God created and redeemed humanity.
Imagine sitting down to write that story. How would you start?
When would you be finished?

Under the inspiration of the Holy Spirit, John opened his Gospel
with the ambition of a man who was going to do his best to give us
as much of the scope of this story as he possibly could. If you don't
believe me, just look at how he begins. He takes us all the way back
to the dawn of time: "In the beginning was the Word . . . " Ambitious.

When John comes to the end of his story, he reveals what every
writer denies at first but eventually acknowledges—he lives in a
world of limits. For any story we set out to tell, we end up telling

only some of it. There is nothing for it. So as ambitious as his opening line might have been, John ends his Gospel acknowledging the reality of limits: "Now there are also many other things that Jesus did. Were every one of them to be written, I suppose that the world itself could not contain the books that would be written."

I believe John's Gospel is exactly what the Holy Spirit meant for him to write, without error and more than sufficient to reveal the one who was the Word, present at creation and solely suited to accomplish our redemption.

I also believe, though, that as John wrote, he grieved the stories he had to leave out for the sake of the narrative he meant to tell. I wonder with joyful fascination what stories ended up on his editing room floor as discarded bits of vellum and parchment. And I wonder what stories remain that he thought about cutting but then just couldn't bear to.

My hope is that this book would serve as a faithful servant of Scripture. I've packed this book with hundreds of Scripture references. Let me explain how I use them. Throughout this book I paraphrase pretty freely in order to maintain a unified voice. Rarely do I quote Scripture directly or at length. This applies to character dialogue. If a character says something and there's a Scripture reference in the endnotes, that doesn't necessarily mean I'm quoting the original text. I'm probably not. More than likely I'm paraphrasing and distilling a larger moment in Scripture to work within the limits of this book. The references I include are there to lead you to the stories Scripture unfolds with perfect sufficiency.

While I'm on this point, I should note that I engage in some speculation in this book, imagining how certain conversations happened, how particular characters felt, and what various scenes looked like. I have tried to limit my speculations to reasonable inferences that wouldn't redirect the Bible's narrative arc. I've avoided inventing characters or manufacturing extrabiblical encounters. I've tried to keep my speculative input within the natural and plausible lines of human nature.

For example, Scripture tells us nothing about how the nobleman from Capernaum felt as his son lay dying. But as a father of four, I imagine he must have felt some of what I experienced when one of my own children had a health scare—helplessness, worry, desperation. I've attributed some of these feelings to the nobleman on the basis that any father would certainly be enveloped in a flurry of emotions like these. When I speculate, it is in the hope that this journey through the pages of Scripture will capture your imagination in ways that will serve your lifelong study of the Bible.

Most of the editorial choices I have made about what to include (and what to leave out) are based on my desire to offer a story that would drive readers relentlessly to the empty tomb by way of the cross. Exploration of the political and religious conditions of the day is crucial for this objective. After all, God in his wisdom sent his Son into the world of Herod Antipas, Pontius Pilate, Caiaphas the high priest, the Pharisees, and the Sanhedrin—who together became the fuel God used to propel this narrative toward Golgotha. I wanted to unpack their significance, and I wanted to show God's providence in sending his Son into our world at that time. So while I have poured myself into the telling of certain stories, I have also left many beloved stories untouched. I've glossed over some better-known characters (like the woman at the well in John 4) while taking pains to expound on others who were given far fewer verses (like John the Baptist). I assure you I did this under protest. I wanted to write about all of it—every person, every conversation, every miracle, every conflict.

Oh, the books that could be written.

The Passion of the King of Glory was written in a world of limits. I set up some rules for myself as I wrote. This book would have forty chapters, one for each day of Lent if people wanted to use it as a Lenten devotional. I would try to find a voice similar to that of John, who was never overtly self-referential even though he was writing the story of own his life as a follower of Christ. As with John's Gospel, my narrative would stay in the third person, making no direct eye contact with the reader until the end.

I developed these rules while writing the first book in this series, *The Advent of the Lamb of God*, twenty-five chapters (one for each day of Advent in December so people can use it as an Advent devotional) following the epic arc of Scripture from the Garden of Eden to the manger in Bethlehem. Together, *The Advent of the Lamb of God* and *The Passion of the King of Glory* tell the story of the need for, the coming of, and the life, ministry, death, and resurrection of Jesus Christ.

The third volume in this series, *The Mission of the Body of Christ*, picks up the story after Jesus' resurrection and tells the remaining narrative of the New Testament, the story of the early church. It is thirty-one chapters long, ideal for reading over the course of one month.

I give my life to the study and expression of Scripture, and it is one of my greatest joys to be able to say that. The story told in these pages is my story. Every picture of brokenness in these pages is in some measure the story of my own brokenness. Every need that rises to the surface is in some way a need I share. Every tendency toward rebellion, every cry of desperation, every prayer for forgiveness, and every hope of redemption rings true in me. I write not as a removed researcher but as an eyewitness to the impact this story has had on my own life and the world I inhabit. This is the story of how God loved and rescued me. I pray the same would be true for you.

PART 1

OBSCURITY

LIFE FOR THE DYING

John 4:43-54

N *O FATHER SHOULD HAVE TO WATCH* his own son die.

The road from Capernaum to Cana ran uphill the entire way, pulling at the already burdened nobleman's steps. He concluded there was only one option that might save his dying son, and that solitary hope had him moving away from the boy as quickly as he could go. It was all he knew to do.

If he hurried, he could cover the twelve miles between Galilee's shores westward to Cana before evening. Though his culture considered it unbecoming of a grown man to run, time was against him. Regardless of what anyone thought, he needed to keep moving, and in this moment neither his wealth, nor his age, nor his position mattered. He was desperate.

From humble beginnings, the nobleman had risen to a position of midlevel importance in Galilee as a servant of Herod Antipas, son of Herod the Great. It was Herod Antipas's world. The nobleman was only living in it. Back before Herod the Great died, he had divided oversight of his part of the Roman Empire between three of his sons: Philip, who oversaw the northeastern lands of the Golan Heights; Archelaus, who became king over Judea, Idumea, and Samaria; and Antipas, who assumed the lesser title of tetrarch over the regions of Galilee and Perea.

Though Archelaus was older and presumed to have the greatest leadership potential of the three brothers, Antipas was driven to command respect. Knowing it would not simply be given, he was determined to earn it. The Galilee he inherited had become politically unstable, a haven for dissidents and outlaws. To Antipas, this was as much an opportunity as it was a problem. He wouldn't just rule Galilee. He would transform it.

Following in his father's footsteps, Antipas did the only thing he knew would gain notice: he built. Early on he rebuilt the war-ravaged Sepphoris into his capital city, which became home to over fifty thousand people. Not too long after that he moved his capital to the glimmering shores of the Sea of Galilee, establishing the great city of Tiberius, with its stadium, hot-springs bathhouse, temple, and royal palace. Under Antipas's leadership the entire region was reborn.

This was the nobleman's Galilee. Though his title was modest, it conveyed that he was a man of influence and affluence—a royal by right of his service to his king. But even if he could call upon all the resources of Rome—all its wealth, its intellectual potency, its political power—the one thing he wanted most, Rome could not provide.

He wanted his son to live.

His mission carried a sad irony. The same Rome that had given him his esteemed position in the world had also been responsible for the deaths of many sons whom fathers just like him would have given anything to save. Only a few decades earlier, Antipas's father ordered the execution of all Israelite boys under the age of two in the hope of killing the one many whispered would be Israel's promised, coming Deliverer—the one they called the King of glory.

Though Herod had no way to know if he had succeeded, his cruelty heaped sorrow upon countless mothers, fathers, brothers, and sisters across the land. How many prayers went up in those days for the sons Rome took? How many fathers searched for a reason to hope and found none?

The world was a hard and broken place. The allure of wealth and power, which always seemed to cost men far more than it gave, didn't matter to the nobleman anymore. Now he was just a father throwing up prayers to whomever occupied the heavens above as he made his way to the little village of Cana, hoping to find the only man on earth he imagined could help—Jesus of Nazareth.

Jesus had made a name for himself at a wedding in Cana not too long before the nobleman's son took ill. Jesus was there with his family when, to the host's great embarrassment, the wine ran out. Knowing her son, Jesus' mother asked him if there was anything he might be able to do to rescue the feast. Jesus gathered the servants and told them to fill the ceremonial washing jars with water. Somehow, though no one could explain it, the water became wine—good wine.

News of this miracle spread quickly. But the miracle itself wasn't what set the nobleman off on his quest to find Jesus. It was how people said he did it: quietly. Had he been a charlatan out to make his living by tricking people, Jesus would have made the miracle primarily about himself and maybe even charged people to see it. Instead, the story went, he sought to deflect attention from himself.

Jesus had been away from the region for some time now. But reports steadily made their way back to Capernaum that Jesus was performing other signs and wonders in and around Jerusalem. It was hard to know which of the stories were true and which were inflated composites of third-party anecdotes. Taken on their own, some seemed more credible than others. But taken together, they presented Jesus as a man who loved the hurting, healed the sick, and welcomed the destitute. This stirred in the nobleman the courage to hope since he himself was hurting, his son was sick, and the entire world around him was a fractured mess.

The nobleman thought that if anyone could save his son, it would be Jesus. As soon as the village came into view he began asking everyone he met if they knew where he could find the man from Nazareth. It didn't take long. When he finally saw Jesus, he realized that the course of his life seldom put him in the position where he now found himself. He was in need. There was nothing he could offer Jesus in exchange for what he was about to ask from him. All he had were his words and a little bit of hope.

The nobleman spoke to Jesus with concise humility: "Sir, my son is dying. Will you help us?"

Jesus looked at the man and then at the people gathered around whose interests were now suddenly piqued. He said, "Unless you all see me perform signs and wonders, you refuse to believe in me. Is this what you want from me? A sign?"

The nobleman hadn't expected Jesus' rebuke. He wasn't asking for a show. Still, Jesus raised the crucial question: What did he want, really? Did he want Jesus to do a trick for him? No doubt many of those gathered hoped for just that. They had heard about the water becoming wine, and they wished they had been there to see it. They would love an encore.

But who did the nobleman think Jesus was? Did Jesus need to come to his son's bedside, put his hands on the boy's head, or speak a blessing? What did he want from him?

The nobleman said, "I want my son to live. That's what I want. I want him to live. I want him not to die. But I can't stop the death that is coming. So please, help me. Come to Capernaum. Please. Save him."

Seeing the sincerity of his hurt, Jesus said, "Yes. Go on home. Your son will live."

Jesus' words alone would have to suffice because his answer made it apparent that he would not be making the trip to the boy's home in Capernaum. There would be no bedside visit, no incantation, no trick. Just these few words. The nobleman would have to accept that Jesus' word was as good as his presence.

So he departed robed in the logic that if Jesus actually possessed the supernatural ability to heal his son, then surely he could bring that healing with nothing but a word.

As the nobleman hurried back, one of his servants met him on the road. Breathless, the servant said, "He's getting better. He's getting better!"

The nobleman's eyes lit up. "What? When?"

The servant said, "Yesterday, about an hour past noon." It was the same moment when Jesus had promised that the boy would live.

For all his nobility and the wealth that came with it, the most valuable title the nobleman held in that moment was "father." His son was alive and recovering, and Jesus of Nazareth had saved him. There was no question in the father's mind about that. When he got home, he told his entire household the story of how he had asked Jesus for this miracle and the way in which it was granted. They all marveled at this Nazarene who had given them such a precious gift. He had given life to the dying.

2

WILD WITH THE HOPE

Matthew 4:1-11

*T*HE DETAILS SURROUNDING *JESUS' BIRTH* became part of the lore of his community. He was born in Bethlehem but raised in Nazareth, west of the Sea of Galilee, and some said he'd been conceived while his mother was still a virgin, that his birth was a miracle from God, heralded by angels themselves. Others assumed that the timing of his arrival—so soon after his parents' wedding—meant that if he wasn't an illegitimate son, then at the very least temptation had gotten the best of his parents before they'd wed. Still, it was hard to deny that there was something unusual about Joseph and Mary's son. Even from a young age, his wisdom, understanding, and learning mystified the religious leaders when they heard him speak. His own community regarded him as a man who had found favor with God. As his parents watched Jesus mature, they couldn't help but see his Nazareth years as a time of preparation for a calling they knew would inevitably lead him away from them.

Jesus was around thirty years old when he left Nazareth to begin his public ministry. The first thing he did was journey to Bethany beyond the Jordan to find his cousin John.

John was a preacher who lived in the wilderness proclaiming a baptism of repentance for the forgiveness of sins. Dressed in a camel hair coat like the prophet Elijah, he looked like the child of a feral, violent land, but he spoke as one privy to the mysteries of God. People from all over were drawn to hear him.

His message was simple and pointed: "Hope is here. The Lord is with us." Many in Israel responded to John's message by coming to confess their darkest secrets—to begin again a conversation with the Maker who promised to never forsake them.

It had been a long time since the people of Israel had reason to think God was near, let alone active. Their recent history was a sad tale of sifting through the rubble of exile. Yes, they had come home. But like Job, though they were able to reconstruct much of what fell to the Babylonians and Assyrians who had carried them off, what they rebuilt could not replace all they had lost. Neither could it take away their grief. They were poor in spirit—mourners, meek and hungry for righteousness. Estranged from comfort and unsure of their inheritance, they wanted to see God, and if not God himself then at least traces of his presence with them.

Generations earlier, when their ancestors followed Joshua across the river where John now stood, they passed from being slaves in the wilderness to a mighty kingdom built on the promises of their God. But now, every Roman sword that clinked against the armor moving through their streets and alleys reminded them that they had again returned to the wilderness of oppression. So when John emerged from the wild, proclaiming the nearness of God, many regarded him more as a guide than a stranger. They came to John, and he led one person after another down into this river that ran through their history as a people—one bank marking who they had been and the other who they would become. And in those waters, between those banks, he baptized them.

John grew up with the stories of how God had opened his own mother's barren womb to bring him into this world. He knew he was born to proclaim the salvation of the Lord. He also knew that the Lord had given his mother's cousin Mary a son of her own—only Mary's miracle wasn't that she overcame barrenness to conceive. It was that she conceived while she was yet a virgin.

Back when Mary was pledged to marry Joseph, the angel of the Lord appeared to tell her that the Lord was giving her a boy and he would be called the Son of the Most High God. God was going to give this child David's throne where he would reign forever over the house of Jacob, and his kingdom would never end. Mary would carry in her womb the King of glory, the Savior of the world.

John's mother, Elizabeth, used to tell him about the time Mary, whom she sometimes referred to as "the mother of my Lord," came to visit and how when she entered their house, John leapt inside Elizabeth's belly. It was as though he couldn't wait to begin proclaiming the Lord's salvation, she told him.

John knew this was his path. He would never be wealthy. He would hold no position of power. He was the courier of the news that God was giving his forgetful creation the Savior he had promised so long ago. John's purpose was to run wild with the hope that the Messiah had come.

Jesus found his cousin baptizing at the river. When John saw him, he stopped and stared.

Jesus said, "Baptize me, John."

John resisted. "Me baptize you? You should be the one baptizing me."

But Jesus said, "John, this needs to happen. We're at the beginning of something new, something greater than you can see. Let me stand in the waters of forgiveness with you. This is part of how we fulfill the reason we're here."

Though John didn't know when, he knew the day would come when the Savior of the world would step from the shadows of his preparation into the public eye. Seeing Jesus wade down into the water toward him, John suspected that day had now come. So he baptized the one whose trail he had come to blaze.

What happened when Jesus came up out of the water was unlike anything anyone had ever seen. A brightness grew and shadows shrank until light flooded the valley and a voice from the sky spoke: "This is my beloved Son, in whom I am well pleased."

Fear and awe gripped those gathered as they then saw the Spirit of God descend like a dove and come to rest on Jesus. Any questions John might have had about Jesus' true identity dissipated. Those gathered witnessed an unprecedented display of divine convergence: the Father sent his Spirit to glorify his Son. The people searched for some way to understand what this meant.

But Jesus understood. He had come to this river as someone unknown to the world. In those waters God himself set Jesus apart in a divine affirmation of a purpose greater than anyone could imagine. When Jesus stepped out of that river, he knew he was entering into a life of opposition and sorrow. As the old cleric Simeon told Jesus' mother years before, Jesus would reveal the hearts of all mankind. The light that flooded the Jordan Valley would go with him wherever he went, shining in every dark corner of every dark heart, exposing every dark secret in a world that had grown quite fond of its shadows. So it would come as no surprise that he would be opposed. Still, the level of hostility coming his way would be greater than anyone could imagine. And it would change the world.

The first opposition Jesus faced when he left John at the river wasn't political or social. It was spiritual, and it was dangerous. The Spirit that descended on him in his baptism drove him out into the wilderness, where he was tested for forty days. The desert had long been a place of struggle and testing for the people of God, as it had also been a place where God often met them. Out among the snakes and wild beasts, this was the sort of solitude that revealed a man's true resolve.

The tempter, sometimes a subtle serpent, sometimes a roaring lion, came to Jesus in the wilderness not as a predator but as a negotiator. He knew Jesus' power well and had no inclination whatsoever to test it. Rather, he came to see if he might strike a deal. There was something Jesus had come to do—something no one else could accomplish. Jesus knew what it would cost him. He had come to offer himself up as an atoning sacrifice for the sins of the people of God—to live the life of perfect righteousness they had all failed to live before God and to die in their place as their sinless sacrifice.

The tempter also knew Jesus' objective, and more than anything he wanted to prevent it. Maybe he could persuade Jesus that there was a way to achieve the better parts of his mission without having to endure the worst. Knowing that Jesus' frame was weakened by hunger, the tempter began to test him by playing to his basest appetites. "Why are you hungry? If you are the Son of God and if you have command of the physical realm, why not eat? Why deny yourself? You should turn one of these stones to bread. You can, you know."

But knowing that his entire life would require continual self-denial on behalf of a people who were governed by their appetites, Jesus said, "I don't live on bread alone. My food is to do the will of my Father who sent me." The tempter considered Jesus' response and then took him to the pinnacle of the temple and said, "You know that if you threw yourself down from here, God would send his angels to catch you. Nothing can hurt you."

The point of this test wasn't for Jesus to imagine the exhilaration of leaping off the pinnacle only to see the angels swoop in to catch him. The tempter was baiting Jesus to speculate about how unnecessary the pain of death really needed to be, if he would only entertain the possibility. Weary as he was, perhaps Jesus would consider, if only for a moment, the appeal of self-preservation.

But this wasn't a game to Jesus. He told the tempter, "It is written, 'You shall not put God to the test.'"

The tempter came back a third time, taking Jesus to a high place where he could see the kingdoms of the world in all their splendor. He said to Jesus, "Bow down and worship me, and all these kingdoms will be yours. They are mine to give, and I will give them to you."

This offer of dominion over the kingdoms of the world was the first time Jesus and the tempter were actually talking about the true nature of Jesus' mission. He had come to establish a new kingdom. This didn't need to be a fight, the tempter suggested. All Jesus needed to do was bow down and worship him, and he would just hand the world over.

Jesus said, "Leave me, Satan. You know what I know—we are to worship the Lord God alone."

The authority Satan offered Jesus wasn't his to give. Jesus had come to establish his dominion over every corner of the world, and through a fierce revolution he would take it all as creation's rightful King. Jesus wasn't there to make a deal with the devil. He had come to defeat him. Forever.

The tempter knew he was getting nowhere. But he also believed there was still time. He and Jesus would tangle again. Maybe next time Jesus' resolve would be weaker. Holding on to that flicker of hope, the tempter departed.

3

BEHOLD THE
LAMB OF GOD

John 1:19-51

IF JESUS' BAPTISM WAS THE affirmation of God's call on his life, then the following weeks in the wilderness were a test to see if he could be enticed to abandon it.

Though physically weakened from scrounging what little food and water the desert had to offer, Jesus did not spend that time alone. The same Spirit who came to rest on him at his baptism remained with him throughout those forty days and beyond. When the trials ended and the tempter left, Jesus began an exodus of his own through the crags and boulders of the Judean wilderness into the purpose for which he had been born.

And once again, he set out to find his cousin John.

While Jesus was in the desert, John stayed at the Jordan, preaching repentance and baptizing any who came to him. An air of expectancy had captured the imaginations of believers who were looking for the redemption of Israel. John's ministry attracted many people who held this hope, and his allure caught the attention of the religious leaders in Jerusalem.

When Rome established control over the region of Israel, it shrewdly granted a measure of religious latitude to the Hebrew people in exchange for their cooperation. Rome conscripted Israel's religious leaders into making sure their people yielded to Rome, paid their taxes, and kept the peace. It became the responsibility of the Pharisees, chief priests, and teachers of the law to investigate any sudden swells of spiritual fervor among the people.

It was fairly common for dynamic personalities to emerge on Israel's fringes, inspiring the curious and hopeful with the promise of something new or the return to something old. Occasionally some of these leaders even took on disciples who would follow them through the better seasons of their influence. John had both popularity and disciples, but he seemed to connect with people through more than his charisma. So the Pharisees sent some of their scholars to ask him who he thought he was and where he hoped his ministry would lead.

"Are you the Christ?" they asked.

"I am not," he answered.

"Then who are you? A prophet? Do you think you're Elijah?"

John said, "I am the voice of one crying out in this wilderness, 'Make straight the path of the Lord.' I baptize the people who come to me with water, but there is one who has come after me who baptizes with the Spirit of God himself. His baptism is like a fire that consumes all that is not eternal. Though I am unworthy to untie the strap of his sandal, I stand here in these waters to announce to you that he has come. You don't know it, but he is here among us now. We've entered a new age. I baptize because the

Christ has come, and his kingdom with him. That is why people come to me to repent of their sins."

The scribes and teachers of the law returned to report that John thought Immanuel had come. John believed God was in their midst, and many people seemed to trust him. On this they would have to keep a close eye.

The next day, as John was baptizing in the river, he saw a familiar figure approach. With astonishment and joy, John pointed at the man and said, "I've given myself to this ministry so that Israel might know the Christ when he comes. Look. Here he is! This is the one I've been telling you all about."

His eyes still fixed on Jesus, John said, "All my life I've known I was born to herald the coming of the Christ. And all my life I've known he was here among us, somewhere. But until recently I couldn't have pointed him out with absolute certainty. I was waiting for a sign. The Lord told me, 'Here's how you'll know the Christ. The one on whom you see my Holy Spirit descend and remain, this is the one who will baptize the hearts of men.'

"Then just a little over a month ago I was here doing what I'm doing today, and Jesus came to me for baptism. As I stand before you now, I tell you I have seen the sign the Lord spoke of. I have seen the Spirit of God descend on this man standing before you now. I have heard the voice of God say, 'This is my Son, in whom I am well pleased.' Look at him, everyone. Behold! Jesus of Nazareth is the Lamb of God who takes away the sins of the world."

This name "Lamb of God" referred to a sober truth: Jesus had come to offer up his life as a substitute for a broken and sinful people. Sharing in humanity's flesh and blood, Jesus had come to die as a sacrificial offering for those who would trust him.

But his death would differ from the thousands of sacrificial lambs that had gone before him in one crucial way: his offering would be sufficient to atone for the sins of the world once and for all. Jesus would satisfy the demands of the law of God perfectly. Just as through one man sin entered the world and death through that sin, so death spread to all men because all men had sinned. But Jesus would set death in reverse through his righteous life and sacrificial death. He would seize the power of death in his hands and deliver those who had lived their entire lives as slaves to sin. His righteousness would reign, and by believing in him that righteousness would spread life to the otherwise spiritually dead.

Very few were equipped to even begin to understand the implications of what John was really saying. Only three, in fact: John, Jesus himself, and the tempter. This was the path John had come to prepare, the ministry Jesus was born to carry out, and the mission the devil so desperately wanted to corrupt. How this would all unfold would remain to be seen, but one thing was certain—the Lamb of God had come and his ministry had begun.

The next day Jesus passed by John again. John said to two of his disciples who were with him, "Look, there he is. The Lamb of God." John's disciples looked at each other. Their teacher had spoken often of the one who would come after him. They didn't understand everything John saw in the man from Nazareth, but in light of his endorsement, they wanted to understand. So they gathered their things, left John, and began to follow Jesus.

When Jesus saw them coming after him, he stopped and said, "What do you want?"

They asked him, "Where are you staying tonight?"

Jesus studied the two men for a moment and said, "Come with me and I'll show you."

Jesus' new disciples were relieved to know they didn't have to explain themselves then and there. They were in no position to articulate what they really wanted because they didn't really know.

By late afternoon they arrived at the place where Jesus was staying. As the conversation unfolded that evening, the disciples came to believe that Jesus was, in fact, the Messiah. One of the disciples, Andrew from Bethsaida in Galilee, was so struck by Jesus that he left the house to find his brother.

"Simon, I have found the Messiah!" Andrew said. "Come with me. Come meet him."

When Simon entered the house with Andrew, Jesus said to him, "You're Simon, the son of John, aren't you?" Without waiting for a reply, Jesus continued, "I'm going to call you Peter the Rock."

Andrew brought Simon to meet Jesus, but neither of them expected Jesus to greet Simon by giving him a nickname. Still, there was something about the way Jesus regarded Simon that suggested he saw something in him that warranted this name, Rock.

In a few days' time there was a wedding in Cana that Jesus and his family had been invited to attend, so the next morning Jesus set out for the land of his childhood, the region of Galilee. His new disciples went with him. Along the way Andrew met up with Philip, another Galilean from Bethsaida, and he introduced him to Jesus.

Jesus said, "Come with me, Philip."

Philip followed, and in only a short time he responded to Jesus in the same way that Andrew and Simon Peter had—he believed. And as Andrew did with Simon, Philip set out to find someone he could tell. He found his friend Nathanael.

Philip said, "Nathanael, we have found the one Moses and the prophets wrote about. We've found the Christ—Jesus, Joseph's son from Nazareth."

Nathanael, a Galilean from Cana, regarded Nazareth as a small, unimportant town. He wasn't alone in this either. Many in that region felt little for Nazareth beyond disdain. Nathanael considered Philip's words for a moment and shrugged. "Can anything good come out of that town?"

But Philip persisted. "Just come and meet him." So Nathanael followed.

When Jesus saw Nathanael coming, he rose to meet him, saying, "Now here is an Israelite who speaks the truth!"

Taken back by Jesus' winsomeness, Nathanael asked, "How do you know me?"

Jesus said, "I saw you under the fig tree, before Philip called you."

Nathanael was speechless. How could Jesus have known where he and Philip spoke? And what did this have to do with knowing him? Jesus was answering a different question than the one Nathanael asked. He was telling Nathanael that he knew more about him than Nathanael could imagine.

Though Nathanael came on strong with Philip, he knew his initial doubts about Jesus were wrong. Something good had come from Nazareth—or at the very least, someone interesting. He sensed that Jesus saw things others missed. Surprising even himself, Nathanael began to believe. He said, "If you are the Son of God, that makes you the King of Israel as well, doesn't it?"

Jesus said, "Nathanael, you believe in me because I told you something about yourself that we both know I shouldn't have known. Isn't that right? But listen, you will see me do greater things than this. Soon enough you will see heaven itself open up and the angels of God descending and ascending on the Son of Man."

Nathanael was struck by the solemnity of Jesus' demeanor. What began as a playful repartee between these two had escalated to an apocalyptic description of Jesus mediating between heaven and earth—between God and man. And now he was telling them that if Andrew, Simon Peter, Philip, and Nathanael stayed with him, they would see the Lamb of God take away the sins of the world. They would see the King of glory open heaven itself.

It was a lot to take in from a man they had all only just met.

4

ONE HUNDRED AND FIFTY GALLONS

John 2:1-12

M<small>ARY KEPT HER EARS OPEN</small>, listening for the news of Jesus' arrival. It had been almost two months since she had last seen her firstborn, and she missed him. Though she didn't know all that had happened in his time away, she sensed that if and when he came back to her, things would be different.

Life weaves a tapestry that ties people together for a time, often to later set them off in different directions. It's the rhythm of relationships. For thirty years, Jesus and Mary walked the same streets and shared the same home in Nazareth. But that season had given way to something new. When Jesus left Nazareth to find John, it wasn't simply to pay his cousin a visit. It was to step into the life of an itinerate teacher.

Just as there are occasions that lead loved ones away from each other, there are also those that bring them together. So when the time for her friend's wedding drew close, Mary gathered up a few things and made the nine-mile journey from Nazareth north to Cana to celebrate the couple's union. They were part of her community, her people, her home. It was sacred when two became one—a man taking the name husband, a woman the name wife. It mattered. They would gain the vision of a sworn partner for life—a loving witness to the joys, fears, hopes, and sorrows buried deep inside each of them. In ways they couldn't imagine, they would get married in order to fall in love. They would discover things about each other they would never have known otherwise.

Marriage was bigger than how either of them felt in any given moment. It was an institution the two would come under. They set aside their rights to themselves for the sake of this new life lived as one. So when the promises were spoken, the community who loved them gathered to bear witness to this union where life's joys would be doubled and their burdens cut in half. They gathered to celebrate.

When Mary and Jesus found each other at the wedding, he had some men with him she had never met. They looked to her son as their leader. She had never seen this before, though she always knew it was in him to lead. Seeing those men, still obviously unfamiliar with her son, following him confirmed what she always knew would happen: Jesus had stepped out of her home and into the world, and he would never come back.

Weddings usually lasted several days. They were festive opportunities for the families involved to get to know each other, so they were not to be rushed. As long as the host had plenty of food and wine, guests would linger, enjoying the bounty and fellowship.

So when, at this wedding, the wine steward bent over to whisper into the host's ear, the host's eyes darted with panic and shame. He had done the unthinkable. He had run out of wine. If he couldn't come up with more, this party would end too soon, though the memory of why it ended would go on and on.

When Mary learned about the situation, she went to find her son. "They have no wine," she told Jesus.

The disciples looked at each other. Did Jesus have a supply of wine they didn't know about? This wasn't even their wedding.

Jesus said, "What does this have to do with me?"

This wasn't a rebuke. It was a fair question. This wasn't his wedding. He was no more expected to tend to the wine than any other invited guest. But Mary knew her son was resourceful and that he cared about the needs of others. He always had. And he tended to carry himself as a willing host, ready to step in and lead when a leader was needed even when the party wasn't his. Mary figured if he understood the need, perhaps he would find a way to meet it.

When she saw that Jesus had taken her request as his own responsibility, she told the servants, "My son can help with the wine. Do whatever he tells you."

The disciples and the wine steward waited for Jesus' instruction. A trace of grief ran across his brow. Something in this request had stirred deep waters. He said, "My hour has not yet come."

They looked at each other, confused.

Jesus knew what power he possessed. It was the power the tempter had brought up—the power to say to the physical world, "Let there be . . . " and see it come to pass. This was an opportunity for Jesus to shine the light of glory on himself. The time had not yet come for this. But it wasn't that far off either. That time was coming, quickly. Just not yet.

Mary couldn't know the passion her request would awaken in her son. To Jesus, she was asking for the world. Yes, he could do something about their lack of wine, but the reason he could was that he was equipped to address every deficit known to man. He had stepped onto a road he knew would lead to his glory being put on full display, but not before unimaginable suffering. He knew that when this was all finished, there would be a celebration—a wedding. His own wedding. His bride would be radiant, perfect, and beautiful, lacking nothing. He wanted to give her much more than wine. He wanted to give her himself—everything he was, everything he had.

All of this was coming. This he knew. Just not yet. There were still preparations to make. And he knew what it would cost.

Near the entrance to the feast stood six large stone jars, each able to hold about twenty-five gallons. Filled with water, the jars were placed there so the arriving guests could wash their hands and so the hosts could wash the vessels they used for the feast, according to their purification customs.

Jesus said, "Fill these jars with water. Fill them to the top." When they had done this, Jesus said, "Now draw some of that water and take it to the master of the feast."

The master of the feast took the cup from the steward and drank. Then he lowered the cup with a look of surprise. Everyone understood there would be various grades of wine at a feast like this. The best would be brought out first to train the taste buds. When that ran out, wine of a lesser quality would be substituted in the hopes that the better wine had done its job to trick the mind and dull the senses. The good wine's job was to make folks much less particular about what filled their cups later as the feast went on.

But here near the end of the feast came the best wine yet. The master of the feast tasted it again. His lips formed a slight smile as he swallowed. He called the bridegroom over and said, "Where did this wine come from? You didn't serve the best wine first? Why have you held this back until now?"

The bridegroom said, "Let me taste it." His first sip went down like a question. The second was not a sip but a long pull that was more like a declaration: "Friends, enjoy yourselves. We have plenty of wine. And you have got to try this!"

The master of the feast asked the steward where he got the wine. The steward said, "It arrived with one of the guests."

"With whom?" asked the master of the feast.

"Jesus of Nazareth, Mary's son," the servant said.

The answer only raised more questions. Where did he get such high-quality wine, and how did he come by one hundred and fifty gallons of it?

"He made it. From water. Just now."

As the wedding wound down, the disciples found their faith in Jesus growing deeper. But it wasn't simply because he'd performed a miracle. It was because he saw something in everyone he met that seemed to stir up traces of grief and love—as though they were captives and he was free, but only he knew it and only he could help.

He could be playful. How could there not be some measure of mirth in the act of bringing one hundred and fifty gallons of fine wine to a party? But he was also a man of mysterious sorrow—and at this wedding it seemed to come awake. It was as though this marriage reminded him of something he needed to do—as though the wine came from a reserve intended for a different wedding.

Jesus spoke of having "an hour," but he said it with a solemnity that left his disciples wondering if they were supposed to be excited for it to come. Whatever it meant to follow him, they were beginning to understand that his path was heading somewhere, and if they were to follow, they would follow him to the advent of his "hour"—whatever that meant.

But his hour had not yet come—this much was clear. What had arrived was the end of the wedding. Jesus introduced his mother and brothers to his disciples, and together they set off for Capernaum, sixteen miles away on the northern shores of the Sea of Galilee, leaving behind a village full of questions, wonder, and a growing appetite for more.

DESTROY THIS TEMPLE

John 2:13-25

A PURPLE ROBE OF IRIS adorned the coastal hills of Galilee, heralding the end of winter. Together with the wolfberry and heather, they knit the fields together in color and scent. When the last petals fell, it meant Passover was just around the corner. Passover was the festival celebrating how the Lord God had delivered his people from their slavery in Egypt.

Jesus and his disciples, along with his mother and brothers, had been staying in Capernaum over the past few days since the wedding. Growing up, Jesus and his family had made regular pilgrimages to Jerusalem for Passover. He would make the journey again, not with his parents this time but with his disciples.

The road took Jesus from the Galilean meadows south through the Samaritan hill country to the crest of Judea where Jerusalem glimmered like a jewel set in a band of desert gold. Jerusalem was so much more than a capital city. It was an ancient promise kept—a promise that God would take his people from their roots as nomads and slaves and make them into a nation ruled by a covenant inscribed by the finger of God himself. He would lead them out of the tyranny of slavery and into a desert. There he would feed them with manna and quail from heaven. He would slake their thirst with water from a rock. He would cover them in a pillar of cloud by day and warm them as a pillar of fire by night. He would deal with those who would meet them for war. And he would whisper into the ears of brave, wise leaders plans for the kingdom he would have their descendants build.

From that desert he would bring them home to the land he swore to their father Abraham—the land of Canaan. Canaan would become a kingdom, replete with tales and songs passed down from the old to the young as they warmed themselves around fires of home. Stories of Egypt and the desert would lose all firsthand accounts and live on in the domain of tales only known through their telling, not their living.

This kingdom would be strong, ruled by the king God himself had chosen: a ruler divinely equipped to shepherd and serve—as protective as a mother, fierce as a warrior, stronger than a giant. The mighty King David would build a capital city that would become the seat of power, and his son Solomon would construct the temple that would be their house of worship.

Jerusalem was beautiful. The palette of desert browns and tans, with traces of green in the olives and figs, could trick the mind into believing this city wasn't built but grown. When the sun rose from behind, the limestone walls shone as though the city were wrapped in a ribbon of Solomon's gold while the structures reaching above the walls testified of the stonemasons David hired to execute the plans Moses drew up in order to realize Abraham's dream. Jerusalem was a promise kept.

But now, she also stood to raise the question in the minds of God's people: "Is the promise broken? Has God abandoned us?" Few would come right out and say it, but many wondered. With the occupying forces of Rome patrolling their streets and the old wounds of the Babylonian and Assyrian exiles still healing, even the most devout among them had their doubts.

The last traces of faith might have disappeared long ago had it not been for one thing: they still had their temple. For all that Rome had legislated away, and for all that had to be rebuilt upon their return from exile, Israel had managed to hold on to the part of this city that mattered more to them than any other.

The temple was like Jerusalem's pulsing heart, drawing in pilgrims with their offerings, pumping out the blood of countless sacrifices. It was the place where God's people came to deal with their sin, their need, and their hope for a future. It was where they came to worship their Creator. They would not have to search the heavens to find him. All they needed to do was go home. And no season drew more pilgrims to this city than Passover. As Jesus approached, the roads crowded with men, women, and children returning again to remember who they were.

Making his way through the city streets, Jesus climbed the steps of the temple complex and entered the Court of the Gentiles, the outer perimeter surrounding the Holy Place. The prophet Isaiah said the temple would "be called a house of prayer for all the nations." This court was where sojourners and God-fearing Gentiles from around the world could come to worship God freely.

But the Court of the Gentiles had taken on a dual purpose over the years. It had also become a marketplace for meeting the practical requirements of the old sacrificial system. Over the years this once-sacred space had been converted into a noisy, cluttered center of commerce where pigeons, lambs, and calves could be purchased by those seeking to make whatever offerings were required of them.

The market was sanctioned and overseen by the temple authorities. The thinking was that the traveler coming from a distance to worship would have difficulty bringing his own pigeons or calves. So the temple offered them for sale upon arrival. It was a pragmatic solution to the problem of worship.

The market was certainly not new. Jesus had been here many times before, and this day's scene was no different from anything he had seen on his previous visits. But this time Jesus walked through the court with authority, like a superintendent on a surprise inspection. He stooped to pick up a few old remnants of rope and walked over to where the money-changers sat. As he began to braid the cords together, he watched the merchants promote their product as the money changed hands. He grew angry at what he saw. They were trying to find the easiest ways to satisfy the rules for worship, as though this were the same thing as loving God. Their bartering voices filled the halls of the court, but their hearts were nowhere to be found.

Without warning Jesus lunged forward, sweeping his arm across the table, scattering coins from all over the world across that ancient floor worn smooth by the feet of a million pilgrims. Next came a table, over onto its side. People jumped back as this unknown lord, whip in hand, began to methodically but forcefully dismantle the marketplace. He opened up coops and unlatched gates. He drove out all who bought and sold. Animals were on the loose, people on the run.

He said, "What have you done? This is not a house of trade! This is my Father's house. It is a house of prayer."

His words dealt a blow to the consciences of the temple authorities. He was accusing them of profaning the house of God, and they knew it. Jesus' indignation was clear. He believed that what he saw was a corruption of worship, so he made a mess of the place under the auspices of cleaning it up. He upended furniture to restore order. This was not how God's people were supposed to be led. This was a holy matter. His actions declared that what was happening in the temple, regardless of what the people thought, was not in fact worship.

What was meant to be a house of prayer had become a den of thieves. But what exactly was being stolen? Though there was some price gouging going on, the far worse crime was the theft of true worship by presenting the great I AM as no different from any other foreign god who demanded tribute in exchange for prosperity.

This was not the God who called them, but it was the god the leaders offered the people. And it was the god the people were seeking to appease. Now a mysterious rabbi stood before them with a whip in his fist, calling it all a lie.

The temple authorities surrounded him, demanding, "Who do you think you are? If you're going to come in here like you own the place, where's your proof? If you're going to speak like a prophet, you show us a sign!"

Jesus said, "You want a sign that proves I have authority here? Destroy this temple, and in three days I'll raise it up again."

They looked at each other, baffled. "Oh, you will? This temple that took forty-six years to build? You could raise it from ruins in three days?"

Knowing their hearts had filled with venom, Jesus said nothing more. But he knew what they were thinking: no act of aggression like this would go overlooked. There would be fallout. There would have to be. This man Jesus had publicly indicted the system of worship his own people embraced, and in so doing he had presented himself as the only one with the authority to make such a judgment.

When that first table landed upside down on that stone floor, Jesus declared that there was something greater in Jerusalem than the temple—someone with more authority than all the temple rulers put together. His zeal for God's house burned his image into the minds of the temple authorities. They would not forget this. If he ever tried anything like this again, they would be watching and ready to act.

6

ZEUS AND THE PHARISEES

John 3:1-21

"H*E DID WHAT?*" Nicodemus asked.

As the temple authorities recounted their confrontation with the rabbi from the north, the Pharisees who had gathered processed what they were hearing. Some were indignant, others shocked. A man from Galilee had come into their temple during the Passover and declared his authority over the place, and he used the Scriptures to take the religious leaders to task.

Most dismissed Jesus as a zealot. But for a few of the Pharisees listening, the story pricked at their consciences. Regardless of who this man was, they knew he spoke at least some measure of truth. The temple had become a house of trade. They could package that reality any way they wanted, but the fact remained the temple was not what it once had been. And if fidelity to Scripture was anyone's responsibility in Israel, it was theirs. Scriptural precision was why the Pharisees existed.

Nicodemus grew up with the stories of Israel's past—its glories and its sorrows. He was raised hearing about Abraham, Moses, David, and Elijah. He had heard how the Babylonians carried the people of Judah off into exile and how, when they finally returned, the high priest Hilkiah found the Scriptures in the abandoned temple. He knew about how King Josiah read the book to the people and made a covenant before God to obey it with all his heart.

Nicodemus resonated with these tales of clinging to Scripture because at his core what he wanted most was to know God. Early on he knew that if he wanted to give his life to chasing that passion, he should become a Pharisee. This was what the Pharisees did. But he also knew that with that title, he wouldn't just belong to a cohort devoted to Scripture; he would join the company of national heroes—men whose origins tell not only of their academic rigor but also of their bravery in war.

In 167 BC, nearly two hundred years before Nicodemus was born, a small pool of blood gathered at the edge of the altar and dripped onto the floor of the Most Holy Place where the Spirit of the Lord was said to dwell. The king of Syria was either too proud or too naive to imagine the fury his sacrifice would awaken in those over whom he presumed to reign. Centuries earlier, the land of Canaan had fallen into the hands of Israel's warring neighbors. In 198 BC, the Seleucid Empire of Syria took control of the Hebrew people, and the Syrian king, Antiochus IV Epiphanes, made it his personal mission to impose Hellenism—the adoption of Greek philosophy, culture, religion, and language—on everyone under his rule.

It had already been a struggle for the people of Israel to hold on to their identity. The challenges of exile ran much deeper than mere matters of place. When they were carried off by the Babylonians and Assyrians, they weren't just taken from their homes; they were brought into the motherland of another people—an established culture with its own moral codes, religious practices, and ways of seeing the world.

As time passed, the exiled Israelites' lives began to look more and more like those of their captors. Without the temple in Jerusalem and without all the freedoms they once enjoyed, they sensed that if they didn't adapt to this new season of wandering, they might lose themselves completely. It was easier to assimilate into a new culture than to hold on to the whisper that said there was still hope of going home, though it would take a miracle. Countless Israelites had abandoned any hope that they would ever return to the land of their forefathers, and with every passing year this number grew.

Those Hebrews who had not abandoned hope had to find a way to preserve their faith. So they established houses of prayer they called synagogues and appointed leaders to oversee them—men they came to call rabbis. In response to Antiochus, a group of scholars and leaders known as the Hasidim came together to build guard rails between the faith of their fathers and the slippery slope of Greek influence that seemed to be carrying so many of their own away. The Hasidim set out to articulate what a strict observance of the Jewish ritual laws and customs should look like for any true Israelite.

It was one thing for the Hasidim to plead with their own people not to forsake their heritage, but it was quite another to contend against the external powers that were committed to ripping it away. The Hasidim's fight eventually turned outward when the king of Syria moved to advance his agenda of Hellenization by abolishing the Hebrew religion altogether. Like stamping out the last remaining coals of a day-old fire, Antiochus wanted to snuff out whatever remained burning in the Israelites, so he made the observation of the Sabbath, along with all of the Hebrew feasts, illegal. He banned the books of Moses, burning all the copies he could find. He made circumcision a criminal act and warned the Hebrews that if anyone dared to disobey any of these mandates, he would have them put to death—a threat he backed up swiftly and often.

Antiochus meant for each of these new laws and the penalties they carried to land like blows to the chins of the Hebrews until they had no fight left. And in 167 BC, on the verge of victory, he threw one final blow he hoped would knock them out. But it didn't. It woke them up.

Antiochus went up to Jerusalem and announced that the temple no longer belonged to Israel's God. It now belonged to Zeus—the god of the skies, the ruler of the entire pantheon of Greek deities. Antiochus entered the Holy Place and set up a statue of Zeus and brazenly formalized his dedication ceremony by sacrificing a pig on the altar of the Lord. Antiochus knew exactly what he was doing. Pigs were ceremonially unclean—not to be touched by the people of God. This was as vile a sacrilege as the foreign king could come up with—a pig sacrificed to Zeus in the Holy Place in God's temple. Surely this would release the Israelite's grip on their heritage and bend them to Antiochus's will once and for all.

Surely this would break their hearts.

Antiochus Epiphanes was wrong. Bands of resistance had been forming for some time, but when he offered his sacrifice to Zeus, a man named Judas Maccabaeus organized enough of a resistance to fight. The Hasidim, among others, joined with him, and in 164 BC they prevailed by taking back most of Jerusalem. Judas Maccabaeus tasked the religious leaders in his company with the job of cleansing the temple and building a new altar unstained by the blood of Antiochus's strange fire.

In the eyes of many Israelites, the Hasidim were among the bravest, most self-sacrificing men in the land. Their devotion to the Lord led to the temple being purified and, in some measure, restored to the people of God. The Hasidim were heroes.

But as the dust settled, the Hasidim, having lost so many to Hellenism and the despair of exile, were left with this dilemma: Should they continue to call their countrymen to follow in their footsteps of fidelity to Scripture, or should they cloister off to preserve what they had among themselves in order to guard against any further dilution amid their own ranks? Eventually the Hasidim split into two groups—the Essenes, whose idea of fidelity to Scripture led them to live as separatists, and the Pharisees, who lived among the rest of Israel, committed to preserving adherence to the Mosaic Law in their communities. The Pharisees had gained the respect of their community not only because of their heroism but also because they made such an uncommon effort to obey the law of God to the letter as ordinary members of their community.

This was the band of hero-scholars Nicodemus had joined when he was younger. He wanted to live well. He wanted to believe he too would have fought Antiochus, given the chance. He wanted to keep the commands of Scripture. He wanted to show others how to do the same. But he knew the corruption that came with belonging to a people who believed they were always right. He knew he and his colleagues had grown arrogant. What may have begun as a fight for the holy name of God now often looked like nothing more than a grab for the glory of the Pharisees. He saw it among his peers. He saw it in himself. Every year they seemed to care less about knowing God and more about being right, and this was robbing them of their childlike sense of curiosity and of their true courage. They traded in credibility, and credibility looked better dressed in answers than in questions.

But as for Nicodemus, he had questions. He heard Jesus could perform miracles. He agreed that the temple had become a house of trade. And he couldn't get past the courage it took for Jesus to stand as tall as he did among the money-changers and temple authorities. He had to know who this man was. So one night under the cover of darkness, Nicodemus went out to find him. He didn't want to draw too much attention to his visit, and neither did he want to lose the upper hand in case Jesus really was nothing more than a madman. He would wade in slowly.

When he found Jesus, Nicodemus said, "Rabbi, we see you are a teacher from God because there are things we know you couldn't have done without his help."

Jesus studied the Pharisee. He was a riddle, coming at Jesus with the confidence of a statement while standing in the darkness like a question.

Jesus said, "Let me tell you something. Unless you are reborn, you cannot see what God is doing."

"What do you mean?" Nicodemus said. "Can a man return to the womb?"

Jesus said, "Unless you are born of water and of the Spirit of God, you cannot enter the kingdom of God. To be born in the flesh is one thing, but you were meant for spiritual birth too. You think you see what there is to see, Nicodemus. The wind blows and you hear it and you feel it on your face, but you don't know where it comes from or where it's going, do you? This is true for anyone born of the Spirit of God. It is a birth that eludes you."

"I don't know what you mean," Nicodemus answered.

Jesus said, "Aren't you one of Israel's teachers? One of the Pharisees? Yet you don't know about spiritual birth? I'm telling you, as someone who does know what he's talking about, that all your scrupulous law-keeping isn't enough to make you right with God. But because you Pharisees are so convinced that you can save yourselves, it will be hard for you to hear me. You believe you have secured eternal life through your piety, but you are dying. Just as Moses lifted up the serpent in the wilderness to deliver the people from the sting of death, the only hope you have for eternal life is to believe in the Son of Man when he is lifted up."

Nicodemus stood in the shadows, thinking.

Jesus continued, "God loves this world so much that he gave his only Son so that whoever believes in him will not die but have eternal life. He didn't send his Son into the world to condemn it, but so that the world might be saved through him. Whoever believes in him will not be condemned. But whoever refuses to believe is condemned already, because he has not believed in the only Son of God."

Though Jesus' words sounded like a rebuke, something deep inside Nicodemus began to wake up—that familiar longing to be close to God. He wanted to believe Jesus.

Jesus said, "People love their darkness, don't they, Nicodemus? They love how their shadows hide them. Do you want to know who I am? Here's the truth: I am the light of God who has come into the world."

7

HEROD'S HALF
BROTHER'S WIFE

John 3:22–4:3

A FTER NICODEMUS'S VISIT AT NIGHT, Jesus left Jerusalem for the hill country of Judea, making his way to where John was baptizing. John's popularity had grown since the last time these cousins had seen each other. Jesus stopped for a while by the river, and his disciples baptized all who came to them.

Though Jesus and John seemed to share a common understanding of why they were baptizing people, John's disciples noticed that people were more attracted to Jesus than to John. They said, "Rabbi, this man you've been talking about, look at how everyone is going to him."

John said, "Listen, when God gives you a mission, that's your mission. No one else can do what has been given to you. God's gift to me is mine to put to use and no one else's. I am here to work with what the Lord has given, and his great gift to me is that I would live my life as the herald of the coming of the Messiah. I serve him; that is my calling. Don't you remember how I told you I was not the Christ? I am not the Bridegroom. I attend to him, and it is my honor to announce his arrival. And I rest in this role, friends. I was made for this. My satisfaction is forever tied to his coming, and he has now come. He must increase and I must decrease."

People continued to flock to John. He spoke openly about sin and about his people's desperate need to trust in something other than their good works to save them. They needed to believe in the Son of God. They needed to know that the Messiah had come. For as long as John drew breath, this would be the theme of his song.

But not all who heard him appreciated his candor. John didn't speak only about the sins of those who came to him. He publicly addressed the state of all things, including the sins of his people and also the sins of Rome. At the intersection of these two parties stood Herod Antipas, for whom John had strong words concerning his particular sins.

Even though his father, Herod the Great, was an Idumean by birth, Herod Antipas considered himself a Jew by faith. He displayed this faith by investing in substantial building projects in and around Jerusalem, including the expansion of the temple. But his erratic and often violent temper, which resulted in the executions of many close to him—including his wife Mariamne—made the particulars of his true beliefs a blood-soaked riddle.

In both his faith and his volatility, Antipas followed in his father's footsteps. He observed the Passover in Jerusalem and took a personal interest in many aspects of the Hebrew way of life. But he was also a politician trying to climb through the ranks of Roman leadership, which was a ruthless game.

Earlier in his political life, Antipas had married a woman named Phasaelis, the daughter of the Nabataean king Aretas IV. Whatever affection there might have been between the two, marriages like this were as much about foreign relations as they were about building a family. Their marriage symbolized a peaceful union between Palestine and its neighbor to the east.

But during one of Antipas's visits to Rome, he met and fell in love with his half-brother Philip's wife, Herodias. The two carried on a secret affair for as long as they could before it became clear that they wanted to be together, regardless of the cost.

It cost a lot. It brought public humiliation upon his brother Philip and it sent the very insulting message to King Aretas IV that the royals of Judea no longer wanted his daughter in their family.

But the heart wants what the heart wants. So Antipas divorced Phasaelis, and Herodias divorced Philip, and the two were married. The list of problems their marriage invited ran long, and it drove a politically explosive wedge between the Nabataeans and Antipas's own brother's rule in the surrounding regions. It strengthened even more the Herodian family's ties to Rome—compromising any hope Antipas might have had of persuading the Hebrews that he would govern in their best interests.

Of particular concern to John was the sin of Antipas's divorce. If Herod wanted his people to see him as a Jew, he should care about Scripture. But his marriage to Herodias stood in direct opposition to the Law of Moses. So John spoke out against Antipas's sin publicly and often.

When Antipas heard of John's protest, he sent for him to hear him out. He knew about John's ministry on the banks of the Jordan and had come to believe that John was a righteous man. Though Antipas's life was filled with extravagance and John's was a life of poverty, John had something that eluded Antipas—he had the affection of the people. Though he wouldn't admit it, Antipas respected John. And if pressed even further, he might even confess that he feared him.

The fortress of Machaerus, which stood atop the steep hills east of the Jordan, served a dual purpose. It was a regal palace but also a prison. When Antipas summoned men to this place, they never knew if they would be permitted to leave.

John followed the guards into the palace, and they led him into the room where Antipas and Herodias were waiting. The ruler had the look of a powerful man in a difficult marriage with a guilty conscience. His wife just looked perturbed.

"I hear you've been talking about us," Herod said. "If you have something to say, we're listening."

John said, "You know what I have to say. Your marriage is a sin. You've divorced Phasaelis and taken your brother's wife, and this makes you an adulterer and a lawbreaker."

Herodias burned with anger. She wanted him dead. But if Antipas killed John, there was no telling how the countless masses who revered him as a prophet would react. Antipas's rule was fragile enough, so although he appreciated his wife's position, he elected instead to seize John, bind him, and throw him into the prison where he would be out of the public eye but also safe within his walls.

Word spread quickly that John had landed in the Machaerus prison. If Antipas was this aware of John's ministry, it was reasonable to assume he had people investigating John's influence in the region, which could spell trouble for those associated with the baptizer. So when Jesus heard that John had been arrested, he and his disciples headed home to Galilee, opting to take the most direct route, which ran through Samaria, a region most proud Israelites would gladly avoid even if it meant going a hundred miles out of their way.

The Samaritans were the descendants of Israel's northern kingdom who had intermarried with their Assyrian captors after they were carried off into exile in 722 BC. The Jews regarded the Samaritans as traitors who had exchanged the bloodline of Abraham in order to settle in a pagan land.

Jesus and his disciples came to the Samaritan village of Sychar at the hottest part of the day and stopped there to rest and eat. The disciples went into the village for food while Jesus stayed by the well outside of town. While he was there, a woman approached. That she came to the well during the hottest part of the day suggested she was a social outsider who had to get water when no one else was around. She was surprised to come upon this man and even more surprised when Jesus asked her for a drink.

"But you are a Jewish man and I am a Samaritan woman," she said. "Why are you even talking to me?"

Jesus answered, "If you knew who it is that asks you for a drink, you would be asking me, and I would be giving you living water."

The woman regarded Jesus for a moment as she processed what he said. Were they even talking about water anymore? She said, "Sir, you have nothing to draw with and this well is deep. How are you going to get that kind of water?"

With that, they were now deep in the pools of metaphor.

Pointing to the well, Jesus said, "Everyone who drinks this water will thirst again, but whoever drinks the water I give him will never thirst again. In fact, what I give will become a spring of water welling up to eternal life."

She said, "Where can I get that water? My life is hard, and I'd love to be able to leave it behind."

Though she was talking about her daily midday trips to the well, her life was full of burdens greater than this. In her wake lay a slew of dead and broken relationships, and with them the pain they heaped on her fragile frame. She put on a brave face to stand her ground and talk like this with Jesus, but he saw right through her.

"Go get your husband, and I'll tell you all about this water," Jesus said.

She said, "I don't have one." She knew he knew better than to imagine she was a married woman.

"I know," Jesus told her. "You've had five husbands, and the man you live with now is not one of them."

This was a personal, painful detail to come from the mouth of a stranger. He was correct, but what would he do with this revelation? Would he shame her? Abuse her? Take advantage of her?

To deflect the intimate light she'd just come under, she started asking Jesus questions about the differences between Jews and Samaritans—specifically about where God wanted his people to gather for worship. But Jesus didn't begin this conversation so they could talk about geography. He disarmed her in order to get to her heart through her wound. He said, "Your people and my people argue about many things. A time is coming and in fact is now here when the true worshipers will worship the Father in spirit and truth. These are the kind of worshipers the Father seeks."

The woman said, "My whole life I've heard that the Messiah is coming and that when he comes, everything will be made plain."

Jesus said, "Listen. I am he."

The woman was shaken. When she'd first encountered Jesus, she'd assumed nothing much would come of their meeting. She came from the wrong race, religion, gender, and moral reputation for anyone like Jesus to care. But in this moment, he hadn't just shown kindness to her. He had exposed her insatiable thirst for comfort and control and revealed her most painful secrets. Then he told her he could satisfy her deepest thirst forever.

Jesus didn't see her the way she saw him. He saw in her a troubled woman longing to be satisfied on a deep soul level. He saw her attempts to slake her own thirst through pluck and a long line of men. But he also saw a person who was created for worship and someone who would always be thirsty apart from it. He saw a woman made in the image of God who wanted something God had put in her heart to desire—himself. And Jesus was telling her that the way to a satisfied heart came through him. It was as though as they sat beside the well, Jesus and this woman were the only two people in the world. He didn't regard her by her reputation but according to what her heart was created to hunger for.

She was a symbol of the world Jesus had stepped into—a world of people created to know and love their Maker. But much in and around them was broken. The brokenness filtered through every single human relationship, from an unnoticed woman alone in the desert to the tetrarch of Galilee who had John the Baptist locked away in his dungeon. But that unsuspecting world was beginning to change as Jesus' ways and words continued to spread.

PART 2

POPULARITY

8

FAMOUS

Luke 5:1-26

C ONTINUING ON THROUGH Samaria to Galilee, Jesus told his disciples he wanted to go back to his hometown of Nazareth. Jesus grew up there with his parents and siblings as the son of a carpenter. Joseph had since died, but Mary and Jesus' brothers and sisters still lived there.

When he was in town, it was his practice to go to the synagogue on the Sabbath and read from the Scriptures. So when the Sabbath came around during this visit, Jesus took his disciples to the meeting. During the time of worship, Jesus stood up and asked the synagogue attendant to hand him a scroll. Jesus then unrolled the scroll of the prophet Isaiah and read aloud:

The Spirit of the Lord is resting on me,
    because he has anointed me
    to proclaim good news to the poor.

He has sent me to announce freedom for the captives
> And the recovery of sight for the blind
> And liberty for the oppressed.

He has sent me to proclaim the year of God's favor.

Jesus then rolled up the scroll, handed it back to the attendant, and sat down to teach. It was customary for a visiting rabbi to read and then expound the Scripture, but the rumors about Jesus had reached the leaders of this synagogue, and there was an air of excitement in the room as everyone waited to hear what he had to say.

"Today," Jesus said, "here in this room in your hearing, this Scripture has been fulfilled."

The people sat in silence, processing Jesus' words.

As he talked about what Isaiah meant by this being the year of God's favor, many were struck by the grace with which he spoke. But for others, the cynicism of familiarity took over. They said, "We know this man. Does he really think he is God's gift to us? Isn't this Joseph's son? Isn't this one of the boys who cares for Mary?"

Knowing their thoughts, Jesus said, "A prophet isn't welcome in his own hometown. Do you remember how God's people rejected Elijah during the famine years? Do you remember how when Israel rejected him, God sent him to care for the Gentiles? When God's people reject his prophet, that prophet moves on."

With those words, the room turned on him. Even those who'd marveled at his words moments earlier were now angry. That he would come into their house of prayer and tell them that God's promises of freedom, healing, and peace were fulfilled in him—a local boy they'd known since he was a child—and then rebuke them for not believing him was more than they could abide. They pressed toward him to drive him out of the synagogue.

"Let's take him to the cliffs and throw him over," some shouted. But Jesus slipped away and disappeared into the streets. So much of his past was tied to Nazareth—his boyhood friends, his family, the sawdust scent of Joseph's shop, the cliffs looking over the Jezreel Valley. Close to three decades of his life happened in that town. But now, the people's reaction in the synagogue raised the question of whether he could ever come home again. So Jesus and his disciples headed northeast to Peter's hometown of Capernaum.

(It was on their way to Capernaum that they stopped in Cana. This was also the visit when the nobleman came to plead with Jesus to save his son's life.)

Soon after arriving in Capernaum, Jesus' popularity began to grow. In the synagogue and in the streets, Jesus taught the people about how the kingdom of God was at hand. He called them to repent of their sins. He spoke with a sort of grace and authority that left people astonished. When the sick and afflicted came to him, he healed them all. His reasoning pricked at their consciences and his hands healed their infirmities. Stories about him spread throughout the countryside, even over into Syria and into the Decapolis beyond the Jordan, and great crowds began to come to see him. There was no other way to say it: Jesus had become famous.

For Jesus' friends Peter and Andrew, Capernaum was home. When they weren't with Jesus, they were back at their work. Some days the Sea of Galilee teemed with fish just waiting to be caught. But not this night. Peter and his brother had been at it all evening, trying every old fisherman's trick they knew, but it was as though the lake had been mysteriously drained of life. They caught nothing.

Jesus found Andrew and Peter washing their nets, looking forlorn. A crowd was already gathering at the shore to hear him teach, so he told Peter he'd like to teach from the boat. Peter set out a little from shore, and Jesus taught from the water.

Peter was a man who wore his heart on his sleeve. It was one of his most endearing qualities, even if it also got him into trouble. Jesus knew Peter's moods, and he could tell that this friend in the boat was frustrated.

When he finished teaching, Jesus said, "Listen, Peter. Let's push out a little deeper and see if we can catch anything."

Peter looked at his brother Andrew. They were experienced not only in the skill of fishing but also in the art of humoring those who couldn't catch a fish to save their life—and who presumed to offer advice. Since the first fisherman caught the first fish, this has been the way of the world. Normally Peter jumped at the opportunity to fish just a little bit more, but he was tired of fishing and tired of failing.

Peter said, "Master, we've been at it all night. I don't know where the fish went, but they aren't here."

He would have left it at that, but he knew mysterious things happened when Jesus was around, so he said, "But since you're asking, let's do it."

As soon as Peter dropped his net into the water, he felt the familiar tug. When they went to pull the net in, they couldn't. It was too heavy for them to manage, to the point that it was beginning to break.

"James! John! Get over here. Help us!" Peter called out. James and John, who were nearby in their boat, rowed over, and the men began to pull the fish into the two boats until both were full to the point of sinking.

When the cup of Peter's joy got too full, it spilled over into other emotions. He looked at the fish and then at Jesus with a smile on his lips and sorrow in his eyes. He fell to his knees and said, "Leave me, O Lord. I'm a sinful man. I do not deserve this."

Andrew, James, and John stood in their boats, speechless and a little afraid of what had just happened.

Jesus said, "Friends, do not be afraid. This is nothing. From now on you will be fishers of men."

The men in the boats were not accustomed to being spoken to in this way. They were men of tables and weights—merchants, tradesmen, pragmatists. All their lives they'd established their significance according to what they could produce. People needed to eat, and they worked to produce that food. This made them valuable to their community. It made them a living. Besides, Jesus could do much better than enlisting lowly fishermen to help him preach the message of God. Wouldn't he be better served taking educated disciples? But as they stood there knee-deep in the catch of their lives, Jesus told them, no, he wanted them.

When they came ashore, the crowds were amazed to see the fish. But Peter, James, John, and Andrew coiled up their gear as though they were preparing to be gone for a while. Somewhere between the site of the catch and the beach they decided to walk away from their lives as fishermen and follow Jesus as far as he would lead them.

It wasn't a bad day to end their fishing careers.

During those months in Capernaum, Jesus lived with Peter's family. Their house became the site of many more miracles and healings—not the least of which was Peter's mother-in-law. She caught a fever that left her bedridden. As the fever rose, her daughter and son-in-law feared for her life. Jesus went and sat beside her. He loved this woman. He reached out and took her hands in his. As soon as he touched her, the fever subsided. She felt it leave and sat up slowly. Taking a quick inventory, she realized she was well again.

As she stood up from the bed, she looked at Jesus and said, "Can I get you anything?"

That night many more came to Peter's house, and Jesus healed them all. "It's just like what the prophet Isaiah said of the coming King of glory; 'He takes our illnesses and bears our diseases,'" the people said.

Every day the crowds continued to gather around Peter's house. Jesus taught and healed as many people as would fit inside—and even those standing at the windows and doors. There was a paralytic who lived in Capernaum. His friends heard about Jesus and wanted him to heal their friend, but when they arrived at Peter's house, the crowds were so large there was no way to get inside.

"Can we take you up on the roof?" one asked.

"What?" the paralyzed man said.

His friend said, "I know how to get you to Jesus right now. But we need to get up there."

The five men climbed up onto the roof, and they began to peel back the tiles until they had made a hole right over where Jesus was sitting. They lowered their friend down in a sling they had made from his bed and some rope. The paralyzed man grinned apologetically at Jesus as he inched his way down through the new hole in Peter's roof.

Jesus looked up at the four faces peering down into the house. He admired their faith and tenacity. "Sir," he said to the man in the sling, "your sins are forgiven."

Everyone close by leaned forward, expecting him to heal the man. But Jesus said nothing more, just that his sins were forgiven.

The religious leaders in the room, some scribes and some Pharisees, grew angry, though they said nothing.

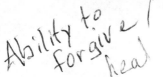

Does he think he can forgive sins? Only God can do that, they thought.

Knowing their hearts, Jesus asked the crowded room, "What do you think is easier to say? 'Your sins are forgiven?' or 'Get up and walk?' To forgive I must possess the authority of God, otherwise my words are empty. But isn't the same thing true about healing? You've seen me doing these wonders. Where do you suppose this ability comes from? These signs are so that you might know that I am sent from God to forgive sins. I possess this authority." So to help them believe that he had the authority to forgive sins, Jesus turned to the paralyzed man and said, "I say to you, get up. Take your mat and enjoy your walk home."

The man stood to his feet, and the room erupted in applause. Tears of joy and praise ran down the healed man's face, and the people wept with him.

"Amazing!" they said. "Just amazing!"

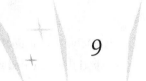

9

LORD OF THE SABBATH

Luke 6:1-11

As the crowd dispersed from Peter's house, Jesus went outside for a walk. He passed by a man everyone knew though few liked. Matthew, a Hebrew man by birth, made his living collecting taxes for Rome. When he chose this career, he knew what it would mean for his place in the community. Most people viewed tax collectors as traitors—men who sold Jacob's birthright to build Caesar's empire. With every coin collected, tax collectors weakened Israel and strengthened Rome. They made themselves rich by taking more than they needed.

Over the years Matthew had grown accustomed to the scorn of his neighbors. The money coming in eased the pain of the community he lost. But he was never fully at peace with the life he had chosen.

As with the rest of Capernaum, Matthew was fascinated by Jesus. So when he saw Jesus passing by his tax-collecting booth, he paused what he was doing to watch. Jesus stopped and looked at Matthew.

"Follow me," Jesus said to him.

Matthew came out from behind his table, and the two men faced each other. Matthew searched Jesus' face for scorn but found none—only a sincere invitation to go with him. Matthew left everything as it was and walked alongside Jesus through the streets of Capernaum.

"Let's have dinner together tonight, Matthew," Jesus said. Matthew looked at him as these words registered. Dinner? Tonight?

"Yes! Let's," said Matthew, and he immediately began to pull together a feast. He invited everyone he thought might come—mostly other tax collectors, along with a few friends who lived on the fringes of Capernaum's good graces. Matthew filled his house with people most folks called sinners. When the Pharisees saw Jesus sharing a meal with Matthew's friends, reclining as though this were a comfortable visit, they asked his disciples, "Why does your teacher eat with such people?"

When the question reached Jesus, he stiffened. "By what rule do you think God measures out his favor? Do you think what he wants is religious precision? Sacrifices to demonstrate your worthiness? Do you think because you have made your rules and then kept them that God prefers you to those who know their lives have fallen apart?"

The Pharisees said, "You act as though we have no concern for their souls. That's not true. We fast and pray for the sinners among us. Our distance is a form of discipline. We're calling them to leave their lives of sin and join us in righteous living. But you and your disciples, you go into their homes. You eat and drink with them. And you even seem to enjoy it. You fly close to the flame. How will they ever decide to change if they see you condescending to make your home among them? How will they ever know that God wants more for their lives?"

Jesus said, "So what do they need? A change in behavior? Is that all? It's the sick, not the healthy, who need a doctor. But you despise the sin-sick among you. Didn't God say through Hosea, 'I desire mercy, not sacrifice'? Will you ever learn what this means? I draw near to the broken so they might hear the voice of mercy. I'm not here to change their minds. I'm here to heal their hearts."

As he listened to Jesus and the Pharisees argue over him and his friends, Matthew quietly decided he would follow Jesus from then on. No one had ever defended his dignity like this before. Jesus knew the ugly truth—he knew that Matthew had chosen money over God. Yet here stood Jesus in his home, defending his right to befriend the marginalized and outcast. Wherever it took him, whatever it cost, he would follow Jesus, even if it meant following him all the way to the end of his own life.

Though the Pharisees in Capernaum had seen with their own eyes how Jesus healed the paralytic, they struggled with his fame and with the ways he so boldly confronted them as though he was somehow above them, somehow closer to God. Whether in Capernaum, Nazareth, or Jerusalem—it didn't seem to matter where—the poor and destitute loved Jesus, and this only heightened the religious leaders' skepticism.

Not too long after the dinner at Matthew's house, as one of the holy feasts drew near, Jesus and his disciples set off for Jerusalem. Entering the city from the northern Sheep Gate, Jesus passed by the pool of Bethesda (an Aramaic word for "the house of mercy"). Bethesda was a gathering place for the sick, the paralyzed, and the blind. It was a strategic place to gather alms from pilgrims whose recent entrance into the holy city had perhaps heightened their sense of charity. But many also thought the place was magical. The pool was fed by an underground spring that released occasional surges of water and air, causing them to bubble. When the waters stirred like this, some said it was the work of angels pouring mercy into the water, and the first worthy people to enter would be healed.

Jesus passed by a man who had been paralyzed for thirty-eight years. The man was a fixture there in Bethesda. He'd been coming to these waters for a long time, always hoping for a miracle but never getting one. The years had taken away some of his sense of urgency because with or without healing, he had found something to fill his days and a means to meet his needs.

"Do you want to be healed?" Jesus asked him.

It was such a strange question. On the surface the answer seemed obvious. Of course he did. Why else would he be there beside the pool? But the man said, "I come here every day. But I'm alone. I don't have anyone to put me into the water when the angels stir, so somebody else always gets in before me. I'm still waiting on my miracle."

This didn't really answer Jesus' question. Why the man hadn't been healed and if he wanted to be healed were two different things. Though it wasn't much, the man had put together a life for himself there at the pool. He knew why he hadn't been healed, but to name what he actually wanted was a bit more complicated.

What if he were healed? This man hadn't taken a step in thirty-eight years. It would be glorious to come and go as he pleased. He would never again take his mobility for granted—not for one single day. But how would he eat? What would he do for work? He was a professional beggar, a lifer at the game of charity.

Jesus said, "Get up. Pick up your mat. Walk."

A sensation ran from the man's head to his feet. For so long his legs had been dead weight beneath him, but as soon as Jesus spoke those words, they came alive. He wiggled his toes, bent his knees, planted one foot on the stone floor, and slowly rose until he could plant the other. He rolled up his bed and walked around, testing his new legs.

By now, everyone was watching Jesus and the man as they stood facing each other. Wiping away a tear, the man turned and slowly walked away, one foot in front of the other. He had no words. People immediately pressed in to embrace Jesus. But not everyone. The religious leaders who had seen the miracle followed the newly healed man. They stopped him. He could see from their expressions that they were upset.

"Is today not the Sabbath?" they asked.

"Yes?" he answered, confused.

They said, "You know you are not allowed to carry your bed on the Sabbath. You know that constitutes work, don't you?"

He wasn't expecting this. Who would? He said, "The man who healed me—the man who, with nothing but a word, bid these legs that have been dead for four decades to live again—he told me to pick up my bed." Could they not see theirs was a ridiculous complaint?

But rules were rules. And the Pharisees had gone to great lengths to establish these rules so that those who wanted to take Scripture seriously could make certain they never violated the command to keep the Sabbath holy and free from work. Nothing about this was ridiculous to them.

"Who is this man who healed you?" they asked.

"I didn't catch his name. There was a lot going on," the man said, suppressing a grin.

With that, the Pharisees left him. He wasn't the only one who might know.

***

Later during the feast, Jesus found the man he'd healed walking around in the temple. Jesus went to him and put his hands on the man's shoulders to get a good look at him.

"Look at you!" Jesus said. "You're doing well, aren't you? Listen. As you walk, walk upright, my friend. Sin no more. There are worse things in this world than being paralyzed."

After this, the man went back and told the Pharisees it was Jesus from Galilee who had healed him. Why he went back to tell them, no one knew. Maybe it was to gloat? Perhaps he feared what might happen to him if he didn't. Regardless, he told them, and they received this information as though it were evidence in a crime.

They wanted confirmation that it was Jesus, because even though picking up a bed on the Sabbath violated the laws the Pharisees had written, there was an even greater transgression at work here. Jesus' fame had so blinded the uneducated masses that they were beginning to look to him as more than a rabbi. They were beginning to put their hope in him in ways they had never done with the religious leaders. And this man the people loved so much seemed to play fast and loose with their rules. If his occupation was to work wonders, then to heal someone on the Sabbath was to work, and to work on the Sabbath was to break the Sabbath, and to break the Sabbath was to sin against God. And that was not permitted.

***

Later, the Pharisees set out to test Jesus to see if he would heal on the Sabbath again. They invited him to meet with them under the auspices of learning from him, but in the middle of the room sat a man with a shriveled hand. Jesus knew they had brought the man there just to see if Jesus would break their law.

Knowing they meant to use this man as a trap, Jesus said, "You're asking me if I think it is lawful to do good on the Sabbath. If any one of you had your sheep fall in a well on the Sabbath, would you just leave it? Of course not."

Then he said to the man with the shriveled hand, "Stretch out your hand." Immediately the hand was restored, as strong and sound as the other.

The Pharisees set this man before Jesus either to force him to yield to their impression of the law or to watch him break it. When Jesus healed the man's hand, many of the religious leaders cringed because they knew he had forced their hand. If they were going to do anything to discipline him, he was daring them to get on with it. When they demanded his contrition, he told them, "Something greater than the temple is here among you. The Son of Man is Lord of the Sabbath."

Whether it was by eating at Matthew's house or healing on the Sabbath, Jesus offended the Pharisees. Religious leaders were called to show the people how to be holy, separate from the filth of the world, clean. It wasn't that the Pharisees misunderstood what Jesus was doing by reaching out to the poor and broken. It was that they understood full well. Jesus meant to associate with the poor and wretched. That in itself might have been tolerable, except that he dared to insist that this was what God wanted from his people—the righteous drawing near to the unclean. His was a ministry of incarnation—touching the infected, dining with sinners, defending the defenseless. The sick needed a physician, and the Physician had come.

10

ONLY SAY
THE WORD

Matthew 8–9

AFTER THE FEAST, JESUS returned to Galilee. Great crowds continued to follow him, and he continued to teach and heal. A centurion in Capernaum sent for Jesus because he had a servant who was dying. The centurion's friends told Jesus, "If there is a man among us who deserves God's mercy, it is this man. He loves our people. He is just, merciful, and generous. He built our synagogue. He is an advocate for our community."

As Jesus approached the house, the centurion came out to meet him. He said, "Lord, I am not worthy to receive you under my roof. Listen. When I speak, my commands are obeyed by those under my charge. My authority grants me this confidence. I know you possess authority too. So please, do not trouble yourself. Only say the word and my servant will be healed."

Jesus marveled at the man's faith. Few bore such confidence in him to believe his word was as powerful as his physical presence. He turned to those nearby and said, "I've never seen such faith in all Israel." The centurion's servants returned to the house to find the servant had fully recovered.

Later, Jesus and his disciples came to the village of Nain, situated at the foothills of Mount Tabor southeast of Nazareth. As they approached the city, a familiar scene unfolded before them. Mourners wept as they trickled like tears from the town gate. Behind them some men appeared carrying a dead man on a stretcher. The man's mother followed, weeping. The disciples looked for the man's father or brothers. There were none. People from the procession said she was a widow and this was her only son.

A loss like this meant the widow would have no one to care for her in her old age. Having buried her husband already, she was no stranger to loss. Many winced at the unfolding scene, but everyone felt the same sting. No mother should have to bury her own child. Such grief felt broken and unnatural in spite of the fact that, eventually, death comes for everyone. But this felt off. Every time death came for a loved one, something in the heart rose up in protest, shouting, "No! This isn't right!" People looked to their religious leaders to make sense of death and the grief it left in its wake. They wanted to know how to hurt less, how to reconcile themselves to this intruder called death.

When the disciples looked at Jesus, they didn't see a man organizing his thoughts into a speech to comfort the grieving. Instead, they saw grief itself. He watched the dead man's mother weeping into her hands and walked over and stood in front of her.

"Do not weep," he said.

Words alone would not stop these tears. They both knew this. Still, Jesus' words interrupted her mourning long enough for her to look up and see his compassion for her. He walked over to the funeral bier and touched the pall.

The bearers stopped. In fact, in that moment, everything seemed to stop. Touching the dead defiled a rabbi's ceremonial purity, so when Jesus touched the board bearing the dead man, several people gasped. What was he thinking? Had he sunk so deep into unfettered empathy that he had forgotten himself?

He whispered, "Young man."

The dead man's mother's sorrow yielded to confusion. Did he just whisper something to her son?

He said, "Young man, listen to my voice. Are you listening? Get up." A huge gasp came from the stretcher as the body jerked like someone startled awake by a clap of thunder. The young man sat up and asked why he was on that board and why everyone looked so terrified.

Jesus helped him down and led him to his mother. Fear seized the crowd of mourners. They weren't sure how to feel. Some wept even more. Others laughed in disbelief. One said what they were all feeling: "God has visited his people and he has given us a great prophet. He speaks and the dead live again."

Reports of this healing, along with many others, circulated around all Judea and the surrounding countryside. Great crowds continued to follow Jesus, so he stayed on the move to manage them the best he could, if only for a while. After the resurrection at Nain, Jesus returned to the Galilean seaside. One day, when the crowds had drained his strength, Jesus asked his disciples to set off in a boat to get some space. Weary, Jesus went to the stern of the boat and lay down. Rocking in the gentle swells of the sea, he fell asleep.

He awoke to a dripping, desperate face inches from his own, shouting over the noise of a sudden storm. "Don't you care that we are perishing?"

A canyon wind had whipped the Lake of Galilee into such a torrent that the waves were beginning to break over the boat. It was taking on water fast. Most of the men in the boat were experienced seafarers, and all but one were at attention, working furiously to keep it afloat and so also their lives. All except Jesus.

"Jesus, we're dying! Don't you care?" screamed Peter.

It was such an ironic question. They were in the boat to escape the crowds. And the crowds had pressed in around Jesus because he had come to be known as a miracle-working healer of lepers and paralytics. The masses sought him because he not only cared about their perishing; he stopped it. He even reversed it.

They were paralyzed on a leprous sea casting its white ruin across their sides, and they knew this could end in one of two ways: death or a miracle. In spite of their best efforts, they were headed for death, and they were desperate. Did Jesus have anything for them like he had for the centurion's servant or the widow from Nain's son? Even if it was only words, they needed something.

Jesus looked at the raging waters as though they possessed a soul and a will. He rebuked the wind and said to the sea, "Quiet. Be still."

At once, the winds vanished and the sea grew still as glass.

The men in the boat were still getting to know Jesus. They had seen him do many things that were hard to explain, and they had made room in their hearts for some of those mysteries. But as stillness overtook the deafening storm for no obvious reason except simple obedience to Jesus' words, they realized they had no category for this. They looked at him as though he had just handed them back their lives, but they didn't know if they'd gotten the safer end of that deal.

Jesus said, "Why are you afraid?"

Authority. This is why they were afraid. They had just learned that the natural world obeyed the command of his voice. And this

lesson came on the heels of learning that he carried the same authority when it came to death.

"Why are you afraid? Friends, don't you trust me?" Jesus asked.

His question hung in the calm, clean air. They whispered to one
another, "Who is this man that even the wind and the seas obey him?"

When Jesus and his disciples returned home to Capernaum, another crowd gathered around Jesus. One of the rulers of the synagogue, a man named Jairus, sat at his daughter's bedside, dabbing
her forehead as her fever grew. Like the nobleman from Cana or the
widow from Nain, he sat in the helpless place every mother and
father dreads more than anything else in the world—the bedside of
a dying child.

"Talitha," he whispered. "Talitha, get better. Please."

When he heard Jesus was nearby, he ran to find him and then fell
at his feet, pleading, "Please come. My little girl, my Talitha—we're
losing her!" He wept as he spoke.

Jesus gestured for Jairus to lead the way. The crowd parted to let
them through, but they followed closely, so that they moved as a
living throng. In the crowd a woman was trying to make her way
to Jesus. She had suffered from bleeding for twelve years, and she'd
spent everything she had in a fruitless quest for a remedy. Her
bleeding only worsened. Her disease was a kind of death. It left her
always unclean, always embarrassed, always avoided.

As Jesus passed her, she reached out to grab the hem of his robe,
thinking if she could just touch him it would be the same as if he
had touched her. She felt her body change as soon as she touched
his robe. Though she couldn't be sure right then and there, she
sensed that her bleeding had stopped.

Jesus turned around, scanning the crowd, looking puzzled. "Who touched me?" he asked.

His disciples said, "Look at this crowd, teacher. What do you mean who touched you?"

"No," Jesus said. "Someone touched me, hoping it would heal them. I felt it."

The woman stepped forward, apologizing nervously. "I'm sorry," she said.

Jesus smiled at her. "Your faith has made you well, daughter. Go in peace. You are free of your disease."

While they were speaking, one of Jairus's servants arrived. His face delivered the news well before he spoke. "She's gone, sir. I'm so sorry. Do not bother the teacher. She's gone."

Jesus said, "Jairus, I want you to look at me. I'm going to ask you to do something, okay? Do not be afraid, but believe in me."

Jesus told Peter, James, and John to come with him, and he told everyone else to let them pass and not to follow. The four of them followed Jairus the rest of the way to his home. They could tell they were getting close by the sounds of the family weeping.

Jesus said, "It's okay. The child is only sleeping."

The people scoffed at his apparent insensitivity. He asked everyone to let him through. Then he took Jairus and his wife, along with Peter, James, and John, into the child's bedroom. The little girl's parents followed Jesus into the saddest, most painful place in their entire world—the place where their daughter lay dead, a room whose walls were stained with the indelible memories of the child's laughter even as the stillness of death hung new in the air. It was at the same time a nursery and a tomb, and the longer they stood there, the deeper their hearts buried themselves in sorrow.

Jesus knelt beside the bed and took the little girl's hand in his and whispered, "Talitha, little one, wake up. Wake up, honey."

The little girl sat up as her parents fell to the ground. She walked over to her mother and father, and the three of them sat on the floor in an embrace that flooded their tomb with the light of joy.

Jesus told Jairus and his wife to keep what happened a secret. This would have to stay between the seven of them. People didn't have categories for resurrection. The community wouldn't know how to treat the girl if they knew what Jesus had done for her.

During those months in Capernaum, the sick, oppressed, and dying came from all over seeking Jesus' help. Each had a story to tell of the way he spoke healing into their lives. Peter's mother-in-law talked about how he took away the fever that nearly killed her. The previously tormented man who screamed at Jesus in Capernaum's synagogue told about how Jesus chased away his demons. The leper who lived outside his community because of a disease he'd done nothing to deserve tried to describe what it felt like when Jesus touched him to heal him. It had been so long since anyone had touched him. Who knew human contact could be so healing?

Such wonders had grown so numerous that people began to preface their stories about Jesus by asking, "Did you hear the one about . . . "

11

THE DEATH
OF JOHN

Mark 6:14-29; Luke 7:18-35

JOHN COULD ALWAYS TELL when Herod was coming to visit by the way the hardened guards would stiffen with fear at the sound of his footsteps. Though Herod had locked John away in the belly of his fortress, he believed John was a righteous man, and Herod took personal delight in these visits—a king and a prophet, a captor and his captive.

Herod's wife, on the other hand, wanted John dead for calling their incestuous marriage a sin against God. But she held no sway over her husband, and whenever the subject came up Herod became protective of his prisoner, partially out of his fear of God but mostly out of his fear of the people who loved John. John wasn't just popular; he had become a symbol of freedom for many in Israel— freedom from Roman rule won through the courage of resistance. Herod's rule was tenuous enough already. Giving his subjects further cause for moral indignation would only spell trouble for Antipas, and he knew it. So he kept John locked away in his prison, but in his mind he was keeping John safe.

Word of Jesus' ministry and teaching spread like a fire after John's arrest. Reports of what happened with the widow's son in Nain, Jairus's daughter in Capernaum, the nobleman's son at Cana, and the man by the pool of Bethesda in Jerusalem had captured the hearts of thousands. With these reports came the hope that the Messiah, who would deliver the people of Israel from the tyranny of Rome, had finally come.

Jesus' ministry wasn't solely one of deeds but also of words. He said, "I was sent for this very purpose—to proclaim the good news of the kingdom of God." The concept of the kingdom of God was a part of Israel's national memory. Their prophet Daniel had foretold that the God of heaven would set up a holy kingdom that would never be destroyed. Destruction, however, was mostly all the people of Israel had known since those words were first given. So to hear Jesus proclaim the arrival of the kingdom of God left many presuming (and hoping) that he was talking about the end of Roman rule in the Promised Land. But there were as many theories about Jesus as there were theorists.

Sitting in Herod Antipas's jail, John himself began to wonder about who Jesus was. He hadn't lost faith in his cousin, but his new life as one of the king's novelties clouded his perspective on the meaning and timing of his suffering.

John's disciples would come to visit him and tell him magnificent stories of Jesus' miracles and boldness. John took courage from the fact that the work begun by the two of them was continuing on. But to silence his doubts, John sent two of his disciples to ask Jesus this simple question: Are you the mighty one God promised would come, or should we be looking for someone else?

John's disciples found Jesus while he was healing the sick and performing other miraculous signs. When they had relayed John's question, Jesus said, "Go and tell John what you're seeing and hearing. The blind regain their sight. The lame walk, the deaf hear, the lepers are cleansed of their leprosy. Tell John the dead are being raised to life. Tell him the poor are hearing the good news of the kingdom of God."

Then turning to the crowd, Jesus said, "You who went out into the wilderness to be baptized by John, what did you see? Did you see a weak man, someone shaken like a reed in the wind? Did you see a rich man? No. You saw a prophet, and I tell you John is more than a prophet. He is the messenger of whom Malachi spoke—the one sent to prepare the way for the Messiah's coming. There has never been a man greater than John, yet he came to you in poverty as one of the least among you."

Jesus looked at his audience. "To whom did John come? To what shall I compare your generation? This generation is like a child who is afraid to be too happy or too sad. We played the flute, but you wouldn't sing. We sang a dirge, but you would not mourn. You don't want your hearts to be moved for fear of what it could cost you. When John came to you, sobered by his call to awaken hope in you, you called him a drunk. When he welcomed the sinful and destitute, you scoffed at him for being a friend of sinners. It may seem easier to numb yourselves against hope for fear that your hope will fail, but God will justify his prophet, and he will be proven true."

What John needed to know and what many feared to embrace was that the kingdom of God truly was at hand. Few could see it, not because they lacked evidence but because they were looking for something very different from what Jesus was showing.

Those who were waiting for Jesus to move on from his time with the sinful and destitute into a more political campaign would forever struggle to receive him as the one sent from God, because Jesus wasn't focused as much on the external problems of his people as he was the internal. He was the friend of sinners—of drunks, gluttons, prostitutes, tax collectors, and all manner of social outcasts. He dignified the lives of liars and adulterers, people who habitually hurt those closest to them, by tending to their moral wounds just as he tended to the lame and the blind. He accepted them, he ate with them, and he seemed to enjoy their company even as he told them to stop their patterns of destruction. The kingdom of God would not be imposed by force but by forgiveness, grace, love, and acceptance. This was the kingdom Jesus was building.

After John's disciples returned to tell him what Jesus had said, crowds continued to gather and Jesus continued to teach and heal the sick, blind, lame, and deaf because he had compassion on them.

After a while Jesus left Galilee to return to his hometown of Nazareth. On the Sabbath he went to teach in the synagogue, as was his custom. But his own people had grown jaded toward the wisdom and wonders he displayed. They whispered to one another, "Lofty words from the carpenter's son."

Knowing their whispers, Jesus sighed: "A prophet has no honor in his own hometown."

Their unbelief made his ministry unwelcome, so he limited his miracles there to only a few before he left. He knew that when he left Nazareth this time, he would never return. He had come to his own but his own did not receive him.

It was around this time when Jesus gathered his twelve disciples, the ones he had personally called to follow him. He said to them, "I'm sending you out to proclaim the kingdom of God to the lost sheep of Israel. I want you to go to your own people, and I want you to call your people to repentance. I want you to do what I have done. I want you to heal the sick, raise the dead, cast out demons, and cleanse the lepers. I want you to bless the homes of those who receive you and shake the dust off your feet when people turn you away.

"You are sheep among wolves, so be wise as serpents but harmless as doves. Be careful. People will reject you and even persecute you because of me. You'll be dragged before kings and rulers because of my message of a coming and present kingdom. When they drag you into court, don't worry about what you should say. God will speak through you.

"Friends, you will be hated on account of me. But don't be afraid of those who can kill the body but not the soul. God will take care of you as sure as he cares for the birds of the air. You are of far greater value to him than they. Whoever receives you receives me. And whoever receives me receives the one who sent me. This is holy work."

So twelve men—Simon Peter and his brother Andrew; James and John, the sons of Zebedee; Philip and Nathanael; Thomas the twin; Matthew the tax collector; James, the son of Alphaeus; Thaddaeus; Simon the Zealot; and Judas Iscariot—went out in pairs and did as Jesus had told them.

John continued to languish in the Machaerus prison, and Herodias continued to resent the way her new husband enjoyed John's company. On Herod's birthday Herodias threw a party at Machaerus. After their guests had eaten and drunk their fill, the music started and Herodias sent her young daughter in to dance for the inebriated king. Antipas couldn't take his eyes off the little girl as she twirled and swept across the floor.

When the music stopped, Antipas called for the child and said, "You have pleased me, young lady. Ask me for anything and I will give it to you. Anything you want."

Knowing this was a great honor, the girl withdrew to tell her mother what the king had said.

"For what should I ask?" she said.

Herodias whispered a single sentence into her daughter's ear. Perplexed, the girl looked at her mother as if to say, "Are you sure?" Herodias gave a firm nod.

The child stood quietly before the king until he noticed she had returned. To impress the girl and amuse his friends, the drunken king said with as much pomp as he could muster, "Well, my child. Have you made your decision? Name your price."

The girl said, "I want the head of John the Baptist on a platter." Such grotesque words to proceed from the lips of a child! But Herod found himself in a room full of people who needed to know, without question, that when he made a declaration, he would follow it to its end. In his heart he hated himself. He liked John, and he feared John for the way the prophet had captured the hearts of those he led.

Herod's captain caught Antipas's eye, as if to say, "Say the word, king. I'll tell the executioner."

Herod nodded, and before the party was over the tetrarch of Galilee and Perea had given the severed head of a beloved prophet to a child, who in turn gave the bloody silver platter to her mother who gave her husband a look that said, "I will not be scorned."

When John's disciples heard what had happened, they came to claim John's body. After they buried him, they went to find Jesus to tell him what happened. Though Jesus had endured some minor scrapes with various religious leaders throughout his travels, up to this point he had been mostly well-received wherever he went. Great crowds continued to follow and people continued to put their hope in him.

But with his rejection at Nazareth, and with John's execution, even Jesus' closest disciples were beginning to sense the changing of a season. Could someone usher in a new kingdom without having to overthrow the current one? Would John's fate eventually find them too?

PART 3

REJECTION

12

THE STORM TREADER

Matthew 14:22-33; Mark 6:45-56

J ESUS DID NOT FEAR Herod Antipas. He did, however, care about where he focused his time. So when he heard what happened to John, he withdrew in a boat to a secluded place beside the Sea of Galilee. Jesus knew that if there was any bloodlust left in Herod after staining his sword with John, it would soon be directed at him.

Jesus withdrew in the boat because the crowds were beginning to overwhelm him and his disciples. The crowds watched them out on the Sea of Galilee and followed their movement from the shore. As the people from the villages saw the crowd passing through, they asked what they were doing. When the villagers heard about the search for Jesus, they began to follow as well, and the crowd continued to grow on the waiting shores.

Jesus' disciples took their boat ashore at a desolate stretch of beach near the village of Bethsaida. Jesus stepped out of the boat into a sea of humanity—men and women who had brought their sick and troubled friends, hoping for healing. Jesus took compassion on them because they were like driftwood, like sheep without a shepherd—people who were supposed to be led well but had found themselves on their own, failed by their own spiritual elders. He stayed and healed all who came to him, and he taught them many things about the kingdom of God.

By evening, the crowd had swelled to around five thousand men plus their wives and children. Jesus' disciples said to him, "Listen. The day is getting late. Send these people into the neighboring villages for something to eat."

Jesus said, "Let's not send them away. Let's feed them ourselves." Then he said to Philip, who was from Bethsaida, "What do you think?"

Philip said, "Feed them with what? Even if we pulled together all our money and then some, we could come up with maybe two hundred denarii, which wouldn't even come close. And who could say if my little village even has that kind of supply on hand?"

Jesus said, "What do we have with us?"

After a quick inquiry of those nearby, Andrew said, "There is a boy here who has five barley cakes and two salted fish." The common seaside fare looked meager in the boy's basket. It appeared that on this night they would forego their meal.

But Jesus said, "Bring the boy's food to me and tell the people to take a seat on the grass."

He took the bread and fish in his hands, looked to heaven, and spoke a blessing. Then he broke it and gave it to his disciples and said, "Take this, all of you, and pass it out to these people. We are their hosts tonight."

The disciples did as Jesus instructed. To their amazement, everyone not only got something to eat, they all ate until they were satisfied.

Jesus then said, "Go gather up what's left. Let nothing be wasted here tonight. Make sure the surplus goes to feed any who need it."

The disciples then went through and gathered up twelve full baskets of broken pieces. When the people saw what Jesus had done, and the twelve baskets of leftover food, they said to each other, "Behold the King of glory! This is the promised one who is to come into this world."

Jesus and his disciples sensed that this crowd, as happy as they had been to receive Jesus there on the shore, was about to turn hostile. Their murmurs of wonder rose to a frenzied zeal to take Jesus and make him their king right then and there. They saw firsthand how this prophet ministered not only to their spiritual needs but also to their physical and material needs. Healing, teaching, and sustenance came from his hand, and all for their good.

They knew of other times when God had fed his people in desolate places. They had grown up on the stories of the manna God rained down from heaven during the days of Moses, and how God sent ravens to feed his prophet Elijah, and how Elisha fed over a hundred men with only twenty loaves of bread.

They understood these to be stories of God sustaining his people as he delivered them from tyranny and oppression. If Jesus was the coming king—the one who redeems and restores, the one who heals the broken, the one who feeds the hungry and provides for his people—they were prepared to forego the king's ceremonial triumphal entry into Jerusalem and hold his coronation right there on the shore beside the no-account village Bethsaida.

But Jesus held no desire to become their king. Not in this way. He would not be a king taken by force. He did not want to be the kind of king who would have to convince his people to praise him. He would be the kind of King who, when seen in all his glory, would leave the watching world with no other response but worship.

These people wanted him as their king because of the wonders he had performed. But they didn't really want him. They wanted more miracles. They wanted someone to step into their broken world and put it right. He knew these sheep without a shepherd were acting on impulse. They wanted to be led into freedom—something they only saw through the lenses of politics. They wanted their lives to be under the rule of a benevolent king who loved them—something they did not have.

But if Jesus were this benevolent king—the second Moses, Elijah come back from the dead—then he could lead them to freedom. To the crowd, it made perfect sense to crown him king on the spot. But to Jesus, their zeal carried a chilling familiarity. The devil himself had tempted Jesus before with this very offer—to have all the kingdoms of the world simply handed to him. And Jesus knew the tempter had promised to come back and try again.

Jesus gathered his disciples quickly and told them to get back into the boat and go on ahead of him. If they didn't remove themselves from this situation, this crowd might become a mob. Jesus began to pick his way through the crowd, greeting those he passed, working his way to the edge of the hills, where he disappeared down a trail and climbed up to a secluded place to pray as the crowd dispersed.

Jesus knew he stood at a crossroads with the people of Galilee. For a long time now, he had moved among them, healing and teaching them. And for the most part they had loved him and received him with great joy. But although they wanted more miracles, they were no longer content with wonders. They wanted to put him forth as their king. Though they were right to pick up on his kingly qualities, their desire to take him by force revealed that they did not truly know him. They only thought they did. Seeing this as a dangerous position for everyone present, Jesus withdrew.

That evening, well after dark, he came down to find that his disciples were a few miles out from shore, struggling against one of the Galilean Sea's sudden gales. They strained to cut through the gusts, but the waves tossed the boat like a toy.

Jesus walked to the water's edge and began to walk out into the water. Though the sea churned and the waves rose, he did not sink but miraculously walked on the surface of the sea. He made his way toward his disciples' boat with the intention of passing them by and meeting them on the other side of the lake.

But the disciples saw him approach. Actually, through the darkness and the swells, they saw a silhouetted figure walking on the water toward them. The figure wasn't just walking on the water, he tread upon the storm. Terrified, they clung to each other and cried out, "It's a ghost!"

The storm treader immediately called out to them: "Do not be afraid. It is I."

Peter moved to the edge of the boat, peering out into the darkness, looking for some telltale sign that this was Jesus. Peter cupped his hands around his mouth and called out, "Lord, if it is you, then call me out to where you are on the water."

Jesus said, "Come."

With the wind still blowing hard and the boat still rocking to its rhythms, Peter swung one leg over the side of the boat, then the other. When he set his weight down on his feet, he did not sink but managed to take a small step on the surface of the sea, and then another. Before he realized the impossibility of what was happening, he had made his way to within only a few feet of Jesus. The reality caught up to Peter when he turned his eyes from Jesus to the raging storms around him. His faith began to fail and he began to sink, which only panicked him more. "Lord, save me! I'm going to drown," Peter said, trying to reach for Jesus' hand.

Jesus took hold of Peter and kept him from sinking. He looked into his friend's fearful but exhilarated eyes and said, "Why did you fear, Peter? Where did your faith go?"

Jesus knew the quality of Peter's faith. He knew Peter was a man whose faith rose and fell and that it could turn on him quickly. But he also knew Peter was the only one who dared to step out of the boat in the first place.

When they got back to the boat and climbed aboard, the wind and the waves became as still as glass. The disciples felt an ever-increasing feeling of astonishment in Jesus' presence. Seeing him walk on water had come right on the heels of seeing him feed well over five thousand people with only a few loaves and fish. They worshiped him, regarding him as the Son of God. But they did not know what that meant beyond a basic comprehension that though he was one of them, he was not like them.

With these two wondrous signs back to back, the disciples were seeing more and more that Jesus was sovereign over everything in the entire world, and nothing about this was simple. Though he had to walk, he could walk on water. Though he got hungry and had to eat, he could create food from nothing. For every new category he added to his identity, he seemed to take others away. He was a man, but not just a man. He was a rabbi, but he connected to God in uncommon ways. Jesus stood fully in their world, but as sure as he sat there among them dripping in the boat, they did not stand fully in his. And this moved them to fear as much as it moved them to awe.

13

BREAD OF LIFE

Matthew 14:34–16:12; John 6:22–7:1

*T*HE PEOPLE OF BETHSAIDA knew Jesus didn't leave in his disciples' boat, and they also knew he hadn't boarded any others either. But when the morning came, search as they might, they could not find him. So they went looking for him, both on foot and by sea.

The men from Bethsaida who sailed west to Gennesaret were confused to learn Jesus had come ashore in the boat with his disciples that morning. It wasn't difficult to find him. Word spread quickly of his arrival, and people from all over the area began to bring him their sick. The hurting and oppressed begged for the opportunity to just touch the hem of his robe. Jesus obliged the crowds, and all who came to him were healed.

The men from Bethsaida found Jesus teaching in the synagogue. They asked him, "How did you get here?"

Jesus said, "What is that to you? You have come all this way because you want something from me. You are not here out of any true fear of the Lord. You are here because I fed you and you want me to do it again."

The people regarded him with a confused incredulity. Was it so wrong to want this man who could conjure bread from thin air to do it again? Was there some offense in wanting a king with unlimited resources to feed his own people in their hunger?

Jesus said, "Did the miracle awaken nothing in you? You want the food but not its source. You're content to come again and again for your daily bread, without which you would perish. But you do not see that I give you more than bread. I give you life."

They said, "We want this life. How do we get it?"

Jesus said, "Believe in the one God has sent to you."

They said, "Do you think we don't? We're here asking you to show us a sign. Moses gave our fathers bread from heaven. You gave us bread from somewhere unknown, and you have our attention. Can you do it again? Can you do it as Moses did every day?"

Jesus said, "You misunderstand. Moses didn't give your fathers bread in the wilderness. God did. And I'm telling you now that God gives you an even better bread from heaven. Though the manna came every day, it only lasted a day. Both it and your fathers perished. But the bread I give is not like that. It comes down from heaven and gives life to the world. Life forever."

The crowd answered, "Give us this bread. Give it to us every day."

Jesus said, "I am the bread of life, and whoever comes to me will never hunger, and whoever believes in me will never thirst."

The religious leaders began to grumble among themselves. They had known Jesus since he was a boy—Joseph and Mary's son. Did he think he was fooling them by claiming to have come from heaven?

Jesus, knowing their hearts, said, "I know you can't see me for who I am. No one can unless the Father who has sent me opens their eyes. But I am telling you the truth. I am the bread of life, and whoever believes in me has eternal life. I am the bread that comes from heaven, and once you eat of this bread, you will never die. The bread I offer the world is my own flesh."

The religious leaders shuddered. "How can this man dare to make such a claim? Does he mean to tell us that we are to eat his flesh?"

Rather than try to clarify this misconception, as they assumed he might, Jesus said, "Whoever feeds on my flesh and drinks of my blood has eternal life. I will raise him up on the last day because he abides in me and I in him. Just as I live by way of my Father's sustaining power, whoever feeds on me will live forever."

While any observer could see that Jesus' words were almost impossible for the people to grasp, what transpired in their hearts ran much deeper. His words scandalized them. The idea that they needed to eat his flesh and drink his blood hit them without nuance. Not only did it seem Jesus was calling for something akin to cannibalism, he was also claiming to be greater than Moses in the process. Moses, they believed, gave his people bread in the wilderness. But Jesus claimed to be the bread itself.

They loved him for the way he fed them. They loved the idea that there could exist a person who could create food from nothing, as God created the universe. But to claim to be the food itself—that they would have to feast not on what his hands had made but on the man himself—crossed a line. If he was referring to his actual flesh, his words were offensive. If he spoke figuratively, his metaphor was impenetrable. Still, Jesus persisted, and the more he did the more their hearts were hardened toward him.

Jesus said, "You think I speak in physical terms. Life comes from the Spirit. The flesh is no help at all. You need the Father to give you eyes to see, or else you never will."

Many of the people who heard Jesus call himself the bread of life turned away from following him any further. It angered Jesus' disciples to see people walking away from their Lord. They had seen so much over the past two years. They trusted him. But they also empathized greatly with those who came to the end of what they could comprehend of this rabbi from Nazareth. He was often hard to understand, and in those moments when he would explain himself in ways they could grasp, it was usually even harder to believe.

Sensing their frustration, Jesus asked, "What about you men? Will you leave now too?"

Peter, who often spoke for the group, said, "Lord, where would we go? You are the one who holds the key to eternal life. We believe in you. We believe you are the Holy One sent from God. We believe everything you just taught. Where else could we go?"

Peter was speaking to the ever-increasing reality that Jesus divided people. Those who needed healing risked hoping in him, but those who didn't were among the growing number who kept their distance. Ever since Jesus had healed the lame man by the pool of Bethesda in Jerusalem on the Sabbath, religious leaders from Jerusalem had been keeping tabs on Jesus' influence and teaching. They resented the way he claimed to be equal with God. This claim that Jesus was the bread of life only added to their consternation.

As for the disciples, Peter said it well when he said, "Where else could we go?" This was more than a declaration of fidelity in the face of opposition. It was the truth. For better or worse, the disciples had publicly associated themselves with Jesus. They did not have the luxury of simply going home. They had made their homes with him.

When Jesus' claim that he was the bread of life reached the religious leaders back in Jerusalem, they were more determined than ever to arrest him. So Jesus stayed away from Judea, preaching along the cities of the Galilean coast instead. Crowds continued to come to him for healing, and since he always accompanied his miracles with teachings on the kingdom of God, he continued to divide people.

As spring gave way to summer, Jesus withdrew from Galilee to the region of Phoenicia along the northern coast of the Mediterranean Sea. Jesus had not spent much of the previous two years outside of Israel. The Phoenician cities of Tyre and Sidon were mostly inhabited by Gentiles who, though they had heard of Jesus, did not presume he would do for them what he had done for his own. But even though Jesus was clear that his mission was to Israel first, as he led his disciples through Phoenicia, he healed their sick and cared for them just as he had done for his own nation. The Gentiles praised the God of Israel.

As summer gave way to autumn, Jesus took his time returning from the region of Phoenicia, passing through the Gentile inhabited lands of the Decapolis to the north of the Sea of Galilee. The crowds continued to seek him, but Jesus and his disciples continued to withdraw deeper into the northern hills.

Under the auspices of seeking a sign from Jesus that he was from God, Pharisees from Jerusalem came to him to test him. Knowing their motives, Jesus said, "You are an adulterous generation to demand a sign when you have seen so much already. No sign will be given except the sign of Jonah. Nineveh's sign wasn't seen in anything Jonah did in particular. The sign was simply that he had come. But in spite of all you have seen, you are blind."

The Pharisees were crafting a narrative that Jesus and his followers were a danger to Israel—men bent on starting a revolution grounded in blasphemous teaching, eager to stir the ire of Rome and undermine the sanctity of the temple. A year earlier the disciples might have brushed off the Pharisees' attempts due to Jesus' overwhelming popularity, but now their Lord seemed to create as much division as inspiration. And Jesus was seeking more solitude than ever in recent months.

Jesus' disciples felt threatened by the persistence and the reach of the Pharisees. Jesus told them that what they needed to watch out for was the Pharisees' influence. A little of their leaven could inflate many things in the eyes of those they led. If they wanted to spin an epic tale about the dangers of Jesus and his followers, no one would be able to stop them.

As for Jesus, he seemed not the least inclined to defend himself. He offered himself not merely as the one who could show the way to God but as the one through whom men must pass to find God. He had not come to point the way. He had come to be the way and to oppose all others. This was a hard teaching—hard to understand and harder still to accept.

14

YOU ARE
THE CHRIST

Luke 9:18-36

*E*VERYONE IN ISRAEL had expectations concerning the coming
Messiah. He would deliver them from Rome and restore the
kingdom David founded. He would be a little more like David than
David himself.

The disciples came into their relationship with Jesus influenced
by these common ideas. But over time, though they may not have
been able to pin it on one particular moment or teaching, their
perspective had begun to transform into something new. During
their time in the Gentile lands north of Galilee, they saw how the
crowds continued to come to Jesus, and they heard how people
talked about him—how they hoped in him.

Needing solitude from the crowds, Jesus led his disciples
deeper into the hills toward Mount Hermon near the source of
the Jordan River. On their way, near the village of Caesarea

Philippi, twenty-five miles north of the Sea of Galilee, Jesus took
his disciples aside to pray privately.

While they were there, he asked them, "Who do people say I am?"

The disciples began to tell him what they'd heard. Some said he
was John the Baptist back from the dead. Others said Elijah, or
Jeremiah, or one of the prophets.

Jesus said, "What about you? Who do you say that I am?"

They looked at each other for a moment before Peter spoke on
their behalf: "You are the Christ, the Son of the living God—God's
appointed leader to deliver Israel."

Jesus regarded his friends. These men had seen so much. The
past months had been difficult. Many in the crowds who had followed out of such fascination reached a point where they could no
longer tolerate the strength of Jesus' words, and they left. But the
Twelve remained because, as Peter said, where else could they go?

Jesus said, "Simon, son of Jonah, blessed are you. No man has
revealed this to you, but my Father who is in heaven. And I tell
you that you are now Peter the Rock—and on you and your confession I will build my church. And the gates of hell itself will not
be able to prevail against it." The disciples stood in silent disbelief at Jesus' words. As the Lord had done with Abraham, the
father of nations, so many generations before, Jesus was now
renaming Peter, not according to who he was but according to
who he would become.

Jesus continued, "Peter, listen to me. I will give you the keys to
the kingdom of heaven. What you loose on earth will be loosed in
heaven, and what you bind on earth will be bound in heaven."

Though the disciples' view of Jesus' identity was more developed
than that of others around them, it was by no means complete. So
Jesus warned them not to tell anyone he was the Christ. People

would not understand what they meant, and they would struggle
to explain themselves if pressed.

This marked the clearest language Jesus had used to describe
himself up to this point. For all the focus on the exaltation of the
Messiah the disciples imagined, the man before them endured an
unexpected measure of humiliation and rejection. The fact that they
themselves did not see this as a contradiction revealed that their
understanding of the Messiah was evolving.

But this change in thinking would not be enough to prepare
them for what Jesus said next. He began to tell them that the Son
of Man would have to suffer many things and be rejected by the
leaders of his own people—the elders, the chief priests, and the
scribes—and be killed, and after three days in the grave, he would
rise from the dead. All this he told them in plain language.

Peter, again presuming to speak on behalf of the others, took
Jesus aside and began to rebuke him. "Lord, you need to stop
talking like this. May these things never be so."

Before Peter could finish his sentence, he knew he had crossed
a line.

The anger on Jesus' face was clear enough for everyone to see.

Jesus said, "Get behind me, Satan. You stand in my way. Peter,
your mind is stuck in the ways of man, not in the ways of God."

Though Peter could not understand what provoked the strength
of Jesus' response, he later came to realize just how satanic his
rebuke of Jesus had been. While he believed his was the voice of
reason, he did not recognize that he was trying to persuade Jesus to
do the very same thing the devil himself had tempted Jesus to do—
to obtain a kingdom without passing under the sword of suffering.

Jesus joined glory and suffering together. The Messiah's path
would lead to glory through affliction. His disciples needed to

recognize that this wasn't only true for Jesus but for them as well, if they were to follow. Jesus said, "Listen to me. If you want to follow me, you must deny yourselves, take up your crosses daily, and then come after me. Whoever wants to keep his life will lose it, but whoever loses his life for my sake will save it."

He continued, "What good does it do a person to gain the whole world and yet lose his very soul?"

Throughout their years together, Jesus spoke to this point: a life of accumulation does not yield the security it promises. In fact, it will cost a man everything in the end. If anyone wants a life that is true, the only true way to live is loyal to God. He taught the disciples to hold this world with an open hand and to be ready to let it all go. A man cannot protect what he cannot keep, and he cannot obtain through his own efforts what only God can give.

Jesus was talking about his own future, and he was talking about his disciples' too. Their glory would be joined to suffering—eternal pleasures arrived at by way of a cross. The defining quality of their lives as his followers would have to become humility, not self-confidence. They would have to empty themselves and accept a life of service, placing their hope not in the praises of man in this world but in the acceptance of God in the world to come. They would have to lose their lives if they were to find them.

It has always been hard for a man to conceive of a world beyond the one he knows. The disciples tried to envision the glory Christ told them was coming, but they were constrained by the limits of their imaginations, and they knew it.

One week later, Jesus led Peter, James, and John up onto a high place on Mount Hermon. Peter, James, and John lay down to sleep while

Jesus prayed. Peter woke to a bright light coming from where Jesus had been praying. Squinting through the brilliance, Peter saw that Jesus was glowing as bright as a flash of lightning and that his face shone like the sun. Searching for its source, Peter realized the light wasn't radiating upon Jesus but coming out from him. Jesus wore the glory without fear or confusion, as though it were a familiar robe he had worn many times before and fully intended to wear again.

As Peter's eyes adjusted, he saw two other men standing with Jesus. The three men were talking. As he listened he realized, to his terror, that these men must be Moses and Elijah. The three men enveloped in light spoke of Jesus' impending departure in Jerusalem. Jesus spoke of his suffering, death, and resurrection with these two men, whose own departures from this world were shrouded in mystery. Elijah had been taken up and out of this world in a chariot of fire with the promise that he would one day return, and Moses had been buried by the hands of God himself on Mount Nebo in a place no man could ever find.

Soon James and John stood beside Peter, silently trying to make sense of the scene. As the conversation ended, Peter, not knowing exactly what to say, said, "It is good for us to be here. Let us memorialize this meeting by setting up three tents in this place."

But as he was speaking, something the disciples would later describe as a cloud of light enveloped them all, and a voice from inside the cloud spoke: "This is my Son, whom I love, and with whom I am well pleased. Listen to him."

Peter stopped talking, and the three disciples fell on their faces in fear. The cloud of light vanished, and Jesus touched his friends on their shoulders and said, "Get up. Do not be afraid."

They looked around to see that only Jesus remained. He told them not to tell anyone about what they had seen.

The disciples struggled to know how to respond. They had seen with their own eyes Moses and Elijah come to meet with Jesus. They had seen that Jesus was elevated over them—that he not only reflected the light of God's glory but that it radiated from him. They had heard the voice of God speak to them from a cloud of light, telling them that Jesus was his Son and that they were to listen to him. Couldn't they now tell the world what they had seen? Wouldn't the world want to embrace him as they did?

They asked Jesus, "What are we waiting for? Is it that the Scriptures say Elijah must come first?"

Jesus said, "Friends, Elijah has already come, and the world did not recognize him. Instead, they killed him. If they did not recognize him, they will not recognize me either. As it went for the second Elijah, the Son of Man will also suffer many things at the hands of men."

How quickly their world went from ordinary to glorious and then back to ordinary again. And how quickly they themselves would follow suit. Though they had seen something no man had ever seen before—this celestial clandestine meeting on the mountain between the representative of the law, the representative of the prophets, and the one called the Son of God by God himself— they would not carry the glory or the wonder of this meeting into anyone else's lives. No one would believe them even if they tried.

15

BEFORE
ABRAHAM
WAS BORN

John 7–8

WHEN JESUS AND HIS DISCIPLES came down from the
mountain, he continued to proclaim to Galilee the coming
kingdom of God. As the crowds continued to gather, Jesus pulled
his disciples aside and said, "Listen to me. I want you to let this sink
into your hearts. Soon I will be delivered into the hands of men."

His disciples still did not understand what he meant when he
spoke of his death, but they were afraid to ask for clarification. They
sensed a looming change on the horizon—that a dangerous tide
was soon to break. And though they were not able to take Jesus'
words much beyond that point, they knew that if trouble lay anywhere, it lay in Jerusalem.

When the Feasts of Booths drew near, six months before Passover,
Jesus' brothers said to him, "Why don't you take your disciples into
Jerusalem so that everyone can see your mighty works in the city

of the Lord? If you are the coming King, then come out of the shadows. Show yourself to the world."

Jesus knew his brothers did not accept him as the Messiah. The world they grew up in expected the Christ of God to be a mighty leader—someone who would deliver his people from tyranny. Up to this point, Jesus shared no brotherhood with men of influence or power but rather chose to invest himself in the sick, the poor, and the outcast. And as much as this attracted people to him, it also challenged the idea that he was the King of glory who was to come.

Jesus told his brothers, "You go on without me."

Soon after they left, he prepared to make the journey in secret. He walked the streets of Capernaum, remembering the past couple of years teaching in its synagogue, ministering to people on its shores, sharing meals in its citizens' homes. He knew that when he left Galilee this time, he would not come back. He set his face toward Jerusalem because he knew his time had come to fulfill the suffering and death for which he had begun preparing his disciples.

Meanwhile in Jerusalem, members of the Sanhedrin, Israel's highest court—made up of seventy-one men from among the chief priests, scribes, and elders of the people—watched for his arrival. Galilee, which was under Herod Antipas's rule, was beyond their jurisdiction. As long as Jesus lay beyond their legal reach, they knew they could not arrest him. But if he came into the city for this festival, they hoped to lay a trap for him.

People other than the Sanhedrin also wondered if Jesus would come; his fame had become a topic of fascination. By this point, though most people had never seen one of his miracles, they all seemed to know someone who had. The crowds were divided. Some esteemed him as a holy man, while others regarded him as a possible devil—an impostor claiming to be from God but secretly seeking to lead Israel astray. He was a polarizing figure.

Halfway through the festival Jesus entered the city and went to the temple to teach. As the people listened, they were amazed at his authority and mastery of Scripture. Most teachers with that sort of ability were associated with one of the great rabbinical leaders of the day. But no one could say who had taught Jesus—only that he handled Scripture with uncommon wisdom and depth.

One member of the Sanhedrin pressed him: "How did you come by this command of Scripture? Did you teach yourself? Are you without a school of accountability?"

Jesus said, "My teaching is not, as you presume, my own. I learned from the one who sent me. If anyone knows the Father, he knows my teaching comes from him. To know the truth of God is not a mere matter of intellect but a matter of the heart. You have the law of Moses, and you claim to love that law. But you don't keep it, because even now all you want is to have me killed. Why do you seek to kill me?"

The members of the Sanhedrin were taken aback. They knew as well as he that they were not seeking an honest discussion. Jesus wanted to pick up what they started earlier when he healed the lame man by the pool of Bethesda. The last time they confronted Jesus, it was because he had healed that man on the Sabbath. When they said this miracle was a violation of God's law, Jesus told them he knew the law of God better than they because God was his Father, adding that Moses himself was a witness against their misapplication of God's Word.

And here he was doing it again.

They said, "How are we breaking the law of Moses, and who is trying to kill you?"

Jesus said, "The last time I was with you, I performed a miracle and you were all amazed. But you were also indignant that I would do such a thing on the Sabbath. If God, in his law, permits circumcision on the Sabbath—the removal of a part of a man—then do you think he would not also permit something that might make a man whole? You use the law of God to justify yourselves, while I use it to justify healing for the broken. Judge for yourselves which is more righteous."

Some who were watching this confrontation said to each other, "Is this not the man from Galilee they were seeking to kill? How is it that he stands before them not only as a free man, but as one who speaks his mind so openly without retribution? Are they beginning to accept that he might, in fact, be the Messiah?"

No one ever imagined the Messiah would come from among them. They assumed he would emerge from some unknown, celestial origin, and be instantly recognizable to all.

Hearing them, Jesus called out so that everyone around him could hear. "You think you know me. You think you know where I'm from. But you don't. I do not come from Galilee or Nazareth. I come from the Father. And I am not here on my own accord. I am sent from God, and my purpose is to carry out his will."

Many members of the high court seethed with anger. They wanted to force Jesus to recant two claims he had made after he healed the man by the pool of Bethesda—that he knew the law of Moses better than they and that he shared a connection with the Father they did not. Now he stood before them again, making the same two claims with unapologetic conviction. So they sent temple officers to arrest him.

When the officers returned without their subject in custody, the members of the Sanhedrin demanded, "Why didn't you arrest him?"

The officers looked at each other nervously and said, "We've never heard anyone speak as he does. Never."

Whatever Jesus had said to them left such an impression that they could not carry out their mission but would rather endure the anger and recompense of their commanders.

Members of the Sanhedrin said, "Have you been drawn in by his words too? We expect those outside the temple authority to lack the discipline to resist his teaching. But you? Your duty is to carry out orders, not to judge them for yourselves."

Nicodemus, who had visited Jesus earlier under cover of darkness, heard the officers' testimony and the Sanhedrin's rebuke. As a member of the Sanhedrin himself, he wrestled in his heart. Early on he was drawn in by Jesus' teaching, and no one had yet drawn him back out. He listened to his brothers' eagerness to condemn Jesus. He remembered how Jesus said his mission was hidden from those who claimed to be wise. He considered how God's pattern seemed to use the weak to shame the powerful. But he also knew that while he was a member of this court, he held a minority position when it came to the man from Galilee, and this required great care.

Caution notwithstanding, Nicodemus wanted to slow the proceedings if he could. He said to the court, "Our law says we may not pass judgment on a man without hearing him first. Can we condemn this man without a hearing?"

His fellow court members were incredulous. "Are you from Galilee too? Who is he to you?"

Meanwhile, Jesus continued teaching about himself and the coming kingdom of God. He did not back away from the issues that angered the Sanhedrin. Rather, he continued to defend his authority. He continued to display his mastery of Scripture, to laud his connection with the Father, and to espouse his view that the religious authorities were leading God's people astray.

The temple authorities accused Jesus of being possessed by a demon. Jesus said, "I am not possessed. Everything I say honors my Father, though everything you say is meant to dishonor me. You seek glory for yourselves while I seek glory for God. Those who hold on to my words will never taste death."

The Sanhedrin said, "Now we know you are of the devil. How can you claim to have the words of life? Abraham is dead. Are you greater than he? The same goes for the prophets. Who do you think you are?"

Jesus said, "You do not know God. I do. And I keep his word. Abraham himself looked forward to my coming, and when he saw it, he rejoiced."

The members of the court struggled to bend their minds around the impossibility of Jesus' claim. They said, "You are not even fifty years old, and yet you claim to know Abraham?"

Jesus looked at his detractors with an expression that bade them to listen carefully. "Before Abraham was born, I am."

To use the name of God himself in this absurd claim of eternal existence was more than they could bear. They picked up stones so they could kill him on the spot, but Jesus quickly withdrew into the crowds and made his way out of the city.

PART 4

JERUSALEM

16

BORN BLIND

John 9–10

WHEN JESUS LEFT THE TEMPLE, he and his disciples passed a man beside the road who had been blind since birth. Jesus' disciples asked, "Teacher, was it this man's sin that caused his blindness, or his parents'?"

This was a prevailing presumption of the times—that affliction was somehow connected to sin, and that the more obvious the affliction, the more acute the transgression. This assumption was born partly out of a simple-minded need to understand why people suffered, but also out of an innate human suspicion that there was always more going on in a person's suffering than met the eye.

Jesus said, "This is neither his fault nor his parents'. This man is blind so that the glory of God might be put on display through him. Men, we are right now in the middle of the light of day, and as long as there is light we must do the work of he who sent me. Night is coming, when no one can work. But as long as I am in the world, there is light because I am the light of the world."

The disciples recognized an increasing urgency in Jesus. Not only did he seem more focused on fulfilling his mission in this world, but he also called his disciples to share in this work with an increasing clarity of call. The disciples knew that when Jesus started to speak in spiritual metaphor, he was likely about to do something the world had never seen before.

Jesus knelt down and spat on the ground and made mud with his saliva. Then he pressed the mud onto the blind man's eyes and told him to go to the pool of Siloam to wash. The act was an echo of creation, when man was formed from the dust of the earth by the finger of God. Only in this case, the man was already mostly formed, but broken—making Jesus' touch more an act of restoration than creation.

The blind man went to the pool of Siloam as instructed, and he came up out of the water seeing for the first time in his life. The man who claimed to be the light of the world had opened the eyes of a man born into total darkness, restoring him to the condition he was meant to know but hadn't.

Not having seen Jesus, the man did not know who to look for to thank. And while he could have asked, the newness of this miracle so preoccupied his thoughts that all he could do was marvel at the world unfolding before him.

Some of his neighbors recognized him but doubted their own eyes. They never saw life behind this man's eyes. To see it now made him look familiar, but different enough that they questioned whether this was the man they knew.

"Is that not the man who used to sit here and beg?" some asked. But others said, "It can't be. The beggar was blind. This man only looks like him."

The man born blind said, "No. I am the man you knew. It's me." But his neighbors still doubted him. "If you are the beggar we know, how is it that you can suddenly see?"

The seeing man said, "The man from Nazareth they call Jesus made mud with his spit and anointed my eyes and told me to go wash in the pool of Siloam. So I did, and when I came up out of that water, I could see."

For a man who had never seen before, the simple act of looking at the world around him was marked by a wonder and joy that made something in his neighbors' hearts ache, though they could not articulate what exactly stirred within. To see the world with new eyes, to be struck by the splendor of the infinite depth of the blue sky for the first time, to have so great a veil of darkness lifted and the splendor of creation unleashed on his senses aroused an elusive jealousy in the hearts of those around him who, though they saw the same things, no longer saw their excellence.

Some men from the crowd asked, "Where is this Jesus?"

They didn't just want to know. They needed to know. A miracle draws attention to the wonder for only so long before yielding to an even deeper fascination with the one through whom it was performed. The work eventually points back to the worker.

"I don't know," the man answered.

So some of the men from the crowd took the man to the Pharisees and told them what had happened. They were irritated with this man, and soon he understood why. They were upset that Jesus had performed this miracle on the Sabbath—a frustration Jesus was accustomed to, but one that baffled the man born blind.

The Pharisees asked the man what had happened, and he told them the same story he told his neighbors: "He put mud on my eyes. I washed in the pool of Siloam, and now I can see."

Before he could finish he saw, for the first time in his life, expressions of displeasure. Some of the Pharisees waved off his story, saying, "No man of God would dare treat the Sabbath this way."

But others could not dismiss the evidence standing right in front of them. They argued, "How could a sinner perform such a wonder?"

They asked the man born blind what he thought of the one who healed him.

He said, "The man is a prophet from God."

Still, several of the religious leaders doubted the man's story. Maybe he was lying about his blindness, they thought. So they sent for the man's parents and asked them if this was their son and if he was, in fact, born blind.

The man's parents shifted uncomfortably. They knew that these leaders had cast Jesus out of the synagogue, and they did not want to suffer the same fate. And as happy as they were for the gift Jesus had given their son, they did not want to appear too sympathetic to the teacher from Galilee, so they gave an honest, but measured reply: "He is our son, and he was born blind. We do not know how it is that he can suddenly see or who opened his eyes. But the man is of age. He can speak for himself. Ask him if you really want to know."

So for a second time they asked the man born blind to tell his story. They warned him to recognize that what he said could either bring glory to God or shame on his own family.

"We know, without question, that the man you claim healed you is a sinner," they said. "So tell us your story again. Think carefully about what you want to say."

The man said, "I do not know if the man is a sinner or not. All I know is that when this day began, I was blind. I had been since the day I was born. But now I can see."

"But how?" they demanded.

He said, "Why do you keep asking me that? I already told you how, but you won't listen. What is going on here? Do you wish to become his disciples too?"

His exasperation only added to their anger. "You may be this man's disciple," they said, "but we are disciples of Moses, the giver of the law of God. We know with certainty that God spoke to Moses. As for this man you claim as your healer, we know nothing about him."

Their attempt to shame the seeing man only strengthened his tenacity. He said, "Really? This is amazing. A healer has come and you don't know where from? You know he opened my eyes, and yet you insist God doesn't listen to sinners. This man has done something this world has never known—he has given sight to the blind. If he were not from God, could he have done that? If he really is the sinner you claim him to be, why would God have listened to his prayer and opened my eyes?"

This was more than the religious leaders were willing to take. They told the man, "Do you who were born into the darkness of someone's utter sin dare now to lecture us about the things of God?"

Then they ordered their officials to throw the man out of their presence, with a warning to stay away.

When Jesus heard that the man had been cast out of the synagogue, just as he had been, he asked around for the man until he found him.

The man born blind saw his healer for the first time. Jesus said, "Do you believe in the Son of Man?"

Finding himself in a place where belief came easy, the man said, "Explain this to me. Tell me who the Son of Man is and I will believe."

Jesus said, "It is the one to whom you speak. Blind man, you have seen him."

Joy swept over the man as his eyes filled with tears. "My Lord, I believe," he said, as he bowed before Jesus and worshiped him.

Jesus said, "I have come into this world for this very thing—to open the eyes that are blind and to call attention to the blind who claim to see. They have chosen their blindness by refusing to see me with honest eyes."

Some of the Pharisees nearby who heard Jesus say this protested, "Are you saying we are blind to the things of God?"

Jesus said, "If you were blind, without any knowledge of the truth of God, you would have no guilt. But instead you claim to see things you do not. You claim to understand things beyond your comprehension and then presume to lead others in your assumed wisdom. This is what makes you guilty."

After this Jesus stayed in Jerusalem until the end of the Feast of Dedication. People continued to come to him—some for healing or teaching, others to try to discredit him publicly. Toward the end of the feast, a group of religious leaders gathered around him and said, "For how long will you keep us in suspense? Tell us plainly. Are you the Christ or not?"

Jesus said, "I have told you. And I have shown you. But you refuse to believe. Everything I do in my Father's name bears witness to who I am, but you are not part of my flock. You want no part of me. Those who do—my sheep—hear my voice and follow me. I give them life, and no one will ever snatch them out of the Father's hand because I and the Father are one."

This was a claim to deity, and everyone knew it. Some of the religious leaders there were so enraged that Jesus would say such a thing that they picked up stones with the intent to kill him. Jesus threw up his hands. "I come to you and show you only good works! For which of these good works are you going to kill me?"

They said, "We will kill you for your blasphemy because though you are only a man, you claim to be one with God. In fact, you make yourself God."

Jesus said, "If I make the claim but have no works to support it, then dismiss me. But if I follow my claim with miracles, even if you dislike me, do not be blind. Believe the works you have seen with your own eyes. Understand that I am in the Father and the Father is in me."

This only angered them more, so Jesus slipped away and led his disciples out of the city and far across the Judean wilderness to the place beyond the Jordan where John once baptized.

17

THE GOOD SAMARITAN

Luke 10:1-37

WHEN JESUS LEFT JERUSALEM, the crowds that followed him included many spectators who saw Jesus as a mere curiosity. But those who were willing to give themselves to his spiritual leadership grew in number and in resolve.

Jesus chose seventy-two of his most devoted followers and sent them on ahead of him into the villages and towns he was about to enter. He told them to tell the people about him and about how the kingdom of heaven was coming with him. He told these followers that the work would be difficult and not without its share of danger. It would require singleness of mind. They would have to set aside their own desires for comfort and rest and follow wherever the message of Jesus took them. Those he sent bore no exceptional qualities save for their devotion, and even that was untested. They were all new to following Jesus and childlike in their faith. Still they went out as he instructed, speaking about the coming kingdom. Following Jesus, they learned, led to a life of proclamation. They were not only learners but also teachers. Followers and leaders. Hearers and heralds.

When they returned to Jesus, they were astonished by what they had seen and done. Whatever they had expected to see happen was eclipsed by what actually transpired. Their message seemed to lodge itself in the hearts of perfect strangers. People were healed when they touched them. Creation itself seemed to yield to their message, and even demons fled when they spoke in the name of Jesus.

They were confounded by the power that flowed through them. They caught a glimpse of what Moses, David, Jonah, and the prophets knew so well—that this power was not their own.

Jesus told them, "I saw Satan fall like lightning from heaven. You have tasted the power of my authority. But don't let the fact that evil spirits yield to you be the thing that brings you joy. Rejoice in knowing that your names are written in the Book of Life."

As much as God had done through them, their real joy would be found in what he was doing in them. Proclaiming Jesus is not a thing a man does; it is the thing a man is. What they did, the stories they told, the catastrophes they stepped into, and the prayers they dared to pray in the hope that everything would be put right flowed out of the power and authority of the man from Nazareth.

Jesus prayed, "I thank you, Father, Lord of heaven and earth, that you conceal your will from the learned and wise but reveal it to those with the faith of children. This is your gracious desire—for your people to know you not as a scholar knows his subject but as children know their father."

Jesus took his twelve disciples aside and told them, "Blessed are your eyes for what they have seen. Listen to me. Prophets and kings have gone to their graves longing to look upon the wonders you have beheld, wishing they could have heard the things you've heard." These men belonged to a new era—that of a kingdom come.

While the newness Jesus brought awakened hope in many, it aroused the suspicions of the religious leaders even more. Under the guise of dinners in his honor or chance encounters along the road, they provoked him to speak about all things sacred and sensitive, hoping to trap him in some inescapable blasphemy they could use to arrest him.

Around then Jesus decided it was time for him and his disciples to make their way back to Jerusalem. As they traveled, one of the teachers of the law came to test him.

The teacher asked, "What shall I do to inherit eternal life?"

Knowing the man's motives, Jesus replied with a question of his own. "What is written in the law?"

Though the teacher of the law did not know it, Jesus had a trap of his own. Jesus knew the answer would be effortless for the teacher, and he knew the answer would be correct, because the religious leaders of the day had rightly distilled the entire law of God down into two basic principles—a love for God and a love for humankind. But Jesus also knew that the lawyer's answer would betray the fact that to him the law of God held no color, no life, no power. It was a subject to study with statutes to be employed, not something to love itself.

The lawyer said, "Love the Lord with all your heart, soul, mind, and strength, and love your neighbor as you love yourself."

Jesus studied the man for a moment before saying, "That's right. Do that and you will live."

Jesus wanted the teacher to see that being an expert in the law of God did not tame the law of God one bit. Jesus wanted the lawyer to be moved by his own correct answer. He wanted this command to love God with every fiber of his being to awaken humility in the teacher's heart—an honest recognition that while his doctrine was precise, his heart was far from his Lord.

But from the teacher of the law's perspective, he felt justified. Had he loved God with every fiber of his being? He had given himself to a life of careful study of God's statutes. Surely therein lay his proof. Had he loved his neighbor? He had given his professional life to serving his countrymen, Israel. Was it not loving to impart his expertise to them in matters of faith and practice?

To justify himself even more, the teacher of the law asked Jesus, "And who is my neighbor?"

But instead of giving the expected answer, "All the children of Israel," Jesus sat down to tell a story.

The Pass of Blood, the desolate route following the Wadi Qilt from Jerusalem to Jericho, was notorious for the crimes committed there in the crags and nooks of its desert walls. Everyone in the area knew it as the place where robbers lay with impunity, waiting to steal, kill, and destroy anyone foolish enough to pass alone.

One day, Jesus told them, a certain man was going down from Jerusalem to Jericho when he found himself surrounded by robbers who beat him, took everything he had, and left him for dead.

As he lay there, clinging to life, a priest passed by. When the priest saw the man, rather than helping him, he moved to the other side of the road. Though people might have expected compassion from a priest, the beaten man found none. Not too far behind the priest came a Levite. Levites were an upper-class clan among the Israelites. Theirs was a life of honor and privilege. The Levite, too, ignored the dying man.

Jesus did not explain why these spiritual leaders passed by the beaten man, just that they did. At this point, since the priest and the Levite were clearly foils in the story, the only person left for the teacher to relate to was the man lying beaten in the road. Unless someone else came along, picked him up, carried him out of his mortal peril, bound up his wounds, and covered the cost of his healing, the man lying in the road would perish. There had to be another coming. Before Jesus could finish the story, the teacher of the law already knew the neighbor would be the man who would do these things.

Jesus played to the irony of the moment. The teacher of the law was attempting to justify his love for his neighbor while he was fully engaged in the process of trying to publicly humiliate Jesus, who was not only a fellow Israelite but one who shared his very profession.

Then Jesus sprung his trap. A Samaritan came along, he told the crowd. This man, they all knew, had good reason to pass by without helping. Seven hundred years earlier, the northern kingdom of Israel had been carried off into exile by the Assyrians. During that period of exile, many of those Israelites intermarried with their captors. After the exile, they returned to their Promised Land as a mixed race who became known as Samaritans. To the southern kingdom of Israelites, who endured an exile of their own but had not intermarried, the Samaritans had done the unthinkable—they had defiled the bloodline of Abraham. To many, Samaritans were worse than full-blooded Gentiles—they were half Gentile, half Israelite, and this by choice.

For the Samaritans' part, there was no love lost. They could be just as disrespectful and indignant toward the Jews as the Jews were to them. They lived in a nationalistic world; individuals represented the nations from which they had come. It did not matter if a particular

Samaritan had wronged a particular Israelite. One Samaritan represented all Samaria, and one Jew all Israel. So it was to great dramatic effect that the Samaritan was the one who stopped to help the man dying in his path. He not only stopped to help; he changed his course to make sure the man would be cared for at that moment, and also in the days and weeks to come, so long as he was still mending.

The Samaritan took the dying man on as his own burden. Eventually he would go on about his business, but not before providing for this man and promising to return to look in on him later to settle any outstanding debts. What a humbling moment that must have been for both when the Samaritan lifted the bloodied, half-dead Israelite onto his own horse.

Jesus asked the teacher of the law, "Which of those three proved to be a neighbor to the dying man?"

The teacher, unable to say the word *Samaritan*, answered, "The one who showed mercy."

It was the act of compassion that answered the teacher's question; beyond race, beyond class, beyond religion, your neighbor is anyone in your path.

Jesus said, "You go and do the same."

The lesson Jesus taught this teacher of the law belonged to the same truth his disciples struggled to understand when they saw God do mighty works through their hands in Jesus' name: God's power, his presence, and his love are inseparable. Theological knowledge without love is nothing but a clanging cymbal. And offers of his love that are not grounded in the truth of who he is lead nowhere. Though they may try, human beings will never isolate the power of God as an impersonal force to be wielded by their own will. To know God is to love him, to yield to his commands, and to delight in his law. This cannot be done without loving others in reply.

When such love is present, the mercy and grace that flows from the heart of God through the hands and feet of his people—those hearers and heralds—is as offensive as it is astonishing.

18

THE LEAVEN OF THE PHARISEES

Luke 11:29–13:35

M ARY AND MARTHA CRIED OUT with joy when they saw his familiar frame darken their doorway. For several years now Mary, Martha, and their brother Lazarus had opened their home to Jesus whenever he came to town. They lived across the Kidron Valley in Bethany, east of Jerusalem. Though many of Jesus' followers regarded him as someone to revere, Mary, Martha, and Lazarus counted him as a friend. He regarded them in the same way and was just as happy to stay with them as they were to have him.

They enjoyed the kind of friendship where they were known not only by the stories they told but by their idiosyncrasies, joys, fears, and vexations. Martha was a doer with a heart for hospitality—sometimes to a fault. But she would go beyond the call of duty to make her friends feel welcome. Mary, on the other hand, loved to linger in conversation. Tears came easily for her, as did an uncommonly open-handed generosity of spirit. Lazarus was a fast friend—loyal, easy to be around, and just as easy to love. He was to Jesus, as the poet-king described long ago, one of the excellent ones in whom was all his delight. As long as Jesus wished to stay, their home was an oasis of comfort and refuge from the pressing crowds.

One morning, as a crowd gathered around Jesus, he began to teach them, saying, "This generation is wicked. They want to see signs so they might wonder at the sign, but not the one who performs it. No sign will be given to this generation except the sign of Jonah. Even when the Son of Man spends three days in the belly of the whale, it will not be enough to soften the hearts of this generation, let alone draw them to repentance. The people of Nineveh will rise to condemn this generation. They repented when Jonah preached, just as the queen of Sheba worshiped God when she saw Solomon's splendor. Yet a splendor greater than Solomon's has come bearing a message greater than Jonah's."

Jesus continued, "A light is shining. It is not a light hidden under a basket but is on a stand for all to see. What does this say about your eyes if you cannot see it? What you accept as light is not light but darkness, so you cannot see me. You need to care about this. Be on your guard against spiritual blindness and hardness of heart."

While he was speaking, a Pharisee asked Jesus to join him for lunch. Jesus accepted the invitation and followed the Pharisee home. When Jesus did not follow the ceremonial custom of washing before the meal, the teacher of the law could not mask his surprise.

Jesus said, "Do you take offense at what you perceive concerning my spirituality? You Pharisees clean the outside of the cup while inside you are full of all manner of greed and wickedness. You are backward with the things of God. Does he who made the outside

People care about appearances and the approval of others

not care about the inside too? You care so much about appearances, but no mercy flows from within. You should give as a mercy to the world the truths you possess, but you don't. Instead, ~~you are en~~ ~~amored with~~ the approval of man, and you somehow manage to get it. But you neglect justice and the love of God. What do you suppose this gets you? It gets you good seats in the synagogue and elaborate greetings in the marketplace, but you are like unmarked graves. People stand right on top of you and never suspect that inside you are full of nothing but death."

The Pharisees looked at one another, stunned and dumb from the precision of their dinner guest's verbal evisceration, until one of the teachers of the law said simply, "Teacher, you insult us."

Jesus received this remark as an invitation to say more.

He said, "You load people down with burdens you yourselves are not willing to bear. You don't keep your own rules, and you certainly don't help those on whom you impose them to keep them either. Through the heartless rule-keeping they called faith, your fathers killed the words the prophets handed down to you, and you have followed right behind them building intricate tombs to keep them dead. And as you have killed them, so you seek to destroy all other prophets who might come to you in the name of the Lord. You do not enter the presence of God, and you hinder anyone else who tries by making yourselves the gate."

After the meal, Jesus took his disciples aside and told them, "Beware of their hypocrisy. The leaven of the Pharisees works its way through the nation, inflating their ideas of true spirituality among those who know no better. One day their duplicity will be exposed in the light of truth, as it shall be for all men. Even with you—those things you whisper in the dark shall one day be known to all. There is no darkness that will not be exposed by the light."

The Pharisees were coming to recognize how risky it was to provoke Jesus to debate. He moved effortlessly from being the defendant to the judge before the prosecution could respond to his indictments. But the elders, scribes, and teachers of the law were not ones to surrender so easily. They began to press Jesus every chance they had into speaking blasphemy or anything else they could twist into a capital offense.

Soon after the feast, Jesus left Jerusalem and traveled to Perea, the area Herod Antipas ruled east of the Jordan. He continued teaching about the kingdom of God, mostly in parable, and crowds continued to flock to hear him teach, hoping for healing.

Someone in the crowd asked Jesus, "Is it true that only a few will actually taste true salvation?"

Turning the theological question into a personal challenge to his hearers, Jesus said, "Why are you concerned about other people's salvation? Be concerned about yourselves. You should strive to enter the kingdom of God through the narrow door. The times are urgent. Many will seek to enter and in fact will expect to. But they will find they are not able. The time is coming when the master of the feast will rise and close the door, locking it behind him. You will stand on the outside knocking to be let in, but the master will say, 'I do not know who you are.' You will be perplexed as you argue, 'Don't you remember me? I ate and drank with you. You taught in our streets.' But he will say again, 'I do not know who you are. Leave, evildoer.'"

The crowd couldn't comprehend what Jesus meant. This was scandalous. Their whole lives they had been taught to consider themselves insiders to the things of God—by birthright, by conduct, and by coming from the line of Abraham. But Jesus seemed to suggest that nationality carried no weight, that the evidence of being a true child of the kingdom was not pedigree but humility and repentance. His kingdom would be for those who truly sought to know him. This, Jesus said, had always been the case. Access to the table of the Lord was for those who didn't merely know about God but who knew him as the host of their lives—the one to whom they belonged.

Jesus said, "The day you stand on the outside looking in will be a sad day, full of weeping and gnashing of teeth. You will see Abraham and Isaac and Jacob at the table of the Lord. You will see all the prophets too. And you will see people coming from all over the world—people you never imagined would belong at such a feast. The least in your minds will recline at the table of the Lord because they, unlike you, truly know him. In the end God's promise to Abraham will be fulfilled—all the nations of the earth will be blessed through him. The question you should be asking is not whether many will be saved. But will you?"

Some of the Pharisees came to Jesus while he was speaking and said, "You had better get out of here. Herod wants you dead."

Jesus showed no fear of the man who had beheaded his cousin John. He said, "Tell that fox that I cast out demons and heal the sick. Tell him I will do what I will do today and tomorrow, and that only when I am ready will I finish my course."

The fearless conviction with which Jesus spoke left everyone wondering if there was more to this man than they imagined. Many hoped he would turn the power of his words into actual political leadership. But Jesus knew that while Herod would not be able to take his life from him, the time was coming when he would lay it down.

Jesus said, "I must go to Jerusalem. I must go to the city where the prophets are killed because my time has come."

Then he said, "O Jerusalem. The tragedy of my life is not my own but yours. When I come to you, you will do to me what you have always done to your prophets. How I have longed to gather you up under my wings. But you would not have me. And because you reject the mothering hand of God, you choose instead your own judgment."

God's own people were created for nothing less than to know and love their Maker—to cast themselves on his mercy in the wake of the catastrophe of the fall. But when the leaders arose to lead the people, they called not for mercy but action—rules over affection, sacrifice over mercy, independence over humility. And while they constructed a system with enough rules to tell people what to do and when to do it, they walked away from the heart of their God.

The ceremonial system was so ingrained in nearly everyone that Jesus' opposition to it led many to dismiss him out of hand. But for some, Jesus' words awakened hope—a familiar breath blowing on the embers of hearts that wanted more than anything else to know and love their Creator.

19

LOST THINGS
FOUND

Luke 14–15

ON THEIR WAY TO JERUSALEM, Jesus and his disciples passed through a town that was home to a prominent Pharisee. Some of the teachers of the law organized a meal at his home and invited Jesus to dine with them.

Jesus watched as the guests came in, carefully choosing their seats around the table. Meals like these offered more than food. They offered honor. The seats at the table were assigned according to a man's rank among his peers. The host sat at the head of the table, and the most honored guests sat closest to him. It was something of a game, but one they all took seriously.

Once the guests had found their appropriate seats, the lawyers and theologians in the room turned their focus to Jesus. They were suspicious of this itinerant miracle worker and of the uncommon affection people held for him.

They brought to Jesus a man suffering from a condition that caused extreme swelling in his legs and arms. The man knew he held no honor among these men, so he did not understand why they would bring him into the middle of this great feast for all to see. It became clear, however, when Jesus looked at the teachers of the law and then at the man and asked, "Is it lawful to heal on the Sabbath? Yes or no?"

The man was a pawn in a theological game. The teachers of the law wanted to see what would happen if they brought together on the Sabbath a sick man and a miracle worker claiming to be from God. If the healer's work was to heal, would he work on the Sabbath?

The religious leaders and Jesus had already been down this road a number of times. He had performed healings on previous Sabbaths, and the general accusation was that he couldn't be from God because he did not honor this day of rest.

Whatever humiliation the suffering man felt was suspended when Jesus took hold of him, healed him, and sent him on his way.

The religious leaders gave each other knowing glances. Jesus said to them, "Listen to me. If any of you men has a son who falls into a well on the Sabbath, what are you going to do? You're going to rescue him."

The teachers of the law said nothing.

Jesus then addressed the entire room. "When you come to a feast, how do you choose your seat? You all came in here hoping for positions of honor. Let me ask you, how do you choose where to sit? If you choose a place of honor for yourself and someone greater than you comes along, you'll endure the humiliation of having to move to a lesser seat—maybe the only one left—a seat of no account at all. But if you come in unassuming and choose a seat of no regard, you leave the assignment of value up to the host. He will place you where you belong, and then you will know the true honor of having worth ascribed to you by another. When this happens, there is no need to posture."

Jesus then turned to his host, the Pharisee, and said, "When you give a feast, how do you decide who to invite and where to seat them? Do you only invite those who can repay you by inviting you to feasts of their own? If this is how you decide, you invite into your home people who bring with them their already established perceptions of where they rank. The man in the middle seat at your table will in turn give you a middle seat at his. But say you go out into the streets and invite the poor, the lame, the blind, and the desperate. Say you give them seats of honor at your table. You give them something they cannot claim for themselves. This is where real blessing lies because these guests cannot repay you. They can only receive from your gracious hand. Your repayment here will not come from them but from above—from the one who can bestow on you what you cannot give yourself: true honor."

The Pharisee and the teachers of the law obtained their prominence in their communities through hard work and birthright. But they were not unlike the rest of the world who wanted so badly to know the answers to life's two most haunting questions: "Am I valuable, and am I lovable?" The world has historically measured such things based on possessions, reputations, influence, or family name. When power tells the story of worth, everyone postures themselves for the best possible seats at the table of life.

But Jesus proposed another way. What if people didn't find their position in this world according to how they compared to others, but rather by what God said of them? What if this were all that mattered—the Father's affection for his children?

One of the guests at the table responded to Jesus, saying, "Blessed is the one who eats at the great feast of the Lord!"

Then Jesus told them a story about a man who set up a great banquet, and when he went to invite his friends, neighbors, and honored guests, they all sent back regrets that they would not be able to attend. Life had gotten in the way. One had a wedding; another had just purchased a plot of land; another had to check on his livestock. They all begged off.

The master of the feast became angry. These reasons did not prevent them from coming. Their lives had filled up to the point that the host's company no longer fit into what they could accommodate. So he directed his servant to go out into the streets and invite the poor, the suffering, the ones with the swollen limbs and blind eyes and broken hearts.

When they had done all that, the servant told his master that there was still room at the table. So the master told him to go outside the city walls and call all who would come. His feast would be full. Of this he would be certain. It would be filled with people who had never dared to assume that they could belong at such a table as this. And because they regarded themselves in this way, every seat would be a seat of great honor.

After the dinner, Jesus left and continued on toward Jerusalem. Along the way he stopped to address the great crowds that were with him. He asked them what they hoped to find by following him. Many were simply curious observers. But some were ready to follow him to the ends of the earth. Had they counted the cost?

Jesus told them, "If you are not willing and able to walk away from everything you hold dear and bear up under your own cross daily, you do not want to follow me."

In a world where people worked hard to establish their worth by way of position and rank, these followers needed to know they would find no honor in this world by associating with Jesus. Instead they would find trouble, sorrow, and persecution. To do this, they would have to be willing to find their worth in no one but God alone. If they could not see themselves as needy and desperate, they did not see themselves as they truly were.

As a result, Jesus attracted fewer and fewer of the prominent and powerful, and more and more of the sinful and broken. This itself was an offense to the teachers of the law. They were incredulous that tax collectors and sinners were drawn to him and that he received them and ate with them.

Jesus stopped and gathered the religious leaders together to tell them some stories about lost things found. He told them about a shepherd who lost a sheep from his fold and how he left the ninety-nine remaining sheep to find the one that was lost. When he found it, he hoisted it onto his shoulders and carried it back to his fold. The return of that sheep, Jesus said, brought the shepherd the kind of joy God finds in one sinner who repents.

Then he told them about a woman who, when she lost a silver coin, turned over everything in her house to find it. When she found it, her joy was uncontainable. This joy, Jesus told them, is the kind of joy God feels over one penitent heart.

Jesus' point was not lost on the religious leaders—God cared about the recovery of the lost. He rejoiced when the hopeless were restored. But then Jesus told them a third story, and this time they realized it was about them.

"There was a man who had two sons," Jesus began.

One day the younger son went to his father and said, "I want you to give me my share of the inheritance now."

Everything about this scene would have ruffled the feathers of the religious leaders. To ask for his inheritance while the father was still alive was the same as saying he wished his father were already dead. But the father agreed and divided his property between his boys. The younger son took his money and left town, chasing every appetite that came his way until he had nothing left. Desperate, he took a job feeding pigs, wishing every day that he could eat as well as those unclean beasts under his charge.

The young man came to his senses, Jesus told the religious leaders, and decided to return home. But he knew what he had done. He had squandered his inheritance. He had spent his future already. Perhaps, he hoped, his father's mercy would extend at least to a position of employment as a hired hand.

The young son rehearsed his speech for when he returned home: "Father, I have sinned against you. I am not worthy to be your son, but would you take me as a servant?"

The young man set out for home. While he was still a long way off, his father, who had watched for him every day, saw him coming and ran out to meet him. The father embraced his son and kissed him as the son began the speech he had rehearsed: "Father, I have sinned against you."

But the father cut him off and said to his servant, "Quick, bring my best robe and sandals for my son's feet. Put my ring on his finger and prepare a feast. Bring the fattened calf, kill it, and let's celebrate. My son who was lost has been found. My son was dead, but he is alive again!"

The older brother came home from the fields during the celebration, and when he found out what was happening, he became angry. He stood outside the house, away from the music and dancing, and refused to go in. His father came out, told him what had happened, and implored him to come in. But the older brother rebuked his father.

He said, "I have slaved away for you all these years, doing everything you ask, and you never offered me anything like this so that I could celebrate with my friends. But when this son of yours, who has squandered his share of your inheritance and now is feasting on mine comes home, you kill the fattened calf for him! Tell me, father. What about this should make me happy?"

The father said, "Everything I have is already yours. But this is your brother. He was dead, and now he is alive. He was lost, but now he is found."

Jesus' implication wasn't hard to figure out. God delights in the recovery of the lost. But somehow over the years, his own people had exchanged that same joy for a self-righteous sense of entitlement to God's favor based on their ability to keep certain rules and avoid certain sins. Their affection for God had died in the process, leaving them callous not only toward the needy but also toward the idea that they were just as sick and broken as those who put their hope in Jesus. The only honor that the younger son carried to his father's table was the honor bestowed on him by the host of the feast. It all seemed so profane. The celebration cost that prodigal son nothing because the host absorbed full expense.

What is an heir to do when he finds no pleasure in the fact that his father's grace has been offered to the undeserving? What comes of him when he does not love in the way his father loves? He will either lay down his pride and come into the celebration, or he will resent his father's grace and stand outside in the darkness of his own self-righteousness.

This was more than a story. It was an invitation to come in to the joy of a grace that the self-righteous have always resented.

20

LAZARUS OF BETHANY

John 11:1-44

"A M *I* DYING?"

It started as a single cough, but his condition deteriorated to the point that Lazarus couldn't get out of bed. He lay there as his sisters cared for him. They told him he would be back to normal in no time, but the sideways glances Mary and Martha gave each other told another story. This illness wasn't good. Everyone in the room knew it. Lazarus was still alive, but he was very sick.

Lazarus and his sisters belonged to a generation that knew that any illness, no matter how small, could very likely end in death. Death had crept into most every home in Bethany at one time or another to claim both the strong and the weak, the young and the old. It was the way of the world. Of course there were remedies for certain maladies, and for those fortunate enough to succumb to one of these, their recovery could be at least somewhat predictable.

But the other side of this cruel coin was that there were also illnesses everyone knew could not be stopped. When loved ones came under one of those, all that was left was to pray and try to make them comfortable.

Over the years Lazarus and his sisters had spent many hours with Jesus, and the four of them had grown close. When he came through Jerusalem, he would lodge with them. They would eat together and stay up laughing late into the night telling stories. They'd encourage one another. He loved that family and they loved him. They were friends.

When Lazarus fell ill, Jesus was still in Perea. For three years Jesus traveled around Israel teaching, healing the sick, and casting out demons. Many considered him more than a teacher. They used words like *deliverer* and *savior*. His popularity grew with every healing, every word of forgiveness, and every teaching on the kingdom of God. There seemed to be no limit to what he could do.

The temple officials knew this couldn't go unchecked. Neither Jesus nor his admirers could be permitted to entertain the thought that he might be there to liberate Israel from Rome. Rome would crush them all. If the chief priests had to quiet him themselves, they would do whatever that required.

Jesus did not shrink from their anger nor did he fear it, and this only heightened their frustration. Jesus knew he wasn't welcome in Jerusalem any longer, so he retreated across the Jordan, where he remained until a breathless courier arrived with an urgent message from Mary and Martha: "The one you love is sick."

Lazarus's sisters knew enough about Jesus to hope that their message might end up being more than an invitation to their brother's funeral. Jesus walked with God, and he also loved Lazarus. Maybe Lazarus could experience the touch of God through the hands of their friend. If only Jesus could get there, if only he could touch Lazarus, if only he could pray over his friend, surely the fever would break and the color would return to his face. He would be well again in no time.

Everything seemed to hinge on time. Who would visit Lazarus first, Jesus or death?

Jesus told the messenger and his disciples, "This illness is for the glory of God so the Son of God might be exalted through it. It will not end in death."

It had been hours since Mary and Martha moved from their brother's side. Over the past few days they'd gone from checking in on him every so often to now keeping a constant vigil. They were witnessing his deterioration as he passed from exhaustion to pain to incoherence to unconsciousness.

Their neighbors knew Lazarus was in his house dying. Few asked anything direct about his condition. Not wanting to impose, they paid careful attention to whatever updates the sisters volunteered, and they passed them along among themselves.

The two women sat watching Lazarus's chest rise and then fall, not knowing which breath would be his last. His breathing slowed. Each inhale became deeper and more labored until in one last, sustained exhale the breath fully and finally left his lungs.

They studied him. Lazarus lay motionless, his color and warmth draining away. Mary took Martha's hands. Their eyes welled with tears. The tremble in their breathing and the beating of their hearts punctuated the silence. Death was an intruder, and it had taken what it had come for. Life was not supposed to be this way.

Neighbors watched the sisters emerge. The sorrow in their eyes and the flush of their cheeks announced what they hadn't the strength to say. Lazarus was dead. Their neighbors hugged the women closely, whispering words of comfort and expressions of sorrow. They promised meals and listening ears, offering whatever help they could give. With that, preparations for the burial of Lazarus, the brother of Mary and Martha and the friend of Jesus, were in motion.

Jesus' disciples knew he hadn't seen Lazarus in a while so he couldn't know his condition. How could Jesus respond so casually to such urgent news? Jesus said this sickness wouldn't end in Lazarus's death, but then he elected to stay where he was for another two days. On the first of those two days, Martha scanned the horizon for any sign of her friend in the hope that he might arrive in time. On the second day, Lazarus died and his sisters' hearts broke to bits.

It wasn't until the third day that Jesus said to his disciples, "Let's go to Bethany." Jesus told his disciples, "Our friend Lazarus has fallen asleep. I am going to wake him up."

His disciples were confused and said, "Good. If he's just resting then he'll recover his strength."

Jesus said, "No. Lazarus is dead. For your sake I am glad I was not there when he died, so that you may believe. Let's go see him."

He was glad Lazarus had died so their faith might be made stronger? What comfort was that? While Jesus delayed his coming, Lazarus's sisters watched their brother struggle for his last breaths. They cradled his lifeless body in their arms. They wrapped him for burial. They wept at his graveside. They endured that lonely feeling only grief gives, like their insides had been hollowed out. If this was meant to be a lesson in faith, it came at quite a cost.

By the time Jesus arrived in Bethany, Lazarus had been dead four days. Jesus used this time to allow his disciples and Lazarus's sisters to question him and even to doubt him. Martha heard he was near and went out to meet him. She said through her sorrow, "If you had been here, my brother would not have died." This wasn't just a lament. It was a statement of faith. Martha believed Jesus could have stopped Lazarus's death. She also believed that he didn't. Not this time.

She continued, "Even now I know whatever you ask from God, he will give it." She was in need of consolation. It was her faith in her friend, not the lack of it, that lay at the core of her turmoil. This man she believed was so great that death itself would have to obey him had not arrived in time.

Martha loved Jesus, but in that moment she wanted him to give an account of himself. "Why didn't you come?"

"Martha, your brother will rise again," he said.

She said she knew he would rise again at the last day, as if to say, "Yes, when these days of sorrow, mourning, and pain are through."

But Jesus told her, "No, listen to me, Martha. I am the resurrection and the life. Whoever believes in me, even if he dies, shall live. And everyone who lives because he believes in me shall never die. Do you believe this?"

Death was such a cruel intruder—this wage of sin. It took her brother and broke her heart. She couldn't stop it. Still, Lazarus's death wasn't some parlor game to Jesus. He wasn't playing fast and loose with his friend's life. He had come to pay Lazarus's wage—to give him life in his name. He had come to banish this intruder forever. He had also come to interrogate Martha's heart.

When word reached Mary that Jesus was just down the road talking with her sister, she ran to him and flung herself at his feet.

"If only you had been here," she said.

"Where is he?" Jesus asked.

They led him to a cave with a stone laid across its mouth. On the other side of that stone lay Lazarus's body. In the sorrowful silence, Jesus' eyes burned and he began to weep. The people of Bethany marveled at how much Jesus loved this family. But some took exception to how he had handled this. If he was a miracle worker, as many claimed, where was the miracle? Why didn't he prevent Lazarus's death? Why didn't he spare these poor women their anguish?

"Open this tomb," Jesus said.

Nearly everyone wondered at first if they'd heard him right. But he persisted, "Take that stone away."

Martha said what everyone was thinking. "Lazarus has been in there four days. His remains are rotting and foul by now. It's too late."

Jesus said, "Martha, trust me. You are about to witness something you've never seen before—the glory of God revealed."

A few of the stronger men nearby rolled away the stone. Every eye was fixed on Jesus as they waited for whatever it was he meant to do. He prayed. Speaking aloud for the sake of those who had gathered, he said, "Father, you are always listening to me. Even now I know you hear me. I'm praying out loud so that those around me might believe you have sent me."

Then he turned to face the open tomb and shouted into the darkness, "Lazarus, come out! Live!"

The man who had died came out. Still wrapped in his grave clothes, he shuffled into the light. Linens bound his hands and feet and a hood covered his head, but there he stood, alive.

Jesus said, "Unbind that man."

Lazarus squinted as his eyes adjusted to the sun. Before him stood his family and neighbors, dumbfounded. People don't die and then come back to life. But there stood Lazarus, as if waking from a deep sleep. And there stood Jesus, the only one not astonished at the sight of his friend.

21

A WORLD
UPSIDE DOWN

Mark 10:35-45

*T*HERE WERE NO INNOCENT BYSTANDERS. Every single eyewitness left Lazarus's tomb with the burden of needing to do something with the knowledge they had been given. Jesus of Nazareth had raised a dead man with nothing but his words. He spoke and there was life. They heard it with their own ears. They saw it with their own eyes. And they had never seen or heard anything like it before.

After this, people put their faith in Jesus by the score. It wasn't just that they trusted what he said. They trusted him, giving their allegiance as one submits to a king. They believed in him in much the same way that they believed in God.

Caiaphas was the high priest over Jerusalem that year. It was his job to lead his people in worship while maintaining peace with their

Roman overseers. When he heard about Lazarus and how people were beginning to regard Jesus as a king, he knew this would not sit well with Rome. He gathered his council and said, "If we let this Jesus perform one more sign, everyone will put their faith in him. Then what? They already regard him as one sent from God. If we don't act, the Romans will close the temple and strip us of any last vestige of national identity we might hope to hold. Men, we must all agree that it is better for one man to suffer and die than for our entire nation to perish."

While his argument resonated with many in his council, they could not simply act on impulse because they lived in a land governed by laws they were bound to uphold. They knew they needed to find a legal way to arrest Jesus if they wanted him put to death. Caiaphas set in motion a plan to do just that.

Some of Jesus' followers caught wind of Caiaphas's plot and warned him that his death warrant had been signed. The first chance the chief priests and Pharisees were given, they would arrest him. So Jesus could no longer walk openly in Jerusalem. He and his disciples sought refuge in a little town called Ephraim, north of Jerusalem.

The story of Lazarus's resurrection spread quickly throughout the region, and with it the speculation that Jesus was, in fact, the long-awaited King of glory.

Jesus gathered his disciples, who were on edge because of their self-imposed exile in the Judean hill country, and he told them, "Listen to me. The day is coming when you will want nothing more than to see the kingdom of God in full force on this earth. People will come along telling you they have seen it. Do not believe them. Yes, the kingdom of God is coming—and when it does, there will be no mistaking it for anything else. The Son of Man will come like a burst of lightning from one end of the sky to the other. But when he comes to usher in his kingdom, it will be as it was in the days of Noah. Few will expect it. Before that day comes, the Son of Man must suffer many things and be rejected by this generation."

Jesus continued, "When the kingdom of God does come, it will look like a world upside down. People want to justify themselves by their actions and then ask God to acknowledge their righteousness. There is nothing more blinding than pride. But the kingdom of God is for those who know they have nothing to offer."

Then Jesus told a story: "Two men went up to the temple to pray—one was a Pharisee, the other was a tax collector. The Pharisee looked at the others praying around him. He said, 'God, I thank you for not making me like these other men with their besetting sins. Thank you for not making me like that tax collector. I fast. I give generously. I thank you that this is who I am.'

"The tax collector, however, didn't notice the Pharisee because he would not lift his eyes toward heaven. He beat his chest, praying, 'Oh God, have mercy on me. I am a sinful man.' That man was the one who went home justified that day. When you exalt yourself, you will be humbled. But the one who humbles himself will be exalted. No matter what comes your way, depend on the mercy of God."

When Jesus left Ephraim for lands east of the Jordan, large crowds followed. He stopped along the way to heal and teach the people. Many brought their children to Jesus for his blessing, but his disciples tried to send them away. Jesus told his disciples, "No, let the children come to me. Don't stop them. The kingdom of heaven belongs to little ones like these—the vulnerable, the helpless, the trusting."

They return to Jerusalem and Jesus tells them what will happen

After a while, Jesus set out for Jerusalem because the Passover was drawing near. On the road to Jericho, Jesus took his twelve disciples aside and told them, "We are going to go into Jerusalem. I am telling you this because when we do, everything that has been written about the Son of Man by the prophets is going to come to pass. He will be handed over to the chief priests and scribes who will condemn him to death. They will deliver him over to the Gentiles, and he will be mocked, spit on, and beaten. They will treat him in unspeakably shameful ways. They will flog him and they will crucify him. On the third day, after this happens, the Son of Man will rise from the dead."

The disciples had heard Jesus speak like this before. Though at first they did not understand what he was talking about, their journeys with him and the conflict that followed began to bring his words into sharper focus, but only by a little. His words rested on them like a burden they could not name.

The gravity with which Jesus now seemed to carry himself got James and John talking. Something revolutionary was on the horizon, and these two brothers had somehow found themselves right in the middle of it. But they could not understand what Jesus meant when he predicted his death. All this talk of a coming kingdom and the perspective one needed to see it, paired with Jesus' apparent determination to go back into Jerusalem, made his words about his own suffering sound counterintuitive to his disciples. Why would this man who seemed to be so focused on ushering in a new kingdom march into the very place he'd been warned to avoid, unless it were for his inauguration?

The brothers talked quietly with each other as they walked from the eastern hills to Jericho. If the coming kingdom of God truly was at hand, they wanted to be as close as they could to their King. So James and John came to Jesus, along with their mother, to present their Lord with a simple request.

"Teacher," they said, "there's something we'd like to ask you to do for us."

"What is it?" Jesus said.

They said, "Grant to one of us the seat at your right hand in your glory and the seat on your left to the other."

Jesus looked at these men he loved. James and John, along with Peter, had enjoyed a proximity to Jesus the other nine hadn't known. Peter, James, and John were with Jesus when he went into Jairus's home to raise his little girl from the dead. They were present when Jesus was transfigured up on the mountain when Moses and Elijah appeared. They, like Peter, led with strong opinions and occasional quick, thunderous tempers. They, like Peter, held the distinction of having been given nicknames by Jesus. As Simon was now Peter the Rock, they had been named the Sons of Thunder. Since they knew they shared an uncommon fellowship with Jesus, they did not think their request, though perhaps unfair to Peter, was beyond reason.

Jesus said, "You don't know what you're asking. Can you drink the cup that I will drink?"

James and John said, "Lord, we can. Of course we can."

It grieved him to give the answer they needed to hear—an answer not for the moment but for later comfort.

"You men will drink the cup that I drink," he said. "But listen, the positions at my right hand and my left are not mine to appoint. Those places are given as an honor by the one who sets the feast."

James and John were now in the company of the religious leaders who always wanted to compete for the best seats of honor—a discovery that came to them through this rebuke. They wanted honor for themselves without thinking much about their holy calling to give all honor and praise to God.

When the other disciples heard what James and John had asked, they became angry with the brothers, revealing they were hungry for honor themselves. Jesus called his disciples together again to remind them of what he had been saying in so many ways on this journey.

He said, "Greatness will not come through honor but through service. You live in a world where honor is given to those who mistreat those under their rule. My kingdom does not work that way, neither shall it be among you. If you want to be great, become a servant. If you want to be first, become the least of all. Even the Son of Man came not to be served but to serve and to offer up his life as a ransom for many."

Jesus spoke not as a philosopher but as a man deep in the process of practicing the very counsel he now gave his disciples. Though they could see the humility in the way he carried himself on that road choked with people who wanted him to make their lives different, they could not see that what he had told them several times already now lay ahead. But he could. He knew not only what lay ahead for himself but for these brothers too. Their world was about to be turned upside down.

PART 5

PASSION

22

THE LIVING LEGEND

Mark 10:46-52; John 12:9-11

W ITH PASSOVER DRAWING NEAR, Jesus and his followers left Perea east of the Jordan and stopped in Jericho to gather supplies for the last eighteen miles of their pilgrimage into Jerusalem. As they left Jericho, a blind man named Bartimaeus, the son of Timaeus, sat outside the city gate begging. Bartimaeus's lot as a beggar was common among the infirmed of his day. His condition doomed him to a life of poverty and darkness. Blindness dictated that he would be a beggar in this world, helpless at the gates, living off the charity of men and women who had better lives than his. The road to Jerusalem outside the city gate was a prime place for a man like him to play off of the heightened sense of charitable duty of those making their way into the holy city to offer their sacrifices to the Lord.

Bartimaeus, who experienced the world through the sounds and the silences of the people around him, sat up when he heard a large, enthusiastic crowd flood the street. He called for someone to tell him what was happening.

"Jesus of Nazareth is coming by on his way to Jerusalem," someone said.

Sitting up, Bartimaeus cried out, "Son of David, have mercy on me. Please!"

Jesus wasn't just a fascination to the masses. He had become a legend among the poor and destitute. Stories of Jesus' teachings and miracles had reached Bartimaeus's ears, and in his heart he had concluded that if anyone was the promised coming King of glory—the heir to David's eternal throne—it was this rabbi from Nazareth. It was this teacher who touched the lepers to make them clean, who gave life to the dead with only a word, and who gave sight to the blind. Bartimaeus believed the Spirit of the Lord was upon Jesus to bring good news to the poor, to bind up the hurts of the brokenhearted, to give freedom to the captives and sight to the blind.

As he cried out for Jesus' mercy, the crowds told him to be quiet. But Bartimaeus believed the prophets of old who said that all who called on the name of the Lord would be saved, so he cried out even louder: "Son of David, have mercy on me!" Though they had never met, Bartimaeus believed this serendipitous encounter on the road outside of Jericho could very likely be the moment when God would exchange the ashes of his life for beauty, and he did not want to let this hour of the Lord's favor pass him by.

The crowds were so dense that Jesus could not see Bartimaeus, but he heard him. He stopped and asked for Bartimaeus to be brought to him. The same people who had rebuked Bartimaeus for troubling Jesus now came to him in a rush of excitement. "Take heart, beggar. The teacher is asking for you. Today is your day."

Springing to his feet, Bartimaeus threw down his cloak which held the proceeds of that day's begging, and took the hand of a man who led him to Jesus.

"What do you want?" Jesus asked.

The disciples knew this question well. Jesus asked it often. The desires of the heart told the stories Jesus wanted to uncover. What drove a man? It was the question he asked James and John on their way into Jericho when they wanted honor for themselves. Whether a man sat blind beside the road or enjoyed a closer proximity to Jesus than any other living soul, Jesus wanted to expose their true desires and hold them up to the light.

Bartimaeus gave no hesitation: "I want to see."

He didn't want money. He didn't want honor. He wanted something no reasonable person should expect another to provide; he wanted his blind eyes opened. Bartimaeus saw Jesus as the one man who could do for him what no one else could. He knew he was asking for more than the gift of sight. If Jesus were to heal Bartimaeus, he would strip away his means of income, his place in the community, his daily routine, even his identity. Many came to Jesus thinking he could do wonderful things for them, but when people came asking for a new life, few realized this meant they would have to leave their old one behind. Few were truly prepared for that reality.

Healing meant the loss of his life as he knew it, but Bartimaeus understood this. Who else could deliver him from his body of decay? Bringing nothing but need and trusting in nothing but Jesus' power, Bartimaeus knew he was asking for a new life.

Jesus said, "You want to see? Then see."

Immediately Bartimaeus's sight was fully restored. The first thing the blind man saw was the face of his healer.

Jesus said, "Your faith has made you well. You can go on your way."

"My way is wherever you go," Bartimaeus said.

This moment was so much more than a miracle for Bartimaeus. It was a conversion. He didn't just put his faith in Jesus. He put his life in Jesus' hands, deciding to leave everything behind to follow him.

Bartimaeus reminded the Twelve of what had become of their lives. They each had their own moment where, after encountering Jesus, they left everything to follow him. Each had left one life for another, trusting that the life Jesus had to offer was better than the one he knew.

Bartimaeus stepped into a journey the others had walked for three years now—a journey that now led to Jerusalem. This pilgrimage would provide the first things he would see. He would see Lazarus, the living legend. He would see the roads swollen with pilgrims leading their sacrifices to the temple in the hope that the blood of the lambs might cause the judgment of God to pass over them for one more year. He would see the sun dance golden off the walls of the temple where the presence of the Lord was said to dwell. And he would see the burden Jesus carried the closer they came to the city of the king. He would see all of this, and if he stayed for the entire feast, he would see so much more.

"I can't see any way around it, can you?" asked one of the chief priests in Jerusalem.

"But he hasn't done anything," another said.

"Yes, but it is on account of him that all these people believe in Jesus of Nazareth. Let's not be foolish. We all know the stakes," the chief priest said.

The temple authorities each tried to come up with a better solution to their problem. The most obvious felt murderous. But it seemed as if it might be their best option.

The chief priest said, "Be assured: the influence of this Lazarus of Bethany needs to be contained. He is more than a man in the eyes of the people. He has become a rallying point for zealots and mystics. Passover is coming, and the last thing we need is a new folk hero."

Soon caravans of pilgrims would fill Jerusalem as families and clans reunited to remember how God had delivered them from their slavery in Egypt. They would tell the old stories of how God sent plagues upon the land, striking dead all the firstborn sons in Egypt, and how the Lord mercifully passed over those homes that had the blood of a lamb painted across their doorposts.

The Passover was God's feast if it was anyone's. He told the people how to observe it: every year they must prepare unleavened bread to remind them of their hasty departure, bitter herbs to call to mind their misery, and a lamb to remember the blood spilled to secure their deliverance. He even told them where to observe it—"in that place the Lord your God will choose." He chose Jerusalem, God's holy hill where the great King David established the kingdom's seat of power and where his son Solomon built the temple.

Every year as the feast drew near, thousands of pilgrims and soldiers flooded into Jerusalem. Rome understood that this holiday focused on God liberating the Israelites from their oppression. The parallels were not lost on them, so they brought in hundreds of additional soldiers to strengthen their military presence. The chief priests were just as devoted to preserving peace as the Romans. It was their own way of life they stood to lose. They would be on the lookout for troublemakers as well, and this year they would be watching for one man in particular.

Jesus did amazing wonders that transformed people's lives. He opened the eyes of the blind. He healed the lame. He brought comfort and peace to the most tortured souls, delivering them from lifetimes of misery. People who came to him found new reasons to hope. They saw a man who, with only his word, could shatter insurmountable suffering.

And then there was Lazarus. The public responded to his resurrection by believing Jesus was the one sent to deliver them from their Roman oppressors. Maybe he would even become their king. These were reasonable hopes, considering they had seen him raise to life a man who had been dead for four days. Lazarus's living after dying had captured the attention of the region, and as sure as Lazarus lived and breathed, there was no explaining this miracle away.

Jesus needed to die. But now, they concluded, so did Lazarus. It would be better for the chief priests to handle this themselves than to let it become Rome's problem.

Jesus stood in Lazarus's door, sweaty and dusty from the road. He had come back. Of all the places he could have chosen for his return from exile, he chose the home of his old friends.

Lazarus asked Martha, "What do you think? Can we pull something together?"

This was Martha's strong suit. With a solemn nod she turned and swung into action. The news spread quickly around Bethany that Jesus had returned and that a dinner was being prepared in his honor. Curious neighbors and longtime friends began to trickle in as the party grew. Bethany had come to life.

During the meal, Lazarus leaned in toward Jesus. "It's good to see you again." Then his smile gave way to concern. "There are people around here who won't be so glad to learn you've come back. You know that, right?"

Jesus knew. But he also knew that his destiny lay within those city walls. For some time now Jesus had spoken about what lay ahead for him—that he would suffer many things and die at the hands of his own people, and that on the third day he would rise again.

Coming back to Bethany was like returning to the scene of a crime, and it couldn't have come during a more volatile week.

23

THE KING'S CORONATION

1 Kings 1; Luke 19:28-36

WHEN THE NEWS REACHED the religious leaders that Jesus was staying with Lazarus, they said, "Why would he come so close to the city if he wasn't planning on coming in for the feast?" Jesus was, after all, a rabbi. It would be uncharacteristic for a rabbi to miss the Passover if he was just across the valley in Bethany. So the chief priests issued orders that if anyone saw him, they should let them know. The sooner they could arrest Jesus and get him out of the public eye, the better it would be for everyone.

Maybe this would be easier than they thought. Either Jesus had forgotten they were seeking his apprehension or he didn't care. Either way, it seemed it was no longer a question of if they could arrest him, but when. They would be waiting. They would dispatch minders to watch his movements, follow his approach, and recommend when and how to bring him in as cleanly as possible—no messes, no outbursts, no choice.

On the morning after the party at Lazarus's house, Jesus said to his disciples, "In the village ahead there is a man who owns a young colt, one that has never been ridden. Go get it for me. We're going into Jerusalem." They had all presumed Jesus would eventually make his way into the holy city, but hearing him say it brought the reality of the danger of their situation home. What did he expect to find but trouble? Still, he was a rabbi, and he was just across the valley on the eve of the feast. Of course he would go into the city.

His disciples began to collect what they'd need for the day. Before long the two who set off to get the colt returned, having found it just as Jesus said.

"Help me up," Jesus said.

This was new. They hadn't known Jesus to ride from one town to the next. Usually only military leaders and politicians rode on beasts of burden, and that was primarily to display their power and importance. Why would Jesus want to enter Jerusalem in this way? Nevertheless, one of Jesus' disciples offered his interlocked hands as a stirrup and hoisted Jesus onto the donkey's back, and they began their slow descent into the Kidron Valley with Jerusalem rising golden before them.

Up on that colt Jesus looked like a king, not because he wore a robe or carried a scepter but because he triggered a memory. He wasn't the first to cross this valley on a colt in a triumphant procession. Centuries earlier King Solomon had ridden this same route to his own coronation.

In those days, the Lord promised Solomon's father, David, that his kingdom would endure forever. God gave the king many sons and daughters, some of whom grew up to be ambitious fools while others revered both their father and his God. Though David had several heirs who would have made fine kings by the world's standards, he knew his throne would go to Bathsheba's son Solomon.

When King David's health started to fail, he lay in his bed covered in blankets, shivering with a fever. As his servants cared for him, his son Adonijah thought about his father's throne. Adonijah said to himself, "I will be king," and he began planning his own coronation.

Adonijah gathered a small army of chariots and horsemen to lend credibility to his claim on his father's throne. He invited most of his brothers and many of his father's military leaders to be part of this historic event. But he didn't invite his brother Solomon. He didn't invite any of David's elite guard. He didn't invite Zadok the priest. He didn't invite Nathan, the prophet who was so gifted at cutting to the heart of the truth when it came to this particular family. And he didn't invite his father, the king.

Nathan was the first to hear about Adonijah's plans. He went directly to Bathsheba, who went to her husband. She said, "Did I not hear you correctly? You swore before God that my son Solomon would inherit your throne after you. Do you know what Adonijah has done?"

David did not know. He didn't know Adonijah had offered dozens of sacrifices to the Lord, thinking this would buy him favor in the eyes of the people. He didn't know Adonijah had invited all of David's sons except Solomon to his coronation. He didn't know Abiathar the priest was there, ready to bless Adonijah, or that Joab, the commander of his army, was also present, ready to swear allegiance.

Nathan entered the room and confirmed Bathsheba's account, adding, "Your sons, your generals, and your priests are feasting with him as we speak, saying, 'Long live King Adonijah!'"

"The eyes of all Israel are on you now, my king," Bathsheba said. "Who will sit on your throne? Decide, because if you don't, when you die, Solomon and I will surely be killed."

The basis of Bathsheba's entire plea rested on one immovable fact: David was still Israel's king. David took his wife's hand, looked at her with his weak eyes, and said, "As I swore to you before God, Solomon will reign after me. I will give him my throne today." David sent for the one general Adonijah had failed to invite, Benaiah. He said, "Round up your men, all those who remain loyal to me. Assemble everyone who will come. It is time to crown my successor. Set Solomon on my colt so the city will know he rides by my authority and with my blessing. Form a procession and lead him down to Gihon, the eastern spring that waters Jerusalem, and tell Zadok the priest and Nathan the prophet to meet you there. Instruct them to anoint my son Solomon as the king over Israel. When they have done this, blow your trumpets and say, 'Long live King Solomon!' Then follow him as he leads you all the way back here to my throne. I will rise and yield my seat of power to him, and he will rule over all Israel and Judah."

Benaiah did as David instructed. The sounds of the celebration echoed through the streets so loudly that Adonijah sent a servant to investigate. The servant found Nathan and Zadok leading the freshly anointed Solomon on the king's colt into David's throne room. He watched as Solomon assumed the crown. He heard the people shouting, "Long live King Solomon!"

When the servant returned with the story of Solomon's coronation, he told Adonijah, "Solomon was riding the king's colt." Adonijah's guests were struck with terror. Their presence at Adonijah's self-appointed coronation put them dangerously close to high treason. So as quickly as they had gathered, they dispersed.

What David remembered and what Adonijah ignored was that man did not appoint the king over God's people. This was the Lord's prerogative and his alone. He established David's throne in his own perfect time. It wasn't David's to take, nor was it his to give. God alone had the right to name David's successor, and he had chosen Solomon.

The people of Israel grew up hearing the stories of King David. They pictured Solomon riding his father's colt into Jerusalem as Nathan the prophet, Zadok the priest, and David the king received him as the Lord's anointed ruler over them. The colt became a symbol of a royal coronation, and by extension a symbol of being under the caring provision of God.

Jesus didn't just summon thoughts of Solomon as he approached Jerusalem on that foal. He also brought to mind the words of the prophet Zechariah, who told the people long after Solomon's reign to look for their future king to enter Jerusalem in this same way. Zechariah said, "Rejoice, daughter of Jerusalem! Behold, your king is coming to you—humble and mounted on the foal of a donkey. He is coming to bring you salvation."

This image wasn't lost on those who saw Jesus riding into Jerusalem.

Like those who joined Benaiah and Solomon's procession, crowds began to gather around Jesus.

The people came because they had heard about Lazarus. Ever since that miracle, those who had witnessed Lazarus's resurrection continued talking about it. Their eyewitness credibility peaked everyone's curiosity. Sure there had been legends of the dead coming back to life through supernatural means. But no one had ever met anyone who had been dead and then come back to life. Nor had they ever seen anyone credited with performing such a miracle. Up until then, stories like these were just stories. But now there were people saying, "I was there. I saw it. I was at Lazarus's burial, and I was there four days later when Jesus called him out of the grave."

Though no one had ever seen a coronation before, some suspected they were seeing one now. If Jesus was the coming king, had God appointed him? And if this was his coronation, did that make him their king? A longing stirred within the people. They felt compelled to praise him. They wanted to cry out, "Long live the king!"

People began to spread their coats on the road, and those without coats tore off nearby palm branches to lay across the path to create a more dignified street to welcome the arrival of the one who might be able to bring the changes they so desperately wanted.

The people shouted the hope of their hearts as he passed: "Blessed is the coming kingdom of our father David! Blessed is the king who comes in the name of the Lord! Peace in heaven and glory in the highest! Hosanna! Come save us now!"

24

HOSANNA

Luke 19:36-40

*T*HE WORLD HAD NEVER SEEN anything like the mighty Roman Empire. When Rome swept through a country, its conquest was so swift, comprehensive, and terrible that the people of those lands were left with two choices—to yield or to die. Most chose to yield.

Israel, however, presented a unique situation. Caesar had resolved to conquer the world, and Israel lay strategically placed between Asia proper, Asia Minor, and Africa. To move freely between the three, Caesar would have to rule Israel. But Israel was complicated. To hold this small country, Rome had to be shrewd. The Hebrew people were very religious. They were a nation defined by their worship, their temple practices, and their history as followers of one God and one God only, Jehovah.

Rome, who acknowledged hundreds of gods, did not conquer the known world by being undisciplined and disorganized. They were calculating, technologically advanced, and powerful. They understood how to make war, how to govern, how to keep peace, and how to intimidate. But they also understood the art of tact in politics. They recognized that Israel's devotion to Jehovah was not something they could take from them by force. In cases like this, it was easier and far less expensive to accommodate than to decimate. So Rome arranged a compromise: Israel could continue to practice their monotheistic religion so long as they obeyed Roman rule, paid their taxes, and kept the peace. Any hint of insurrection, however, would be dealt with swiftly and without mercy.

It was a clever arrangement. Rome had persuaded many in Israel that their right to worship the God who gave them their national identity was a privilege now granted to them by Caesar, who could take it away if they fell out of line. In doing this, Rome divided the temple court's loyalty between the God of their Scriptures and the ruler of their occupying force. This left the religious leaders with the charge of maintaining a peace. Allowing Israel to continue their worship on the condition of their submission to Rome virtually guaranteed that the religious leaders would insist that their own people behave themselves, lest Rome try to take this freedom away. This being the case, the religious leaders were very sensitive to anyone who could possibly upset this delicate balance.

Jesus did nothing to turn the people's hope away as he rode on the coats and palms they laid out before him. He accepted their praise in full view of anyone who cared to see. This made the religious leaders very nervous, especially on the eve of the Passover.

Who was this Jesus? The whole city wanted to know. For Jesus' disciples, this question had come up often. It seemed that Jesus was usually reluctant to provide much in the way of a clear answer, at least publicly. And when people began to draw accurate conclusions about his identity, he often instructed them not to tell anyone, saying, "My time has not yet come."

Even Peter received this warning. When Jesus asked his disciples who they believed he was, Peter said, "I know who you are. You are the Christ, the Messiah of God." Jesus told them Peter was correct. He told them he was, in fact, the Savior sent from God to deliver his people from their slavery to sin and their bondage to brokenness. But he warned even his own disciples to keep that information to themselves.

This day, however, was different. Here the people shouted their praises calling Jesus their king, and he said nothing to quiet them. In fact, he appeared to take it all in as though they were right to regard him in this way. Could the difference now be that the time had finally come for the world to know who he really was? And what would the world do if it did know? The religious leaders in Jerusalem said, "Look, the whole world has gone after him." Jesus was gaining momentum. What he might do with it could be disastrous. What if he tried to lead a rebellion? What if he rallied the people as an army to rush the citadel? Amid the shouts of "Hosanna!" his followers looked like people drunk on the euphoria of hope. What had become of their self-control? Who did he think he was to permit them to praise him in this way?

Some Pharisees appealed to Jesus: "Rebuke these disciples of yours. Tell them you are not a king. Tell them they're wrong. Tell them you are not coming to save them."

Surely, they assumed, Jesus appreciated the delicacy of their political position.

But Jesus said, "If these people fall silent, I tell you the very stones will cry out in praise."

Jesus accepted the praise of these people because though they
didn't really recognize the King he was meant to be, the rest of
creation did. This was a coronation, and if the people wouldn't
praise him on this journey into the capital of his kingdom, the
stones within her walls and lining her streets would cry out, "Rejoice, daughter of Jerusalem! Your King is coming to you; humble
and mounted on a donkey. He is coming to bring you the salvation
your hearts have always desired."

As Jesus crested the rim of the Kidron Valley, there stood Jerusalem
glistening in the sun. In his ears echoed the words of the people
pleading with him to bring them peace. He thought about the travail
of his kindred, of their constant struggle to receive the love of their
Maker, of God's strong hand of discipline in their lives, of the way
their hearts broke when Babylon and Assyria carried them off into
exile, and how hardened they had become to the idea of hope.

Jesus stopped the colt and began to weep. "If only you had
known the things that make for peace, dear city. But now they are
hidden from you. The day is coming when not one stone will be
left upon another in you because you didn't know the time of
your visitation."

This was the hour of Jerusalem's visitation. Jesus loved this city.
He wept because what the people wanted and what they needed
were so far from one another. He knew the full extent of the salvation these people required, and he also knew what it would cost.
He knew salvation was unfolding before them in that very moment.
The punishment that would bring them peace was about to be laid
upon him. He knew that the religious leaders would play a role in
bringing this punishment to him because they feared Rome more

than they feared God. He knew they would be willing to kill one of their own if it meant preserving the privilege of worship that Caesar had granted.

With tears in his eyes he rode on into the city and made his way to the temple while the people parted like a holy curtain, crying, "Please save us."

Jesus had said a lot about his imminent death. Though he had told his disciples that no one would take his life from him, he told them he would lay it down. The last day's actions revealed a man inching ever closer to the snares set by his adversaries. Coming back to Bethany and attending a party in the home of the man he had raised from the dead was inciting enough. Now he was riding into the holy city to the sounds of his own people praising him as their King.

Within those city walls stood the temple of the Lord. In that temple were the most respected and powerful religious leaders in the land. And they wanted him dead. Still, Jesus entered the city and went to the temple. He and his disciples toured the area, looking at all the preparations underway for the big feast. As the hour grew late, Jesus returned to Bethany for the night. His disciples were relieved to have the day behind them. Maybe they were done with the temple and its authorities for a while. Maybe tomorrow they'd just stay in Bethany.

25

THE VINEDRESSER'S TREE

Matthew 21:18-22; Luke 13:6-9

*I*F *JERUSALEM WAS A BEEHIVE,* on Sunday Jesus hit it with a stick, and the buzzing inside grew angry as it got organized. Early Monday morning Jesus woke his disciples with the news that he wanted to go back into the temple to teach. It sounded risky given the entrance he had made the day before, but it wasn't surprising.

Before breakfast Jesus and his disciples were up and moving. They crested the eastern edge of the Kidron, looked across the valley, and there before them, dignified and tall, stood the city of God. But it was also a city of man, built one brick at a time, and when invading armies toppled its walls and leveled the temple, the people of God eventually returned and, brick by brick, put Jerusalem back together. Was there ever a more glorious city? Such an ancient place. Such well-worn roads packed and swept by the feet of a million pilgrims. If they were anything at all, these disciples of Jesus' were just that—pilgrims. Three years on the road with their itinerant leader had brought them to the rim of this valley many times. But today was different, and everyone felt it.

On their way across the valley Jesus saw a fig tree, and for the first time that day, it occurred to him that he was hungry. It would be another month or so until the season for figs, but the leaves were developed, which meant there might be a crop of *taksh*—the little green almond-shaped forerunners to the summer figs. The *taksh*, which grew in early spring, were bitter but edible, so Jesus went to have a look.

No *taksh*. This tree had nothing for his hunger. Nor would it for anyone else's hunger later either, because no *taksh* in the spring meant no figs in the summer. That year that fig tree would bear no fruit, so Jesus cursed it. His disciples heard this, and it called to mind what Jesus had said about fruitless trees back when they had first set out for Jerusalem a couple weeks earlier.

As they had made their way through Galilee to Jerusalem, Jesus had been scattering parables like seed across the towns they entered. In one town he told the story of a man who had a fig tree planted in his vineyard. One day he came seeking fruit and found none. For three years the man had been coming to this tree hoping to find fruit, but every time he returned, the tree stood bare.

He said to his vinedresser, "Why should this tree even take up space? Cut it down and throw it in the fire."

But the vinedresser said, "Sir, let me tend to it another year. I'll fertilize it and keep it watered. One year is all I ask. If it bears no fruit next year, then we'll cut it down, but let me try one more time."

Jesus' disciples had followed him for three years. Everywhere he went he sought evidence that the people who claimed to represent

God actually knew him. He was looking for the fruit of true faith. Had he found any? What makes a fig tree a fig tree? Maybe that was a discussion for the philosophers in Athens, but everyone knew what made a fig tree significant: figs. A man keeps an orchard not for the love of foliage but for its fruit. If all he gets from his grape is the vine, he'll have no wine. If all he gets from his olive is the branch, he'll have no oil. And if all he gets from the fig is the leaf, he'll have no fruit. Why bother tending to such a plant?

Maybe the tree was having a bad year. Maybe next year the absent crop would return and the leaves would bud and the *taksh* would cluster and all would be forgotten. After two years with no fruit, the third year would be a mercy. Still, there was mercy. After three years of searching for the figs the tree refused to yield, the landowner began to doubt the tree's integrity. Everything about it claimed to be a fig tree. Even a lush, healthy fig tree. But the landowner knew that the tree bore no fruit. He also knew that this had become its habit.

To its owner, the tree was nothing more than a land-occupying, resource-wasting weed. But the vinedresser interceded for the poor tree: "Give me one more season. I'll dig around it. I'll fertilize it. I'll do everything I know to awaken this tree to its purpose."

The landowner agreed. All the while the tree had no idea that it was being contended for. It could not feel the shovel turn the earth around it. It could not smell the dank methane or see the rich blackness of the dung heaped beneath its drip line. And it certainly could not know how personally the vinedresser undertook all of this.

It could not hope so it would not hope. But the vinedresser hoped for it. And more than that, he worked. He did his best work. He pruned in the fall. He kept careful watch in the winter. He fertilized in the spring until the moment of truth arrived. The tree, which for a winter had looked all but dead and barren, began to bud. Something was stirring within—life. The buds took on a furled look, waiting to unravel into a canopy of green. If everything went according to plan, and if the tree responded to the vinedresser's care, he would find more than leaves. He would find the telltale evidence of a transformed tree. He would find *taksh*. Bitter but beautiful *taksh*. Or he would find only leaves. Either way, the truth about that tree would be told.

Jesus inspected the tree that grew along the way to the city and found only leaves. The disciples remembered what he had said through tears just yesterday about how Jerusalem did not know the time of her visitation. Apparently neither did this fig tree.

Jesus walked over to the tree as if it were one of his trees and as if things were not well between the landowner and this struggling plant. What would make for peace? Fruit at the time of the vinedresser's visitation. But there was none, so he cursed it. "May no one ever eat fruit from you again."

Time was up and something new began to stir in that tree—death.

Jesus approached Jerusalem in the same way he approached the fig tree, with all the authority of the vinedresser coming for his final inspection. Things were not well between the landowner and this city. What would make for peace? Fruit at the time of the vinedresser's visitation. But there was no fruit. To Jesus, everything about this was sad. O Jerusalem, it wasn't supposed to be this way.

To the astonishment of everyone present, the fig tree withered away down to its roots. Peter called Jesus over and, searching for something profound to say, simply said, "Look!"

Jesus said, "If you have faith and do not doubt, you will not only do what has been done to the fig tree, but if you command a mountain to be raised up and thrown into the sea, it will happen. Whatever you ask in prayer you will receive if you have faith."

Jesus had stressed this point for years now. The life of faith is a life of limitless possibilities. The faithless life, on the other hand, is doomed to be found out for what it is—fruitless and therefore useless. Life should be saturated with purpose.

The lesson with the fig tree was a lesson in faith. But Jesus was also telling a parable. That tree grew from the same earth as the city of God. The time of visitation had come for both, and both put forth an impressive display. But neither bore fruit. For three years the vinedresser had visited both for inspection but the results never changed.

Jesus turned from the cursed tree to the city before them as if they were of the same substance. The stories Jerusalem could tell. The city was older than the collective memory of its citizens. Here Israel had housed the ark of the covenant, David had penned his psalms, and Solomon had hosted the queen of Sheba. It was the destination of millions of pilgrims over hundreds of years, and it had the highways and the tombs to prove it. Its beauty was second only to its significance. Was there ever a more glorious place—the city of God, the city of man?

Up the western slope they walked toward the temple gate.

26

INDIGNATION

Matthew 21:12-17

THE LIFE-SUSTAINING, INNER WORKINGS of a nation pulsed
within Jerusalem's walls. Those charged with maintaining order
kept a close eye on anyone who threatened to upset the balance. To
the religious leaders, Jesus was unpredictable. When they heard that
he and his disciples were approaching the city that Monday morning,
they wondered what he would do. Would crowds again gather to lay
their coats and palms at his feet? Would he blaspheme the name of
the Lord by accepting their praises as he had done the day before?
Would he incriminate himself in a way that would make an arrest
appear justified and thereby meet with no opposition?

Later that morning, word came to the religious leaders that Jesus
had entered Jerusalem and was on his way to the temple. Venturing
into the epicenter of their ongoing conflict took a lot of nerve. Was
he that obtuse? Or was he spoiling for a fight?

Coins from all over the world spilled across the temple floor as a table came to rest on its side. Confused and startled men jumped up with a shout as Jesus overturned a second table. The men who sold pigeons backed away to get out of his path, and Jesus knocked over their chairs before heading to the main causeway where the merchants brought in their wares.

"Get out of here, you and your beasts!" Jesus said. "Have you no respect? It is written, 'My house will be a house of prayer for all the nations.' But you have made this sacred place into a den of thieves."

His voice echoed down the long hall. Everything happened fast. The merchants, Jesus' disciples, and even the temple authorities who saw the whole episode unfold watched in relative passivity, unsure of what to do. Jesus stood in the center of the mess looking like a man full of authority. He would yield to no one who would reduce the house of the Lord to a cheap temple. Nor would he tolerate religious leaders who approved of such empty displays of worship.

Jesus was indignant. This is not how God's people were supposed to be led. The temple was a sacred space, and worship was a holy matter. The propriety and dignity of approaching the presence of God had found an advocate in this visiting rabbi. Jesus had cleared the temple like this once before, back before anyone knew his name. Then he had warned the merchants to remove the money-changers' tables and stop making his father's house into a den of thieves. If the first time Jesus cleared the temple served as a warning, this time it served as a judgment. Whatever anyone might say, this was not an eruption of blind anger. This was premeditated. Jesus saw nothing today he hadn't seen many times before. He had stood in this very place as recently as yesterday. Nothing he saw came as a surprise. He did what he meant to do.

From the triumphal entry to the cursing of the fig tree to this, Jesus presented himself as a man with authority and an inscrutable perspective on what God expected from his people—and they had missed it. It wasn't just that he had the nerve to carry out an act like this. It was his unflinching commitment to stay in the conversation he had started. If an average man had mustered the courage to do what Jesus did in the temple, he would probably get out of there as quickly as he could. But after overturning those tables, which brought the temple market to a halt, Jesus stayed right where he was and spoke with those who would listen.

When people saw Jesus, they whispered, "It's him! It's the man who rode on that donkey yesterday, the one who raised Lazarus of Bethany from the dead!"

Children who had gathered to watch the spectacle picked up on the cues of the excited grown-ups around them. They remembered the little song they had heard the day before, and they began to sing as children do, delighting in the repetition of the refrain: "Hosanna to the Son of David! Come save us, Son of our greatest king. Prince, assume your throne. Become our King of glory and deliver us. Hosanna, Hosanna, Hosanna. Save us now."

Jesus listened to their song just as he had listened to the singers outside the city the day before. He gathered a crowd and taught from God's Word. He encouraged the people with God's promises. He presided as their priest, and before long the lame and the blind began to come to him because they knew he welcomed the downcast. They knew he ate with those on the fringe. They had heard of Lazarus, so they knew Jesus was a healer. To their great comfort and joy he received them, healing their infirmities with just a touch.

These were people beyond any physician's help, but when Jesus touched them, he reversed what had been otherwise irreversible. Women who had never seen the crystal blue sky over Jerusalem and men who had never seen their own mothers came to him, and he opened their blind eyes. Those who had never gone anywhere without being carried stood on their own atrophied legs and danced. People came to Jesus because they wanted to be close to the priest. The children wanted to watch him work. The sick hoped to feel the touch of God through this man with authority in his voice. But the blind and the lame and the children were not Jesus' only audience. Every eye was on him now, including those of the temple authorities, and they were not pleased. They were embarrassed and angry.

The chief priests and the scribes were not known for getting along with each other, but in response to Jesus, they had become a unified front. While the children sang their songs and the lame danced to them, the chief priests and scribes together insisted that Jesus take responsibility for this situation and silence those children.

"Do you hear what they're saying?" they demanded.

Jesus' reply was as strong as it was succinct: "Yes."

Jesus let his answer register. He had heard them, and he knew why the chief priests and scribes were so troubled. For Jesus to let these children sing this song to him came dangerously close to accepting a level of praise that belonged only to God. Jesus walked a fine line toward blasphemy here. He needed to end this and end it right away.

Jesus broke the silence by quoting from the Psalms: "Have you never read, 'Out of the mouths of infants and nursing children you have prepared praise'?"

The entire day had been building up to this moment. This was the level of blasphemy they'd thought they might hear. The psalm

Jesus quoted was from their songbook. Of course they had heard it. They knew it well. These words spoke of praise out of the mouths of babes intended for God himself. That was what the psalm said. But Jesus now claimed that these children in the temple fulfilled that prophecy by singing their praises to him. No one misunderstood his meaning. Anyone who wondered who this Jesus thought he was just got an answer from the man himself. Jesus put himself on the same level as God.

As the day gave way to night, Jesus and his disciples went back across the valley to Lazarus's house. Many had come to the temple that morning to meet the sacrificial obligations God delineated in his Word. If their sacrifice required a pigeon, they purchased a pigeon and gave it to the priest, who offered it on their behalf. They regarded this as worship, though there was little to distinguish it from the rites of their pagan neighbors who shoveled meat into the bellies of their gods while they prayed for fertility, rain, abundance, and victory over their enemies.

But when the blind and lame came to Jesus, they hoped he might change their lives. They didn't want him to simply note their presence and approve. They wanted to be near him. They wanted this man of God to transform them, to give them new life. And he did.

While many came to the temple that day to offer their prayers or present their sacrifices, Jesus drew a distinction between doing worshipful acts and being a true worshiper of God. One was the business of ritual, but the other had to do with what lay at the core of a man.

The Sanhedrin was the highest Hebrew court over Israel, consisting of seventy-one men from among the chief priests, scribes, and elders of the people. Caiaphas, the high priest, presided. Rome had given the Sanhedrin a fair measure of autonomy to rule over the civil matters of Israel so long as they kept the peace. It was a role the Sanhedrin took seriously. They were the gatekeepers of the temple. It was their job to assess a teacher's credentials; it was also their prerogative to grant or withhold permission to teach in the temple.

When Jesus entered the temple that morning and turned over the money-changers' tables, declaring that this place appointed for worship had become a den of thieves, he assumed a posture of authority over the people, and he did this without the Sanhedrin's permission. Jesus had taken over the temple so that no one could come to God the Father that day except through him. He took up the role of the priest, the mediator between God and man. What troubled the Sanhedrin most was that the people they were supposed to lead now sought Jesus in droves.

That night and into the next morning, the members of the Sanhedrin met to discuss what needed to happen. They distilled the matter down to a single question they wanted Jesus to answer—a question that would either put him in his place or trap him in blasphemy. Either way they figured he would give them what they needed to silence him. When he arrived at the temple on Tuesday, they would find him and demand a response.

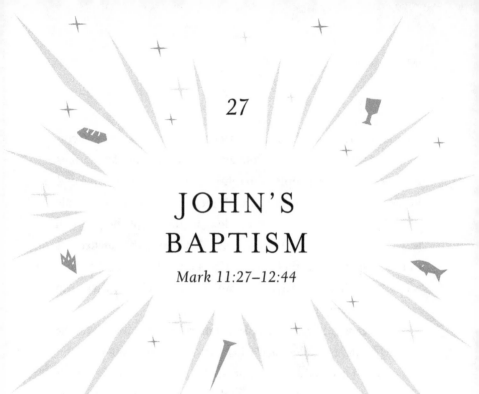

27

JOHN'S
BAPTISM

Mark 11:27–12:44

WHEN THE RELIGIOUS LEADERS learned that Jesus had returned to the temple area on Tuesday morning, a group from the Sanhedrin set out to meet him. When they found him, they asked their question: "Who gave you the authority to act as you have these past two days?"

It was a strange question. They weren't asking him to explain his behavior. They wanted to know who had granted him permission to act as a man in authority. The question betrayed their wounded pride. They were the keepers of civil and religious affairs in the city. Jesus certainly hadn't asked them if he could descend like a whirlwind on the temple the day before. Did he presume to appeal to a higher authority? Would he say his authority came from God? They wanted to know.

Jesus answered with a question of his own: "I will ask you one question. Answer me and I will answer you. John's baptism: was that from heaven or from man?"

To a casual observer, this might have sounded like a random question, but it wasn't. Nor was Jesus attempting to be clever. His life was closely joined to John's. They were cousins, and John gave his life testifying that Jesus was, as the prophet Malachi had said, "the Lord suddenly come to his temple." John proclaimed Jesus to be God's Messiah, the one and only Savior of Israel, and he called the people to repent and trust in Jesus. If the Sanhedrin didn't believe John was from God, they certainly wouldn't accept that Jesus was either. On the other hand, if they did see John as one sent from God, why did they oppose the one whose coming John had heralded?

Jesus' question challenged a simple presumption. If the Sanhedrin were going to judge Jesus as being out of line in God's temple among God's people, could they demonstrate that they could tell the difference between something that was from God and something that was contrived by man? The question was anything but simple for the Sanhedrin. There were only two options, but no matter which they chose, they would be exposed as duplicitous.

They said to Jesus, "Give us a minute to confer."

Jesus had backed them into a corner, and they knew it. If they said John's baptism was from God, why weren't they the first to be baptized by him? More importantly, why weren't they following Jesus, whom John had proclaimed was the Christ?

But to say John's baptism was contrived by man brought an entirely different set of problems. The people loved John, and to speak ill of his memory was not advisable with all the Passover pilgrims around. He was a martyred Jew whose head was served on a platter to a child by Herod himself because the wife of his adulterous union hated John's incessant call to repent.

The members of the Sanhedrin gathered not to discuss what they believed but rather which answer would frame them in the best possible light. If they said John's baptism was from God, they would have to accept that Jesus held authority in the temple. But if they said it was of man, they would have to dismiss the martyrdom of a national hero, and they feared how the people would respond.

They returned to Jesus and said, "We don't know."

Though this third option seemed to be the safest in terms of saving face, it stripped them of the authority to demand an answer from Jesus because it revealed a complete collapse of integrity. Either they didn't know the truth or they wouldn't speak it, which showed they weren't really after the truth but instead a desired outcome. And if they weren't concerned about the truth, what was the basis for their authority? Their answer was a lie and everyone knew it. Why should Jesus yield to the agenda of liars?

Jesus said, "Since you won't answer my question, I will not tell you by what authority I do these things."

This entire confrontation was an attempt to put Jesus in his place by forcing him to yield to the Sanhedrin's authority. But their judgment of Jesus made less sense with each passing day. Jesus asked smarter questions and gave clearer answers than his opponents. They tried to discredit his ministry, but there were people walking around in the temple who only days earlier had been blind and lame.

When the Sanhedrin tried to question his motives, he exposed their hearts. When they attempted to intimidate him by coming to him in numbers, he showed not the slightest sign of backing down. He had literally turned the tables on them the day before, but today he had done it again—this time with further-reaching implications. When they demanded he submit to their authority, he exposed them as liars. If they had no integrity, they held no real authority.

If they wanted to contain his influence among the people, they would have to rely on more than warnings and bravado. They would have to remove him because he would not yield.

Jesus wasn't ready to move on yet. Turning to those who had gathered to watch this confrontation, Jesus told them a parable about a man who owned a vineyard. It was a nice vineyard with a fence to protect it. It had a winepress and a tower. The owner leased it to some of the locals and then left the country. When harvest came around, he sent a servant to inspect the vineyard's fruit. But the tenants took the servant and beat him and sent him away empty-handed. The owner sent another servant, and the tenants did the same to him, sending him away in shame. The tenants killed the third servant the owner sent. Every servant who came to inspect the vineyard was either beaten or killed by the wicked tenants.

The owner of the vineyard was very concerned. He said, "I have no servants left. If I send them my beloved son, surely they will respect him." But when the tenants learned that the owner had sent his only son, they said to each other, "If we kill him, the owner will have no heir. He will have no one to give this inheritance. The vineyard will be ours."

In those days if a person could prove three years of uninter-rupted possession of a place, they could legally claim ownership. With the owner's servants destroyed and his only heir dead, he'd have to personally return if he wanted to keep the vineyard as his own. For this vineyard that had already cost him so much, surely the owner would relinquish his rights rather than absorb any further expense.

The tenants killed the owner's beloved son and threw his body over the vineyard wall like a piece of garbage.

"What do you think the owner will do?" Jesus asked.

The members of the Sanhedrin listened with nervous agitation. When Jesus began this story, they suspected it was a thinly veiled analogy about them. By the end they were certain, but they couldn't show it because Jesus had revealed a secret they were working hard to keep. They thought they were the only ones in the room who knew about their plot to kill him. But the masterful storyteller revealed, as though speaking in code in the form of a parable, that he knew their plan and what drove them. He knew they meant to kill him, and he knew they planned to do it in a way that looked completely legal.

Jesus said, "That owner will surely come. He will destroy what those wicked tenants have attempted to build, and he will give the vineyard to others. Have you never read this Scripture: 'The stone that the builders rejected has become the cornerstone. This was God's doing, and it is marvelous in our eyes'?"

By rejecting the authority of the Sanhedrin, Jesus was saying that everything about who ruled the temple and how a person gained access to the holy presence of God was about to change. As he had done the day before, Jesus stayed in the temple long after his initial confrontation with the chief priests, scribes, and elders, teaching the people.

The range of topics Jesus touched on that Tuesday afternoon served as a sort of manifesto. This was the last day Jesus would speak in the temple as a free man. Though no one noticed, Jesus used this opportunity to speak directly to the baseless charges that would be brought against him only two days later—charges of blasphemy, of opposing paying taxes, and of upsetting the people.

As he taught, a widow came into the temple treasury. Many wealthy people had come and given large sums of money, but this widow put two small copper coins into the offering box. Jesus said to his disciples, "This woman has given more than any of the others. They gave out of abundance, but she gave out of her need."

The widow was a picture of what the people desperately needed to see. God didn't care about how much money they gave or how much power they presumed to possess over others. All he wanted— all he had ever wanted—was their whole hearts, minds, souls, and strength. He wanted them, but they couldn't see it.

This was a day of turning the tables on common thought. God's people had become pragmatists. They saw everything in terms of an economy—they made deposits and took withdrawals and measured their standing in the world according to how well they balanced the good with the bad in their lives. This had become their religion, and God had become another creditor come to settle debts.

The Sanhedrin saw this God who delivered them from their slavery in Egypt, this God who had led them through the wilderness into a land flowing with milk and honey, this God who had made a promise to keep them as his own forever, as a disinterested landlord who didn't deserve the vineyard he planted. They wagered he would not come. So on that Tuesday, two days before the Passover and the Feast of Unleavened Bread, the chief priests and the scribes conspired together on a plan to arrest Jesus. They required discretion because they feared the people. This would have to happen out of the view of the public.

At the end of the day, Jesus and his disciples left the temple to return to Lazarus's house in Bethany. As they left the city and crossed over to the Mount of Olives, one of the disciples stopped and turned around to look at Jerusalem rising high above them. He said to Jesus, "Look at that city, teacher. The buildings and stones, they're so beautiful."

The crowds were gone. It was just Jesus and his disciples now. The disciples regarded the city in silence for a moment. It had been a stressful day. Although they had stood by Jesus throughout his confrontations with the religious leaders, they didn't fully understand everything he taught. What they did understand made them feel they were close to the end of something.

Jesus said, "Look at it, friends. Soon the whole city will be thrown down. Not one stone will be left on another."

Peter, James, John, and Andrew pulled Jesus aside and said, "We don't understand. Please tell us what you mean. When will these things happen?"

Jesus had spoken like this before. In the earlier days, his strong assertions stirred them awake with excitement. But the events of the past few days had left them weary and afraid. They needed a word of consolation.

Jesus said, "I know you're afraid. Let me tell you what is coming so that no one leads you astray."

28

THE SCENT OF OPULENCE

Matthew 26:6-13; Mark 13:3-13;
John 12:1-8

*L*ATE *TUESDAY AFTERNOON* on the Mount of Olives, Jesus told his disciples how this gospel of the kingdom of God would unfurl. He told them that many would come claiming to be the Savior and that many would be deceived. Tribulation and persecution would escalate to proportions beyond their wildest imaginations. Men would hand their own brothers over to death, fathers their children, and children their fathers. Earthquakes were coming, as were famines, wars, and rumors of wars. Jesus' life and message would break this world in two.

But in the end the gospel would prevail. The good news concerning the coming kingdom of God would make its way across the nations, Jesus said, but it would cost his disciples everything. The time was coming when they would be arrested for their association with him. They would be beaten. They would stand before governors and kings, on trial for their lives.

"You will be hated by all because of me," Jesus told them. "But do not be afraid. The Holy Spirit will give you the words and the strength for every trial you face. It will not be you who speaks, by my Spirit speaking through you, so do not fear. Heaven and earth will pass away but my words will remain forever."

Jesus' words landed heavy on his disciples' threadbare hearts. They were hoping for some insight into what was coming so they could prepare themselves. But this was not what Jesus offered. What he gave instead was a promise. God would give them everything they needed for everything he had called them to do and to be, regardless of what happened. It was a strange consolation, but a consolation just the same. His plans for these men were gilded with a greater glory than safe, uneventful lives. They would light up like a city on a hill and burn with the brilliance of the gospel until it was God's will to bring them home to where the light of his glory would render the sun itself obsolete.

Their lives were infused with divine, eternal purpose, and God would preserve them according to his perfect will. If they were going to find any consolation from Jesus, they would have to find it there.

Though Sunday, Monday, and Tuesday had been filled with harrowing experiences that seemed to be drawing him ever nearer to his death, on Wednesday Jesus was still. He and his disciples went to the home of a man in Bethany known as Simon the leper. Simon belonged to a growing part of the population known not for their accomplishments but for what was wrong with them. It was a difficult life, but also strangely liberating since the first thing people learned about Simon was his broken past. Simon lived among the few who did not have to pretend to be what they were not. He was Simon, the leper. People could choose his company or reject it, but that was who he was.

His history with leprosy made Simon's home a relatively safe place for the ostracized and destitute of the community. Simon invited Jesus and his disciples to his home for a feast. Bethany was festive as pilgrims arrived by the score to stay with old friends and relatives in preparation for the Passover. It was both the command of God and the joy of Israel to celebrate how God had delivered them from their slavery in Egypt into this land flowing with milk and honey. The extravagances of a feast were a statement to the senses that they no longer lived in desolation but in abundance. The feast at Simon the leper's home was no exception. They ate, drank, and laughed to their hearts' content.

After the meal, Simon and his guests settled in for some conversation. The levity was good for the disciples' hearts. Through Jesus' more recent actions and words, he had led his followers into a deepening understanding of what he meant when he spoke of his coming arrest and execution. At first his statements on the matter were veiled, either by design or by the disciples' own dullness of mind and heart. But in the light of his most recent clashes with the temple authorities, those words had taken on flesh and come alive to them. Though the feast was festive, there lurked a sober foreboding in the back of the disciples' minds—as though they were nearing the end of something and uncertain of what that end would bring.

While they reclined around Simon's table, Mary, Lazarus's sister, came into the room carrying a stone-hewn bottle. She handled the flask as though it were a rare and precious jewel. Knowing what it was, her brother leaned forward in his seat. His sister had been saving this bottle for a long time. Many times she had told Lazarus and Martha what she meant to do with it.

The sealed stone bottle was made of Egyptian alabaster. It held a pound of an exotic Arabian perfume called nard. The costly scent fetched close to a day's wage for a day's supply, so it belonged mostly to the wealthy and powerful. Arabian nard was the scent of opulence—the fragrance of those whose needs had been met and wanted for nothing. Over the years Mary's family had saved a half-liter of the exotic fragrance, equal to a full year's wage, and now Mary was its keeper.

Mary took a seat on the floor beside Jesus, turning the bottle in her hands as the men talked. Gripping the bottle with both hands, she broke the stone neck and the scent of kings wafted up, filling the room with a fragrance that brought an instinctively reverent silence. Then, with every eye now on her, she began to pour the oil-based perfume on Jesus' head so that it saturated his scalp, filtered into the sides of his beard, and wicked through his garments onto his shoulders and back. After this she used what remained to anoint his feet.

This was an intimate moment between friends. Jesus had given Mary so much, not only by saving her brother but also by being her friend. Though her sister, Martha, expressed her love through cooking and serving, Mary was a woman of extravagance when it came to giving the gift of unhurried time. The perfume gave her time with Jesus, and she wanted to spend it all.

Many regarded the perfume Mary poured over Jesus' head and feet as her only security for the future. They immediately began to question her judgment. But this was no whim. It was Mary's response to what Jesus had given her. He had brought her brother back from the dead and then promised to do the same with her. In this promise she sensed that Jesus meant to give her something more and wouldn't stop until he was finished. So in return she gave Jesus everything she had. She anointed her King's head with oil in the presence of his enemies and made lovely the feet of this one who had brought her so much good news.

The disciples reacted as men often do. They thought about the value of her perfume. It seemed a waste. They thought about how they might have capitalized on the nard's value if it were theirs. To voice such dreams seemed vulgar, but something needed to be said, so they dressed their indignation in the noble auspices of concern for the poor.

They said to each other, "Think of the poor people who could have benefited from the sale of this perfume."

Hearing this, Jesus came to Mary's defense. "Leave her alone," he said. "What she has done is beautiful. You will always have the poor but you won't always have me."

The men in the room regarded that alabaster bottle as a commodity Mary should have held on to in the event that she needed to trade it in. But what were such fragrances for? Perfume was meant to be spilled out and evaporated in order that it might fill a room with its beautiful and startling aroma. As the scent electrified the senses of everyone present, Jesus called it beautiful. Creation testified to a Maker who delighted in beauty for beauty's sake. So many things in their world were beautiful that didn't need to be because God opted to make them that way. This could be for only two reasons: because beauty pleased him and so that he might arrest his people by their senses to wake them from the slumbering economy of pragmatism.

Jesus said to Mary's critics, "She has given me this gift because she is preparing me for my burial, and history will never forget her act of beauty. Wherever stories are told of me, people will remember her."

For three years Judas Iscariot kept (and stole from) the purse that supported Jesus and the disciples as they traveled. He made his way through life by determining what a thing was worth and functioning within that economy. At first Jesus seemed to carry the power of a warlike king. But lately Judas's days with Jesus had brought more suffering than notoriety. Mary's lavish act and Jesus' response were more than he could bear. As that perfume dripped from Jesus' beard, Judas saw his life, as with those drops, being wasted.

Judas appeared to be invested in Jesus' ministry. He had even gone out and proclaimed the kingdom of God when Jesus sent out the Twelve. He had seen miracles, signs, and wonders. But Judas was ready to do the unthinkable without a second thought. He had spent years with Jesus, but he never loved him. He was close to Jesus, yet he was lost. At the time, no one but Jesus knew the true heart of Judas—or any of the Twelve, for that matter—because a man's thoughts are often hidden.

After dinner Judas slipped away from Simon the leper's house and crossed the Kidron Valley, this time on his own. He was going to have a very different meeting with the chief priests than those Jesus had been having.

"How much will you give me if I hand him over to you?" Judas asked. It chilled him to discover they had an answer: thirty pieces of silver—about four months' wages. Jesus' life and Judas's betrayal added up to one-third of the value of Mary's perfume—just enough to make it through the winter.

Judas agreed. He hoped he could salvage the time wasted following this man who proved to be something other than what Judas had thought. But even before he took one step back toward Bethany, his plan, like venom, had already begun to liquefy his soul.

Jesus put everything now in the context of his pending death. The scent that covered Jesus' body, filling the room, would remain on him for the next several days before the scented oils dissipated and were spent. He knew well what those days would bring. Mary's perfume would stay with him through everything Judas had set in motion: his arrest, trial, death, and burial. Judas's and the chief priests' plan would not be able to escape Mary's gift. Every lash of a whip would release the scent of nobility into the air. With every blow to his face, every rub of the crossbeam, every tearing away of a garment from a wound, the scent of opulence would fill the air and linger wherever he went as though a king had passed through this violent world and left behind his spirit.

29

THIRTEEN MEN

John 13:1-35

*L*ATE AFTERNOON ON the Thursday before the Passover, thirteen men sat around a table in a room on the second floor of a home on the southern edge of the Old City. They had been together for three years now—years filled with wonder, struggle, honor, and rejection. They were about to eat their last supper together, though only two of them knew it. Partway through the meal, Jesus wrapped a towel around his waist and made his way around the room, washing the feet of each of the twelve men he called his disciples. It was one last demonstration of his deep love for them and a foretaste of what he was about to do to make them clean.

He began with Andrew, a fisherman by trade, who was the first to hear Jesus say he would make them fishers of men. Andrew had been a disciple of John the Baptist before becoming the first disciple Jesus called. Though Jesus called the other disciples soon after he called Andrew, this follower had been with Jesus the longest.

Beside Andrew sat James and John, the two brothers Jesus nick-named the "Sons of Thunder" due to their fiery personalities and competitive spirits. They were among the most loyal-hearted of the group. These men who loved to be first would lay down their lives for Jesus because they loved him.

Next there was Matthew, son of Alphaeus. Matthew first met Jesus while he was working in his tax-collection booth. He invited Jesus to his home for dinner where tax collectors and sinners, a necessary sort of fraternity, joined them. Matthew's life with Jesus began at a table filled with sinners, and now three years later not much had changed except Matthew's understanding of who fit under that label.

James the Younger, seldom the center of attention, sat beside his brother Matthew. Though James's place among the disciples was rather quiet, he took his seat at that table because Jesus wanted him to be part of this group, which was enough.

Philip from Bethsaida was the third disciple Jesus called, after Andrew and Peter. When they first met, Philip ran his opinion about Jesus through the filter of what he knew from the Scriptures. He came to enthusiastically believe that Jesus was the Messiah Moses and the prophets spoke of. Once he believed this, he became a man who wanted everyone else to know Jesus too.

Beside Philip sat his friend Nathanael, who carried himself with confidence and sometimes even an air of superiority, as seen in his first encounter with Jesus. When Philip told Nathanael that he had met a man from Nazareth whom he believed was the Christ, Nathanael shrugged. "Can anything good come from Nazareth?" Jesus pursued Nathanael until he believed whole-heartedly that something good had come from Nazareth. But as Jesus washed his feet, Nathanael sensed that Jesus' goodness would be punished before it would be rewarded.

Thaddeus, the son of a man named James, was there too. He was one of the men Jesus sent out to care for the lost sheep of the house of Israel. Thaddeus saw the gospel transform lives, but he also saw many reject not just the message but Thaddeus himself for speaking it.

Beside Thaddeus sat Simon the Zealot, who saw his world through the lens of its political climate. At one point he had belonged to a revolutionary sect of Idumeans who hoped to incite their people to expel all Romans from the Promised Land. He didn't know what to make of Jesus, who had turned out to be far different from the political hero he'd imagined. But when any thought of leaving came to his mind, he remembered Peter's eloquent point: where else would he go?

Next there was Thomas, a pragmatic man who made decisions based on the information in front of him. Though he was inquisitive, he was also brave. Thomas knew that the religious leaders wanted Jesus dead. When Lazarus died and Jesus said he was going to Bethany, it was Thomas who said to the others, "Let us go with him that we may die too."

Then Jesus came to Judas Iscariot. By the time he took Judas's feet in his hands, Judas had already struck a deal with the chief priests. He would hand Jesus over soon, maybe even this night if it worked out. Judas had spent three years with Jesus, but he never loved him. Though Jesus knew what Judas was about to do, he washed his feet anyway, just as he had done with the others, giving him one more chance to repent of his treachery. Judas said nothing.

Last, Jesus came to his dear friend Simon Peter, the second disciple to follow Jesus after his brother Andrew. Peter was both a hero and a mess. In one moment he refused to accept that Jesus had to die, and in the next swore he'd die with him if he had to. Peter was insightful yet dense, hot-tempered yet tender-hearted.

His confidence that Jesus was the Messiah and his zeal to speak his mind established him as a leader and spokesman for the Twelve.

As Jesus went to take Peter's feet in his hands, Peter objected. "This is out of place. You shouldn't be washing my feet."

Jesus said, "Peter, you don't understand what I'm doing right now. But soon you will. If I don't cleanse you, you have no share with me."

Though Peter was quick to rebuke his teacher, he was also quick to repent when corrected. Raising his hands in surrender, Peter said, "Then by all means. Not just my feet, but wash my head and hands as well."

Jesus quieted the room and said to them all, "Do you understand what I have just done? You call me your Teacher and Lord, and you are right to do this because this is what I am. Follow my example. As I have washed your feet, do the same for each other. Serve each other well."

Jesus' heart was heavy. The disciples saw the weight of the burden he carried pulling at his frame all day.

"One of you will betray me," Jesus said.

Sorrow cut the disciples' hearts as Jesus' words hung in the air. Jesus reached for a loaf of bread, tore off a piece, and began to eat.

The disciples soon did the same as little conversations resumed around the table. Still, tension and sadness clouded the room.

John had chosen a seat next to Jesus. Peter stared hard at John until John noticed. Peter pleaded with his eyes, "Ask him who he means." So John leaned in close to Jesus as they ate and whispered, "Who will betray you?"

Jesus said, "Watch. It's the one to whom I'll give this bread."

Jesus dipped his bread in the oil and herbs and handed it to Judas, who reached for it without a hint of suspicion. Before Jesus let go of the bread, their eyes locked and Jesus said, "What you are going to do, do now."

Judas froze. Most of the disciples assumed he was going to make preparations for tomorrow's feast. But Peter and John understood exactly what was going on, as they searched their teacher's face for some sign of what to do next.

These thirteen men had been through so much together. They had spent countless nights under the Galilean stars, eating, drinking, and laughing themselves to sleep. They knew each other—Thomas's pragmatism, Simon's love of politics, Nathanael's endearing self-importance, John's compassion, Peter's ability to wield words like a blunt object. They knew the same battery of parables Jesus told when he entered a new town—the lost son, the sower and the seed, the ten virgins, the friend at night, and Matthew's favorite, the Pharisee and the tax collector. Though they were mostly strangers when they first came together, they were now more similar than different.

The thought that one of them could be capable of the kind of betrayal Jesus suggested shook them because they had walked with Jesus long enough now to know that if any of them were capable of such treachery, they all were. Their first question wasn't, "Is it him?" but rather, "Is it I?" Judas was a riddle—part pretender, part conspirator, part disciple.

He had gone into the hills of Galilee, just as the other disciples had done, healing and proclaiming the kingdom of God. But Judas was also greedy, and as the keeper of the disciples' common purse he was known to skim off the top. Thirty pieces of silver seemed hardly enough to repay three years of service. The economically minded Judas would have been the first to do that math.

But Jesus knew Judas. He knew the tempter from the wilderness had taken hold of Judas's heart. He seemed to belong to the Twelve in every way, so when Jesus told them one of them would betray him, no one assumed he meant Judas. Though he would go on to become the archetype of all traitors, when Jesus handed him the bread, none of the others suspected a thing.

Jesus released his grip on the bread, and Judas slowly raised it to his mouth and ate. Still chewing, Judas rose, crossed the room, and disappeared through a blackened doorway, abandoning the light of the world and stepping irreversibly into darkness, not knowing that his actions would lead not only to Jesus' death but also to his own.

He went out, and it was night.

30

THE LAST CUP

Mark 14:22-42; John 14

THE PEOPLE OF GOD WERE unapologetically traditional. Theirs was an ancient faith, and they were slow, if not unwilling, to introduce new practices to old feasts.

Loaves of unleavened bread sat on the table in the upper room, along with bowls of bitter herbs and four cups of wine, each representing one of the four main promises God made to his people when he led them out of Egypt. During this Passover meal, Jesus and his disciples shared the first cup as they read from the Torah: "I am the Lord, and I will bring you out from under the burdens of the Egyptians."

The disciples felt the tension that had been building over the past few days, as though they were on the cusp of losing something they couldn't name. Jesus could see the weight on their sloping shoulders and the fear in their eyes. He knew they were burdened.

"Don't let your hearts be troubled," Jesus said. "Believe in God; believe in me also. I am going to prepare a place for you, and if I do this, then you can know that I will come back for you and take you with me." The disciples looked confused but no one said anything. Jesus said, "You know the way to the place I'm going."

Thomas spoke up, "Lord, we do not know where you are going. How can we know the way?"

Jesus said, "I am the way, and the truth, and the life. No one comes to the Father but through me. If you know me, you know the Father. You have seen him."

Philip said, "Show us the Father, Lord. That will be enough for us."

Jesus replied, "Do you not know me, Philip? If you have seen me, you have seen the Father. We are one. Believe in me. Believe the works you have seen with your own eyes. Believe me because after I'm gone, you will carry on in my name. The Father will send a helper, the Spirit of Truth, and he will never leave you."

They leaned in, trying to understand.

Jesus said, "I will not leave you as orphans. I will come to you. The Helper, the Holy Spirit, whom my Father will send in my name, will teach you all you need to know, and he will cause you to remember the things I've said to you. I leave you peace, not as the world gives peace. I give you my peace, so do not be afraid. Don't let your hearts be troubled."

Jesus lifted the second cup, the cup of deliverance, and recited the second promise: "I will deliver you from slavery to the Egyptians." He passed the cup around the table, and when it made its way back to him, he took a loaf of bread, gave thanks to God, broke it, and handed it to his disciples. The bread symbolized how their forefathers had fled Egypt in haste, leaving no time for their bread to rise. It was a reminder of the knife's edge they had walked along for so many generations. It was the food wanderers ate as they roamed the desert searching for a home. The disciples held the bread until everyone had some. They were all in this together.

Jesus said, "This bread is my body. Take it. It is for you."

The disciples ate slowly, never taking their eyes off their Lord. It was highly unusual to deviate from the Passover tradition. Jesus had assigned a new meaning to the bread. This now wasn't the bread of the narrow escape of their wandering forefathers in a vast desert, but the bread of the presence of their Lord who had given them a seat at his table.

Then Jesus took the third cup, the cup of redemption, and returning to the Torah said, "I will redeem you with an outstretched arm and with great acts of judgment, says the Lord."

Then, as the disciples passed the third cup around the table, Jesus said, "This is my blood—the blood of the covenant which is poured out for the sins of many. Drink this in remembrance of me."

When the cup made its way back to Jesus, the disciples waited for him to conclude the ceremony by passing the last cup around— the cup of the fourth promise, which said, "I will take you to be my people, and I will be your God, and you shall know that I am the Lord your God who has brought you out from under the burdens of the Egyptians." It was the cup of being kept.

But Jesus didn't reach for the fourth cup. Instead, he told his disciples, "Listen to me. I will not drink of the fruit of the vine again until the day comes when I drink it new in the kingdom of God."

Then Jesus rose to his feet and asked his disciples to stand with him to sing a doxology over their suspended, unfinished Passover meal. Though Jesus' voice carried the tone of a troubled heart, he

led them in the ancient song about how the stone the builders rejected had become the cornerstone and how the steadfast love of
the Lord endured forever. When they finished singing, Jesus led
them out to the Mount of Olives to one of their regular meeting
places, the garden of Gethsemane.

The fourth cup, the cup of being kept, sat full and untouched,
waiting to be emptied.

As they crossed the valley, loose threads from their conversation
over supper tangled up in the disciples' minds. Jesus told them that
one of them would betray him, and each believed it could be him.

Jesus gathered them close and said, "Tonight is going to be a hard
night for you—for all of you."

It already had been.

He continued, "You will all fall away from me tonight. None of
you will be able to stand strong."

Jesus had a way of saying hard words in a manner that brought
strange but sure comfort. He knew what lay ahead, and he knew it
would prove too much for them. They were going to do the unthinkable—abandon Jesus in his greatest hour of need. There was
no stopping it.

So, because he loved them, he named their failure before it happened and framed it in the context of history. He said, "Zechariah
was talking about you when he said, 'I will strike the shepherd, and
the sheep will scatter.'" Their pending failure had been foretold long
ago and was as inevitable a part of this story as anything they had
seen or heard up to this point.

Jesus did not leave them alone under their pending collapse,
however. He said, "Listen. After I am raised up, I will go ahead of

you into Galilee. We will meet again there." Though failure was coming, it would not be enough to overrule his love for them or his call on their lives.

As they reached the garden of Gethsemane, Jesus asked Peter, James, and John to stay with him as the others went back to Bethany. Entering the garden, Jesus said, "I want you to stay here and pray. Pray that you won't enter into temptation."

Jesus went a stone's throw deeper into the garden and knelt on the ground.

He prayed, "Father, if you are willing, please take this cup from me." Jesus wiped his dripping forehead with his sleeve, which came down red. He began the night troubled in spirit. Now, after all that had unfolded, he was in agony. His pores had begun to bleed from the stress, mixing his blood with his sweat, staining his garments.

He whispered to his Father, "If there is a way, let this cup pass from me. But if there isn't, may your will be done."

This was not a prayer spoken into a void. An angel appeared and began to comfort him, revealing two immovable facts: that the Father cared about his Son's agony so much he would not leave him alone and that the course was set. Jesus would be poured out like Passover wine—emptied until there was nothing left.

Jesus rose from his knees and walked back over to Peter, James, and John, all of whom he found sleeping. They didn't sleep because they were lazy. They were exhausted in the way a person feels at the end of a day spent crying. They slept for sorrow because for all that their minds could not comprehend, their hearts understood well that they were about to lose their friend.

Jesus said, "Wake up. Stay alert. Pray that you won't fall into temptation. Your spirit is willing, but your flesh is weak."

Peter, James, and John rubbed at their eyes, wanting to stay awake but losing the battle even then as Jesus stood before them.

Jesus left them and went back to where he had been praying. Twice he returned to find them asleep. The last time he woke them and said, "Enough sleeping. The hour has come."

In the distance a serpent of torchlight snaked its way up the hillside into the garden. Through the trees a soft orange glow flickered as the faint sounds of clanking armor grew to announce the advance of a small army.

31

TRIAL AT NIGHT

Matthew 26:47-68

*T*HE FIRST SILHOUETTE TO APPEAR walked with a familiar gait. Others followed behind. Torchlight filled the clearing as the sounds of shuffling feet, clanking armor, and quiet orders rose to a crescendo. Peter, James, and John snapped out of their slumber, alert like sheep who had caught the scent of the wolves but had not yet seen them.

"The one I kiss is the man you're looking for," Judas whispered to the commander of the Roman detachment.

Jesus stood facing the arresting party, peaceful and still as a statue. As the last of the group came into view, Jesus and his disciples saw a collection of soldiers, Pharisees, and officials from the chief priests. It was a rare sight, Romans and Pharisees working together.

Judas emerged from behind the soldiers. Though his lips were bent into a smile, his eyes showed only fear. Peter, James, and John recognized his treachery as soon as they saw him, but things were unfolding far too quickly for them to be much beyond confused.

Judas walked directly to Jesus. When he was a few steps away he opened his arms for an embrace.

"Hello, Rabbi!" Judas said.

"Friend," Jesus said, "do what you came to do."

Judas wrapped Jesus in his arms and kissed him on his cheek. As he pulled back, the two of them stood face to face. Search as he might, Judas found no fear or surprise in the eyes of his teacher— only pity, sorrow, and strength.

A couple of soldiers stepped forward and grabbed hold of Jesus as the rest spread out to flank the disciples to keep them from running. They were many, and they were armed. They were not here to argue. Big men in body armor had come to bring a wanted man into custody. Jesus and his disciples were clearly outmatched. The soldiers expected this arrest to take place without incident. They knew Jesus was a man of peace and that his disciples were untrained in the art of war. Beyond that, they cared little about the man in the garden. He was an assignment on their duty roster—another zealot upsetting the festival in Jerusalem.

But no one, not even the disciples, expected what happened next. Jesus asked, "Who do you want?"

"Jesus of Nazareth," they answered.

Jesus said, "I am."

Immediately everyone in the garden fell to the ground, as though they had been slain by some unseen spirit. Jesus stood among the stunned soldiers and panicked disciples. As they began to pick themselves up, Jesus asked again, "Who do you want?"

Reluctantly, the captain of the guard said, "We seek Jesus of Nazareth."

Jesus said, "I told you, I am. Now listen to me. If I am the one you are looking for, let these men go." He said this to fulfill what he had prayed earlier that night in the upper room when he said, "I haven't lost a single one of those you have given me, except the son of destruction."

Agreeing to deal with Jesus only, the soldiers moved forward to bind him. James and John backed into the shadows, but a spirit of indignation seized Peter. Before he knew what he was doing, he reached for his sword and he let out a cry. He swung his blade at a man named Malchus, the high priest's servant. Peter didn't land a fatal blow, but he did cut off Malchus's right ear.

Whatever calm there might have been up to this moment nearly evaporated completely. Each soldier instinctively reached for the hilt of his sword, ready to fight. Jesus stepped quickly between Peter and the guards, yelling, "Stop, Peter! Stop. Put away your sword. Shall I not drink from the cup my Father has given me?"

Then Jesus said to the soldiers, "And you, what did you think you would find here? You know me. You have seen me day after day teaching in the temple. You could have arrested me at any point. Were you coming after a thief? Is that why you brought swords and clubs?"

Jesus reached out and touched Malchus's wounded head and healed him. This calmed the soldiers enough for Peter to withdraw to where James and John were standing, and with them to disappear into the shadows of the Mount of Olives.

Jesus submitted to the arrest, but he carried himself like a man who was yielding to a greater purpose than that of his captors. From receiving Judas's kiss to permitting the soldiers to arrest him after they had fallen to the ground from the power of his words to healing poor Malchus in order to calm an escalating battle, Jesus stood as a man set apart from the proceedings in the garden. He didn't only accept his arrest. In many ways he facilitated it, even choosing to wait for Judas in the same place he and his disciples had gathered during the previous nights.

The watchmen on the ramparts of the old city walls saw the arresting party come into the clearing at the bottom of the valley, and they summoned the chief priests, scribes, and elders of the temple who had been anxiously awaiting the report that Jesus had been taken into custody. These members of the Sanhedrin gathered at the home of Annas, the former high priest. Annas had ruled the Sanhedrin for eight years before passing his title down to his son-in-law Caiaphas. Though Annas no longer acted in an official capacity as the Sanhedrin's leader, his influence ran deep. He had either built upon or personally laid the foundations for their current means of mediating justice.

The arresting party brought Jesus to Annas's house for two reasons: to give the council time to assemble for trial since it was the middle of the night and to discuss in advance the charges they meant to bring against Jesus when his official trial began. They knew they had to bring substantial charges if they wanted to force a conviction that carried the appearance of justice. Their own legal system clearly stated that no man should be put to death unless there were at least two witnesses who could testify in full agreement of a capital crime, and those charges had to be proven beyond doubt. So serious was this law that if someone brought false charges for corrupt reasons, they were to receive the punishment they falsely sought.

Annas presided over the improvised court to help the council articulate the charges. Annas questioned Jesus about his ministry, his life, his disciples, and his teachings.

Jesus said, "I have lived my life out in the open. I have hidden nothing. I have always taught in the synagogues and in the temple here. So why do you ask what I am teaching? Ask those here who have heard me. They know what I have said."

Jesus was exposing Annas's attempt to trap him in his words. He was suggesting that Annas was either ignorant of the man he meant to execute or willfully attempting to deceive him. Jesus did this without giving Annas a single word of actual testimony.

Embarrassed, Annas fought to conceal his anger. One of the guards struck Jesus across the cheek and said, "Is that how you talk to the high priest?"

Jesus lifted his swelling face and said, "If what I said was untrue, then bring a charge against me. But if I spoke the truth, why did you hit me?" Jesus' anger was enough for Annas to send him across the courtyard to the home of his son-in-law Caiaphas, the current high priest.

Before the proceedings could be called to order, Caiaphas had already made up his mind what needed to happen. He had been waiting for this moment. He pressed for it, framing the need to execute Jesus as a matter of sacrificing one man to keep the rest of the nation safe from Rome's ruthless determination to cut insurgencies off at the root.

Caiaphas would speak his piece soon enough, but lest he appear too eager as the sole judge and jury, he asked the gathered crowd to make their charges known. One by one, men came forward to testify against Jesus, but no two of them could agree on their testimony, which rendered their testimonies inadmissible. As the false witnesses argued over the details, Caiaphas's frustration mounted until he rose and silenced the moonlit courtyard.

Looking at Jesus, Caiaphas said, "Have you nothing to say? Answer the charges before you."

But Jesus, as a sheep before its shearer, did not open his mouth. What could he say? Substantial charges had yet to be brought. So far only liars had spoken.

Caiaphas took Jesus' silence as an insult. He said, "Tell us all. Are you the Christ, the King of glory and the Son of God?"

There in a room full of experts on the law and the prophets, Jesus lifted his eyes to meet Caiaphas's. He knew the high priest's question was meant to bait Jesus into speaking blasphemy.

"Well, are you?" Caiaphas demanded.

Jesus said, "I am."

He spoke with an authority that had been attracting people for three years. A couple of the guards who had arrested Jesus in the garden gave each other a nervous glance, thankful to still be on their feet.

Before Caiaphas could say anything, Jesus continued, "I am, and you will see the Son of Man seated at the right hand of power, coming down on the clouds of heaven."

The scholars in the room did not miss the fact that Jesus was applying the words of the prophet Daniel to himself. Daniel had prophesied, "Before me stood one like a son of man, coming down with the clouds of heaven. He approached the Ancient of Days and was led into his presence where he was given authority, glory, and sovereign power. And all peoples from every nation and tongue worshiped him."

Caiaphas couldn't believe his ears. He tore his garments in a show of incredulity. How could Jesus' answer be anything but the blasphemy he wanted to hear? Who could actually believe that this man, swollen from the fists of the guards and abandoned by his own disciples, was in fact the Lord of all, the King of glory, the one worthy of the worship of all creation?

Caiaphas had heard enough. Blasphemy was a capital offense. He polled the council, and they agreed that Jesus needed to die. To demonstrate their consensus, they began to spit on Jesus. Then one of the men pulled a hood over Jesus' head, and they began to strike him in the face, saying, "Prophesy, prophet! Tell us who hit you."

They spun him over to the guards who rendered blows of their own. Jesus did not defend himself. He offered his back to those who beat him and his cheeks to those who pulled out his beard. He did not hide from their mocking and spitting. He was reviled, but he did not revile in return. He suffered, but he did not respond with threats. In the face of injustice, he entrusted himself to the one who judges justly. After they had beaten him, the guards led Jesus away to the court of Pontius Pilate, the prefect of Judea.

Peter and John, who had followed the arresting party from the garden and made their way into the courtyard, saw everything as they hid in the shadows.

32

THE RECKONING

Matthew 26:69–27:2; Mark 10:17-31

A FEW WEEKS EARLIER while Jesus and his disciples were returning to Jerusalem by way of Jericho, they met a young man
with a question. It was common for people to come running when
they heard that Jesus was in the area. But most often those who
came to him did so because of a sickness or a particular need. This
young man, however, appeared to need nothing. He was young,
wealthy, and powerful. People treated him with honor. They spoke
of him as a faithful and upright man—honest, fair, and mindful of
the way he lived his life.

The young man ran up to Jesus, fell on his knees, and said, "Good
teacher, what must I do to inherit eternal life?"

Jesus regarded the man for a moment. In his culture, men did
not run. Neither did they prostrate themselves as this man had. His
haste and his posture conveyed sincerity.

Jesus said, "Why did you call me good? Is anyone but God good? Yet you come to a man you know only by reputation and you assume a goodness in me you have no way of knowing."

The young man took Jesus' reproof without apology.

Jesus said, "You know the commandments: Do not murder. Do not commit adultery. Do not steal, bear false witness, or defraud others. Honor your parents."

Surely it wasn't this simple. The young man weighed Jesus' words before he spoke: "I have kept all these since I was a boy."

Jesus looked at the rich young man and loved him. In all his naivety and innocence, the young man believed every word of his own confession.

Jesus said, "There is one thing I see you lack."

The young man's face lit up, eager to receive whatever Jesus would say next.

"Sell all that you have. Everything. Let it all go and give what you earn to the poor. Let the treasure that gives you assurance be in heaven. When you have done this, come follow me," Jesus said.

The young man's face fell. He was a man of great fortune, and the idea of emptying himself of everything he owned this side of heaven in order to gain heaven itself was more than he could embrace. Crestfallen, he turned to leave. Jesus said nothing to stop him but let him go. Then, turning to his disciples, he said, "It is difficult for the wealthy to enter the kingdom of God."

The disciples were amazed that he of all people would say this. He had come preaching that the kingdom of heaven was at hand, and now he was saying it was hard to enter, at least for the wealthy.

Jesus continued, "It is indeed very difficult. In fact, it would be easier for a camel to pass through the eye of a needle than for a rich man to enter the kingdom of God."

The disciples said, "That isn't even possible."

"I know," Jesus said. "It is impossible for man. But with God, anything is possible. Still, it would take a miracle."

Peter watched and listened, keeping his eye on the wealthy young man until he could no longer see him. He thought about all he had left to come follow Jesus and how Jesus was right to tell the young man that the cost of being his disciple was steeper than he might imagine. Peter thought about the day he and his brother had set down their fishing nets for the last time, unsure whether they would return to that life again. He thought about how he had left his home in Galilee and how he missed the heather fields blooming by the cliffs of Arbel. He thought about the miracles but also the tension, the conflict, the uncertainty.

Bringing Jesus and the others into a conversation he was already well into in his own heart, Peter said, "See, we have done that. We left everything to follow you."

Jesus said, "Listen, I'm telling you the truth. Those who leave everything to follow me will get their reward, but this life will be filled with persecution."

Peter swelled with pride. He could deal with the persecution when it came. No one in the world believed more deeply in his own loyalty than Peter.

That's why it had stung Peter when, earlier that night on their way to Gethsemane, Jesus told his friends they would all fall away. He said they would do what the rich young ruler had done; they would walk away. They would be asked to hand over a treasure too great. Some would walk away sad, others perhaps in anger, others still in confusion. But to a man, they would all walk away.

This was hard for them to hear. Peter was convinced Jesus had underestimated at least one of his followers. He said, "Even if the others fall away, I will not."

Jesus looked at his friend—the rock, the mouthpiece, the leader. Peter believed every word that came out of his mouth. He believed he was the exception. He loved Jesus with abandon. But Peter did not know his own weakness. Self-confidence felt strong so long as it wasn't tested. But trial yielded the true verdict.

Jesus said, "Peter, hear my words carefully. Before the rooster crows twice, you will have already denied me three times."

Peter grew angry with his Lord. "No, I will not. I will die with you if I have to. I will not deny you." Of this Peter had no doubt. While the young ruler of Perea took comfort in the excess of his wealth, Peter found comfort in the abundance of his sacrifices.

Peter had followed Jesus' arresting party at a distance, hoping the darkness in the garden would make him unrecognizable but staying out of sight just the same. It was a cold night. When the arresting party came to Annas's and Caiaphas's courtyard, they built a fire to keep themselves warm while they waited for the trial to end and orders to be issued. Peter slunk to the fire, attempting to blend in. One of the servant girls near the fire looked at him.

"I know that man," she told the others. "I think he is one of Jesus' followers."

Peter dismissed her. "I don't know what you're talking about." Nearby a rooster crowed.

One of the men from the arresting party, a relative of Malchus, whose ear Peter had taken off with his sword, studied the disciple for a few minutes and asked, "Didn't I see you in the garden with him?"

The shadows softened the worry on Peter's face. He said, "No, sir, you did not."

As casually as he could, Peter stepped back out of the light. The fire had grown too hot for him, but it was too late. He had already drawn the interest of his audience. Another man said, "You most certainly are one of his followers. You speak with a Galilean accent."

Anger grabbed hold of Peter. He swore at them: "May I be cursed if I'm lying. I swear before God that I do not know the man."

Before Peter had finished his sentence, the rooster crowed again. Peter remembered how Jesus had told him this would happen. The sound tore at his heart like a talon as he stepped into the shadows again. Only this time he could not hide from the one he feared the most—himself.

While Jesus stood trial in the courtyard of the high priests, Peter faced a trial of his own before the priests' servants, and he failed. He broke down and wept bitterly. Heaving with sobs of defeat and self-loathing, Peter could not believe what he had just done. He had promised Jesus, who at that very moment was taking the vicious blows of scoffers and false witnesses, that he would never abandon him.

This collapse of loyalty, Peter knew, was the worst thing he had ever done. The rich young ruler they met on the road was incapable of leaving his security to follow Jesus. But it wasn't until the rooster's crow that Peter realized his precious confidence lay not in money but in the wealth of his sacrifice. He had trusted in himself more than anything else. It had felt good when his hand touched the hilt of his sword in the garden. His sense of valor swelled when he first slipped out of the shadows and dared to draw near enough to the high priest's fire to feel its warmth. But under the scrutiny of a servant girl, Peter traded in all his courage for the sinking sorrow that the cost of following Jesus was more than he could afford. He had taken a low view of Jesus' warning and a high view of his own devotion, which he now suddenly found desperately wanting.

If all Jesus had said was that Peter would deny him, Peter would have abandoned hope then and there. But Jesus had prepared him for this moment. After telling him that this was coming, Jesus had pulled Peter aside and said, "Simon, listen to me. Satan has demanded to have you, that he might sift you like wheat and upend your life like Job's. But I have prayed for you, that your faith won't fail even when you do. You will fall away. Know this. But when you come back, I want you to go find the others and encourage them. They are going to need you."

Though this didn't feel like much to hold on to, it was something—this idea that even though Peter had let go of his Lord, his Lord had not let go of him. It was a strange but real comfort to hear that his future sins, great though they were, were not only known by his Lord but were also forgivable.

The rooster signaled the morning. It was Friday. The trial concluded with a consensus among the chief priests and elders of the people that Jesus would be handed over to die that day. For this they would need Rome, since it was beyond the scope of their authority to put a man to death. So with the charges hammered out and the sun coming up, they bound Jesus and led him across the city to the home of Pontius Pilate, the governor of Judea.

33

WHAT
IS TRUTH?

John 18:28–19:16

*E*ARLY *FRIDAY MORNING*, the members of the Sanhedrin stood outside Pontius Pilate's headquarters with Jesus bound and beaten. They waited for one of Pilate's servants to acknowledge them and summon the governor. Pontius Pilate and the Sanhedrin shared a past neither cherished. On this morning, the chief priests needed Pilate, but they did not like him. Although he alone held the authority to legally call for a public crucifixion, he was nothing more to the chief priests than an unclean Gentile. So rather than defile themselves on the eve of the Passover by entering his home and possibly coming into contact with one of the unclean, they waited outside for Pilate to come to them.

Pilate went outside, and seeing the bloodied prisoner he asked, "What is the accusation you bring against this man?"

Indignant, they asked, "Do you think we would be here if this man wasn't guilty of a great evil?"

Pilate said, "What does this have to do with me? He is your prisoner. If it is your own law he has broken, deal with him yourselves."

They persisted. "It isn't just our law he has broken. He has been misleading our entire nation, claiming to be a king. He calls himself the Christ and forbids his followers from giving their taxes to Caesar. That, governor, is a capital offense. But it is not legal for us to put a man to death for breaking your law."

It has always been the case that what a politician thinks and what a politician does often look very different. Pilate could clearly see that Jesus posed no threat to Caesar. He wanted to release the man. But this moment was about more than the accusations against Jesus. This was politics, and Pilate was a politician who governed a fragile peace.

The scope of Pilate's power lay somewhere between that of the foot soldier and the king. He hoped, as any midlevel politician would, that his personal stock was rising. He believed power and money made the man, and he lived his life navigating those waters for the purpose of gaining more of both. Judea was a step along the way to the power, stature, and respect he hoped to one day possess.

In Judea, however, Pilate had a few things working against him. Early in his rule, he severely damaged his relationship with the Jews he governed when he put to death some Galileans and mixed their blood with the blood of their sacrifices. This was a desecration the Jews never forgave.

No midlevel politician could hope to gain the favor of his superiors when the people he governed detested him. That didn't make for long-term peace. The happier the Jews were with him, Pilate understood, the sooner he could be rid of them.

As it happened, Herod, who held a higher rank than Pilate, was in town for the Passover. Pilate was being asked to preside as a judge over what was, to him, a religious matter between the chief priests and their prisoner. Though this was an opportunity to show his wisdom and leadership, it was also an opportunity to expose weakness. Either way, Pilate knew Herod would hear about how he dealt with the captive accused of claiming to be king. There was only one king—Caesar. Pilate's chief responsibility was to enforce that rule above all. The suggestion of disloyalty to Caesar, together with Pilate's history of trouble with the Jews, could quickly cost him every bit of favor he might have accrued in the eyes of his king. He knew he could not ignore the charges. But that didn't mean he had to let the chief priests manipulate him either.

Using their self-righteous superiority to his advantage, Pilate brought Jesus into his headquarters and shut the door, leaving them outside. If the Sanhedrin were going to force his hand, he would not give them the pleasure of witnessing his interrogation.

"Are you the King of the Jews?" Pilate asked, offering Jesus an opportunity to defend himself.

Jesus said, "Are you asking this because you suspect this yourself, or because this is what you were told?"

The absurdity of the scene was plain to them both. Jesus had no followers, and his own people were the ones who wanted him dead. Still, Pilate did not appreciate being addressed as a peer.

"Am I a Jew? Your own people handed you over to me. What have you done?" Pilate asked.

Jesus said, "If I were after their throne, wouldn't I have a band of rebels fighting for my release? Where are they? My kingdom is not of this world."

Though Pilate didn't understand what Jesus meant, he caught the implication loud and clear. Jesus did, in fact, claim to be a king—and not just any king. He claimed to be king of a kingdom higher than Rome, implying he was a greater king than Caesar. His kingdom would outlast Rome, and his rule would be defined by truth—the absence of which led him to this very conversation.

Pilate was frustrated. He didn't want to convict, let alone crucify, Jesus. He had brought Jesus in behind closed doors to give him an opportunity to persuade the governor to release him—something Pilate wanted to do. If Jesus would give Pilate what he needed, Pilate could spare his life and save political face. But Jesus would not cooperate, and Pilate was losing control of the moment.

Then Pilate had an idea. Jesus was from Galilee, which was Herod's jurisdiction. So he sent Jesus over to Herod, who was in Jerusalem at the time. Herod received Jesus as a curiosity. He had heard much about the miracle worker from Galilee.

When Pontius Pilate's wife learned that her husband had sent Jesus over to Herod, she pulled him aside and pleaded with him, saying, "Have nothing to do with this holy man, husband. He has plagued my dreams. Leave him alone."

Herod questioned Jesus at length but found no more guilt than Pilate. His fascination turned to scorn as he and his soldiers mocked Jesus and dressed him in kingly robes before sending him back to Pilate.

Jesus stood before Pilate weak and bloodied, a living contradiction decorated with fresh wounds and royal robes. Pilate said, "So you do still claim to be a king?"

Jesus said, "You say I'm a king. Hear me. For this purpose I was born into this world—to bear witness to the truth, and everyone who cares about the truth listens to my voice."

Pilate had had enough. Turning to leave, he said, "What is truth?"

The truth, as far as Pontius Pilate was concerned, was that he had an accused insurrectionist without a single follower talking about ruling over a kingdom not of this world. He went out to meet Jesus' accusers and said, "I find no basis for your charge against him. Will it be enough to leave him marked by Rome's whip? Let me flog him and release him back to you in shame."

It would not. The crowds wanted more.

Perhaps he could persuade them into pardoning Jesus themselves by appealing to an old custom that allowed Rome to release one Jewish prisoner during the Passover. Pilate offered them the choice between Jesus and a notorious prisoner named Barabbas, a convicted murderer and thief. Jewish law taught that the Lord detested the condemnation of the innocent and the acquittal of the guilty. Pilate hoped that given the choice they would choose Jesus over the murderer, thus setting the governor himself free from this unseemly injustice.

"Who do you want? Jesus or Barabbas?" Pilate asked.

"Barabbas! Barabbas!" they chanted.

As Barabbas came squinting in the light of his new freedom, Pilate looked at his guards and nodded at Jesus. They seized Jesus, led him into an open courtyard, and began to whip his back with the cat-o'-nine-tails. Seeing the blood saturate the royal robes, one of the soldiers twisted together a crown of thorns to complete the ensemble. Then the soldiers took turns bowing in mockery, saying, "Hail, King of the Jews!" as they struck him on his face with their fists.

Pilate went out to the mob, hoping yet again to persuade them that the suffering Jesus had already endured was enough.

"Behold the man!" Pilate said, as a soldier led Jesus in his bloody robe and thorny crown to Pilate's side. Pilate let the people take in what they were seeing. What Pilate hoped might soften the mob only hardened them. They began to shout, "Crucify him! Crucify him!"

Putting up his hand, Pilate said, "I find no fault with him. Crucify him yourselves!"

Pilate looked to Jesus for help. "Speak. Defend yourself."

Jesus could have defended himself. The primary charge, the one that mattered most to the high priests, was blasphemy. But earlier that Tuesday, while Jesus was teaching in the temple, the scribes had asked him to clarify his understanding of the law of God. Jesus said, "The most important law is that you should love the Lord your God with all your heart, mind, soul, and strength. And the second is like it; love your neighbor as you love yourself. There are no commands greater than these."

The scribes agreed with Jesus' summary of the law. How could a blasphemer be so theologically aligned with those accusing him of heresy? The lesser charge, but the one that would have mattered most to Rome—that Jesus opposed paying taxes to Caesar—was as flimsy as it was deceptive, and everyone knew it. After Jesus was questioned about his understanding of the law of God, he was also questioned on the matter of paying taxes. Taking a coin, Jesus had asked whose image was embossed on the surface, saying, "Render unto Caesar what is Caesar's, and unto God what belongs to God."

Jesus had a case. Pilate suspected he had committed no sin that pulled any weight with Rome. Only three days earlier Jesus had publicly and clearly addressed the accusations now brought against him. But now when given the opportunity, Jesus did not defend himself even though his case was, in fact, utterly defendable.

Pilate urged, "Don't you realize what's happening here? Just as I have the power to crucify you, I also have the power to release you."

Jesus answered Pilate with quiet strength: "You would have no authority over me at all unless it had been given to you by my Father."

The crowd cried out to Pilate, "If you release him, you are no friend of Caesar."

Pilate feared the mob would riot if he didn't act soon, so he washed his hands in full view of everyone, saying, "Fine! I wash my hands of this man's blood. That is what you want, isn't it? Behold your king!"

The mob shouted back, "He is not our king! Let his blood be on us. Let it be on us and our children!"

Pilate shouted, "Shall I crucify your king?"

Though the city was lit by the morning sun, a darkness crept over everyone present as the people of God—the heirs of his covenant gathered within the walls of the city of their great King David— answered Pilate with all their hearts, minds, souls, and strength: "We have no king but Caesar."

34

CRUCIFIXION

Luke 23:26-46

*T*HE JOURNEY FROM CYRENE in northern Africa to Jerusalem gave Simon plenty of time to build anticipation in the minds of his sons, Rufus and Alexander. They set out from their home with images in their minds of the gleaming gold City of David, expecting it to come into view with the cresting of every ridge. They knew they were getting close when the roads became choked with pilgrims like them flooding in from all over the world. Simon warned Rufus and Alexander to stay at his side. It would be easy to get separated.

Early Friday morning on the day of the Passover feast, Simon and his sons heard a commotion and saw a throng of people pressing in to catch a glimpse—though of what, he couldn't say. Curious, Simon tried to see what was happening, only to find that the throng was moving toward them.

The crowd sounded angry, shouting impassioned pleas and scornful rebukes. Roman soldiers cleared the way to keep this procession moving. Simon saw what looked like the top of a large beam of wood rise occasionally above the heads of the approaching crowd, and with it the sound of scraping stone.

Before they could get out of the way, Simon and his sons were enveloped in the mob and swept along. Then Simon saw an unrecognizably bloodied man with the wooden beam on his back stagger toward him and fall to the ground. The man lay on the stone street gasping for air, unable to stand.

Simon gathered enough from the pleas and jeers of the crowd and soldiers to realize that this man was a political prisoner from Nazareth named Jesus on his way to Golgotha, the Hill of the Skull.

The soldiers treated their prisoner with impersonal contempt. They had only just reported for duty when Pilate handed Jesus over to them. They knew their job. Political prisoners accused of insurrection received the same basic treatment. The soldiers would crucify him, but first, they would humiliate and abuse him in order to create a public spectacle that would serve as a warning to any who might oppose Rome.

Mockery and scourging were part of the process. The soldiers learned early to keep their hearts out of this work. They were simply following orders. Nothing more. When they stripped Jesus naked and flogged him with the cat-o'-nine-tails, when they covered his shredded back with Herod's royal robe and pressed the crown of thorns into his brow, when they took turns pretending to bow to him, shouting, "Hail, King of the Jews," doubling over in laughter, and then spit on him and hit him with sticks, they were only in the first phase of their task—humiliation and abuse.

After this they put his clothes back on him and marched him out into the streets to carry his cross to the mount of crucifixion outside the city walls. The sight of Jesus—the man Simon saw breathing heavily on the ground—moved the people around him to a horrified lament. He looked so despised and rejected, so crushed by God, that people had to hide their faces from him.

The soldiers could see they had taken the last bit of their prisoner's strength too soon. If they were going to make it to Golgotha, someone would have to carry Jesus' cross the rest of the way. The captain of the guard looked for the nearest able-bodied pilgrim to relieve their broken prisoner of his burden.

"You there," the soldier barked at Simon. "Take up that cross and follow us."

When they arrived at Golgotha, one of the soldiers produced a sign he had been carrying—the sign that would hang over the dying man's head, detailing his crime. The chief priests were upset when they saw the sign Pilate had made. In three languages—Greek, Latin, and Aramaic—the sign read, "The King of the Jews." The chief priests went to argue with Pilate, demanding that the sign should say that Jesus only claimed to be the king of the Jews, not that he actually was. This was a matter of clarity. The whole world would read this sign. Precision mattered, they argued. With a hint of satisfaction, Pilate shrugged and said, "What I have written, I have written."

While the chief priests were arguing over the wording of the sign, the soldiers were preparing Jesus for crucifixion. Two other men, convicted thieves, arrived at Golgotha with Jesus, each carrying a cross of his own. John was in the crowd, along with Jesus' mother, Mary, Mary's sister, and Mary Magdalene. They gathered their courage as they went along, watching helplessly as the guards peeled Jesus' tunic off his bleeding back so they could fix him to his cross.

The soldiers drove large nails through each of Jesus' wrists into the crossbeam. With both hands nailed in place, they set his beam on the post in the ground and drove another nail through his gathered feet into an angled platform. The platform required the dying man to bend his knees, turning his legs to one side, contorting his torso. Once the soldiers had Jesus in place, they nailed Pilate's sign above his head. "The King of the Jews." They did the same with the other two condemned men.

As the first waves of agony swept across Jesus' hanging body, he prayed, "Father, forgive them. They don't know what they are doing."

The soldiers turned their attention to the pile of garments on the ground. They began to divide them among themselves. Jesus' clothes landed in a pile with the other two thieves' garments. One of the soldiers picked up a tunic John recognized immediately. He could have picked it out of a pile any day—seamlessly woven from one continuous thread from top to bottom. How many times had he handed that tunic to Jesus over the years? John watched as the soldiers handled it as though it were a prize. They didn't want to tear it, so they cast lots to see who would win it. Few things seem more final than giving away a man's clothes.

The chief priests focused on the wording of the sign. Pilate focused on the priests' displeasure. The soldiers focused on doomed men's clothes. John and Jesus' mother, Mary, focused on the one they loved as their hearts broke.

Mary thought about how the old cleric Simeon had told her years ago that her son would grow into a man who would cause the rising and the falling of many in Israel and how through him the thoughts of many hearts would be revealed. She remembered how serious Simeon looked when he drew her close and said, "And a sword will pierce your soul too, dear woman."

She thought of that night in Bethlehem and how her sweet husband had made the best he could of an empty manger-room, how he wiped the sweat off her brow as she pushed and pushed until her baby boy was born. She thought about Herod's paranoid attempt to rid the world of the rumored king the sign over Jesus' head declared him to be. Now with every labored breath, that sword was pulled a little deeper through her broken heart.

John, who had fled in fear from Jesus in the garden, had traded his fear for grief over the suffering of his closest friend.

Jesus looked at Mary and John, wrapped in each other's arms. He said to his mother, "Woman, here is your son."

To John he said, "John, she is your mother now."

Even as they wept over losing him, he gave them to each other.

The soldiers continued their public humiliation. They shouted, "If you are the Son of God, come down from there. Save yourself, King of Israel. Come down and we'll believe in you!"

One of the soldiers lifted a sponge soaked in sour wine to Jesus' lips and said, "You must be thirsty up there. Would you like a drink?"

Then one of the thieves started in with contemptuous words of his own, saying, "Are you not the Christ? Save yourself. Save us!"

But the gravity of the scene settled on the other thief. Jesus had taken the brutality of his captors to God in the form of a prayer for mercy. He had given his own grieving mother his treasured friend. The crowds were mocking the idea that Jesus could have been a king, and yet he endured this travail with a strength for which no one could account. Seeing the grace by which Jesus received this death, the second thief broke into sobs, saying to Jesus, "Forgive me. I am here for the wrongs I have done. But you have done nothing. Please, remember me when you pass from this place into your waiting kingdom."

Jesus answered, "Today you will be with me in glory."

The weight of Jesus' body pulled down on his arms and shoulders, compacting his twisted torso. In this position he could breathe in, but to breathe out he would have to straighten himself to relieve the tension on his diaphragm and relax the torque on the muscles he used to exhale. To do this, he had to pull himself up by his wrists and push with his feet, both of which were fixed to the cross by nails.

Every breath cost precious strength and delivered unbearable agony, resulting in shallow breathing, which limited the supply of oxygen to his blood, which in turn caused muscle cramps, spasms, and fatigue, all of which made it even more difficult to come up for another painful breath, creating a cycle of searing pain and suffocation.

Death by crucifixion normally took at least a day. The combination of the trauma and blood loss Jesus had already suffered left him close to death by the time he was lifted up to die at nine that Friday morning.

By noon, three hours into his crucifixion, a strange darkness crept over the land. The darkness stayed for the next three hours, filling the crowds with an eerie apprehension. The few words he spoke came in short, terse bursts of hard-won breath. As three in the afternoon approached, Jesus cried out, "My God, My God! Why have you forsaken me?"

Startled by this outburst, people said, "Listen. He's calling for Elijah." They watched him to see what he would do.

Jesus whispered, "I thirst."

Someone lifted another sponge of sour wine to his lips, and this time he sipped what he could draw. Swallowing was almost as difficult as breathing. After taking the wine, he pushed up for another breath as a look of excruciating pain spread across his face.

He looked at the remaining crowd and said, "It is finished."

A spasm seized his body, straightening his frame as much as his wrists and feet would allow. He screamed out in agony and gasped again, "Father, into your hands I commit my spirit."

After this, his body relaxed. He hung his head and breathed his last breath and died.

35

THE FORGOTTEN DAY

Matthew 27:51-66

A<small>T THREE IN THE AFTERNOON</small>, as the last bit of breath left Jesus' lungs, an earthquake shook Jerusalem. The blanket of clouds that had rolled in at noon remained. The quaking darkness struck many present at the crucifixion as creation's groan over what had just taken place on the Hill of the Skull.

Back inside the city, the slaughter of the Passover lambs—numbering in the thousands—was well underway. The priests were bathed in the blood of an endless line of unsuspecting creatures offered by pilgrims hoping to deliver from their unclean hands a sacrifice pleasing to their holy God. The iron scent of the blood mixed with the dung and dander of the dying beasts filled the courts of the temple. It was the scent of separation from their Maker, and of the hope of one day being restored.

The earthquake shook the temple, from the outer courts to the Most Holy Place. The Most Holy Place was a kind of new Eden: the sanctuary in which the presence of God dwelled while his image-bearers inhabited the world outside. Between the Lord and his people had hung a curtain like an angel with a flaming sword.

During the quake, the priests near the Most Holy Place crouched in fear as they heard the ripping of a heavy cloth. Looking up, they watched as the curtain tore from top to bottom. They were struck with terror, because as much as they feared what would come of a man who entered the holy place unprepared, they feared even more what would come of them if the power inside were unleashed on the world. If that happened, who could stand?

Fear gripped those outside the city as well. As the earth trembled, those gathered at Golgotha instinctively looked at Jesus as though he may well have been the source.

One of the centurions began to beat his fist against his chest in sorrow. He watched as the darkness spread across the land. He had heard the way Jesus cried out to God with his dying breath. He felt the earth shake beneath his feet. The power of the moment was too much for him.

"Surely this man was innocent," he said. "Surely this man was the Son of God."

Back inside the city, the chief priests were concerned about the coming Sabbath, which arrived at sundown. Their law stipulated that if a man was guilty of a capital offense and was sentenced to death and his body was hung on a tree, they were not to leave his body up overnight. This would defile their holy day. The chief priests did not want the three convicted criminals hanging outside their city to become a blemish on their Passover.

The cruel reality of crucifixion was that death came slowly. Even though the chief priests wanted to take down the bodies, they had to wait until the men were dead. There were, however, some methods that hurried the dying process once the governor deemed the criminal had suffered enough. The chief priests went to Pontius Pilate and asked him to instruct his soldiers to break the dying men's legs so that they wouldn't be able to push up for air.

The soldiers broke the legs of the two thieves first, but when they came to Jesus, they saw that he was already dead. To be sure, one of the guards thrust the tip of his spear into Jesus' side. A pulseless trickle of blood and water ran freely from the wound, so they did not break his legs. They took his lifeless body down from the cross.

While this was happening, one of the council members, Joseph of Arimathea, stayed back to have a private word with Pilate. Pilate regarded the nervous priest who seemed willing to risk one more request of the already exasperated governor.

Joseph said, "Would you please turn over Jesus' body to me and let me bury him?"

Pilate tried to hide his surprise. Was this lone priest actually a believer in the man his council had labored so hard to kill? With a wave of his hand, Pilate granted Joseph's request.

Joseph arrived at the site of the crucifixion to find Jesus' body ready to be taken away. Looking up, he saw his colleague Nicodemus carrying a large bundle of spices used for burials. It appeared the two men shared more in common than just their positions as members of the chief priests. What Joseph paid for the tomb and what Nicodemus gave for the burial spices revealed that they were both wealthy men. They also both believed in the coming Messiah.

They believed Jesus was in some way a man sent from God, and both of them, on different occasions, had attempted to defend Jesus before their own council. They were by all accounts decent, upright, and respected men.

But there on the Hill of the Skull, they discovered they had something else in common. They were both secret disciples of Jesus. Throughout Jesus' ministry, many Jewish leaders had put their faith in him, but few would confess it for fear of being put out of the synagogue. So it was for Joseph and Nicodemus. Joseph's fear kept him silent until that Friday afternoon. Nicodemus had sought Jesus earlier, but only under the cover of darkness to avoid becoming known as one of his sympathizers.

The two men picked up Jesus' body, which still bore the faint scent of Mary's perfume, and took it to a newly hewn tomb in a nearby garden. They wrapped his body in layers of linen and spices. Then they wrapped his head and lay him on a stone table where, according to their custom, the body would stay for a year until only the bones remained, which would then be gathered up and placed with the bones of the dead man's fathers. Mary Magdalene and James the Younger's mother watched on, grieving as the men worked.

It was dark when the two men left the tomb. They had handled a dead body on the Sabbath during the Passover week, which made them ceremonially unclean on their highest holy day of the year. But in the process, they found each other—two reluctant believers, grieving over the injustice of Jesus' death, sorrowful for their part in it, and now joined together in that lonesome, sacred, intimate act of laying to rest the body of the Messiah they had been too afraid to acknowledge.

Pilate awoke the next morning to another request for a meeting with the chief priests. This time they came into his headquarters, so he knew whatever they wanted was important to them.

"When this imposter was still alive," the council told Pilate, "he kept saying that after three days, he would come back from the dead. If his disciples attempt to steal his body in the dead of night and claim he has risen, this last fraud would be worse than the first when Jesus claimed to be the Christ."

Resurrection from the grave would establish Jesus as divine. This would have been undeniable evidence that Jesus was not constrained by the limits of mortal man. The chief priests and Pharisees wanted Pontius Pilate to give them a guard of soldiers to watch over the dead man to make sure no one tried to stage a hoax.

This request struck Pilate as odd. Were these men really afraid that Jesus' followers, who had scattered in fear when he was arrested, had suddenly regained their courage and hatched this plan to steal his body just one day later? Is this what moved the chief priests to violate their own Sabbath by walking into his house?

It was clear that the chief priests and Pharisees were shaken. Though they had gotten what they wanted, this trial had not gone as they expected. They had thought it would be an open-and-shut case. They knew Jesus was a miracle worker—there were blind men who could see and lame people who could walk. They knew Lazarus was alive and well in Bethany just on the other side of the Kidron Valley. But they had not expected the covering dark that spread across the land at high noon or the earthquake that shook the city later that day when Jesus died. They had heard Jesus declare that the temple would be destroyed and that he himself would rebuild it. When the temple curtain tore in two from top to bottom, they shuddered to themselves, saying, "It's happening." The burden of proof against the divinity of Jesus was getting heavier to lift.

Pilate told the chief priests, "I'll give you a guard of my soldiers. Go make the tomb as secure as you can."

The chief priests went and sealed the stone that had been rolled over the mouth of the grave and the guard stood watch. If anyone wanted to come and tamper with this tomb, they would have to get through the soldiers and the seal. But even with these layers of security the chief priests felt unsure that the tomb was secure. They had seen too much to dismiss Jesus. They were prepared for anyone who might want to tamper with the tomb from the outside. But what if a seal and a Roman guard were not enough to keep this tomb from opening? What if the real threat lay inside the tomb? If Jesus did what he promised—if he rose from the dead—who could guard against that?

36

HE IS NOT HERE

Matthew 28:1-10; John 20:1-10

M ARY MAGDALENE WOKE EARLY. She had first met Jesus a couple of years earlier when he set her free from an affliction. When Jesus healed her, something had come awake in her heart—a whisper to her soul that there might be hope amid the wreckage of this world. That hope had forged a deep longing in her heart, a longing she shared with every other living soul since the first parents were put outside of Eden. It was a hope that told her she was made for a life where things were meant to be good. From the day Jesus set her free from her suffering, Mary followed him, helping to care for his needs and those of his disciples as they traveled.

Mary Magdalene and Mary the mother of James had witnessed Jesus' crucifixion with their own eyes. They had seen Joseph and Nicodemus claim Jesus' body, and they had followed them to the garden tomb on Friday evening to help with Jesus' burial. They were the last to leave his side on the Friday of his death, and their hearts were broken.

In the early traces of the new dawn on Sunday, the two women gathered their balms and perfumes and made their way to Jesus' tomb to grieve their sorrow and to anoint his body. They knew the tomb lay sealed by a stone they could not move, but they went just the same. If they could slow the decay of Jesus' body and mask the stench of death perhaps they could hold on to him a little longer— just enough to cry their tears and say their goodbyes.

As they drew near to the tomb, the earth began to shake beneath their feet. This was the second quake in the past three days. The first had come the moment Jesus died on the cross. That Friday, when he let out a loud cry and gave up his spirit, the earth began to shake, rocks split apart, and the curtain in the temple tore from top to bottom. Now, on their way to Jesus' grave, it was happening again.

When the women reached the tomb, they found that the stone had been rolled away. On top of the tomb sat an angel dressed in a brilliant white. The women were stunned by the power of the seraph who seemed to have opened the tomb not by moving the stone itself but the earth on which it rested.

The ground around the tomb was littered with unconscious soldiers who had fainted at the sight of the angel in white. These men charged with guarding the tomb were not hapless, untrained cowards. Rome did not conquer the world by accident. These were strong, brave, well-trained, hardened fighters who did not shrink in the face of opposition. But they had never seen anything like this angel. And when they did see him, they swooned with fear.

The women were filled with fear too. Their world was fragile enough. Now, after so much loss, it seemed the ground itself was crumbling beneath them and God was somehow responsible for it. His messenger dressed in white looked like someone who could consume them with a snap of his fingers. But the angel did not consume them. Instead, he spoke.

"Do not be afraid," he said. "I know why you have come. You seek Jesus, who was crucified. He is not here. He has risen."

The women stood in stunned silence. The angel knew why they had come. He knew their fear, their sorrow, and their mission to anoint their friend. But the women could not make sense of what was happening. If the angel had just now rolled away the stone to reveal an empty tomb, then the angel did not open the grave to let Jesus out but to let the women in. Jesus had apparently left the tomb in another way at another time. This whole display was too wonderful for them to behold.

"He has risen, just as he told you. Come see where he lay," the angel said.

The women remembered how Jesus had told them this would happen. He had spoken with such clarity. But they could not understand. He had told them several times, "I must go up to Jerusalem and suffer many things from the elders, chief priests, and scribes. I will be handed over to the Gentiles to be mocked, flogged, and crucified, and on the third day I will rise again."

These very predictions were the reason the chief priests had asked Pilate for soldiers to guard the tomb in the first place—for fear that something would happen with Jesus' body.

Was this a dream? Hope began to rise in the women's hearts, coming as hope often does—bringing with it bewilderment, fear, alarm, joy, and trembling. This was such an otherworldly moment for these earthbound creatures. Of course they trembled. Of course they feared.

But the angel's words breathed life into the hope that all of humanity's frailty, brokenness, struggle, grief, and mourning might have a remedy—that mankind's ability to wound one another by their own sinfulness and their ability to absorb pain and grief from the sins of others might in fact be reversible. If what the angel told them was true, death had been beaten. This, the angel reminded them, had been Jesus' plan from the start. Everything happened exactly as he said it would, which meant that no one had taken his life from him. He had lain it down of his own accord and everything now was just as he had said.

If Jesus had risen, everything had changed. Mary Magdalene felt what all people feel in the grief of death. She didn't want death to be the end. No one did. Deep within her lay the sense that death was an intruder. People were made to live, not die. If Jesus had overthrown the power of death itself, the curse had been reversed.

This was more than these women could bear alone. Every story they knew of encounters between angels and human beings included a moment when the angel told the image-bearers of God not to fear. It wasn't simply their otherworldliness that struck fear. It was the fact that if a heavenly dispatch had come, it was to deliver a message about something God was doing that no mere mortal could initiate or stop.

More than that, the women were afraid because they did not understand what they had come upon that morning. The open tomb, the unconscious centurions, the man dressed in lightning, and his words to them only heightened their confusion and fear. So the women ran from the tomb to try to tell Peter, John, and the others what they had seen.

"They have taken my Lord," Mary Magdalene said, weeping breathlessly. "Please, I don't know where they have put him."

At first the disciples did not believe the women, but there was a conviction to their pleading. The prospect that they might be telling the truth hit Peter and John at about the same time, and they took off running toward the tomb. John, who was faster than Peter, did not wait but raced ahead. He arrived to find the grave open, as the women had said, but he did not go inside. Instead, he peered in, nervous, confused, and exhilarated. He saw the linen grave clothes lying on the stone slab where the body of Jesus once lay.

Peter arrived, brushed past his friend, and entered the tomb. John followed. They saw the linens and the spices the clothes had held lying on the stone bed as though Jesus' body had simply passed through them. Their scent gave the dark stone room the aura of a garden in bloom. And they saw the linen cloth that shrouded Jesus' face neatly folded where his head had been.

John and Peter looked at each other as they began to understand what they were seeing. Their confusion over the occasions when Jesus had told them he would suffer, die, and rise again moved to comprehension. They did not know what to do with this information, but they did believe that Jesus had in fact risen from the dead.

They knew they needed to tell the other disciples. As they left the grave they passed Mary Magdalene, who had followed them back to the garden. She stood outside the open tomb, still wrought with grief.

"I do not know where they took him," she wept. "Someone tell me where he is. Someone tell me where they took him."

37

FLESH
AND BONE

Matthew 28:11-15; John 20:11-29

WHEN THE ROMAN SOLDIERS woke to discover they had failed to guard the tomb, they knew that fainting with fear would not excuse them before their commanding officer. The captain of the guard, realizing that the lives of his men hung in the balance, knew he needed a plan. So before going to his own commander to report what had happened, he went to the chief priests.

His story chilled the chief priests' blood. Pilate had granted them the best security detail the world had to offer. But as the centurion ventured deeper into his story—when he told of the earthquake and how the last thing any of them could recall before losing consciousness was the appearance of a man dressed in lightning rolling away the massive stone—the picture became clear. This was no simple grave robbery. Something supernatural had happened at that tomb.

The chief priests conferred and said to the captain of the guard, "Listen to our proposal. We need you to tell people that Jesus' disciples came and stole his body under the cover of darkness. Make your story as convincing as possible. And if Pilate hears about this and wishes to discipline you, we will defend you to help keep you out of trouble. We won't let him have your heads for it. In exchange for your cooperation, please accept this modest offering."

The chief priests handed the captain of the guard a large sum of money. The centurions told their tale, and the chief priests did what they could to make it believable.

Mary Magdalene had arrived at Jesus' tomb that morning weary with grief, tender from tears that seemed to keep flowing. When Peter and John left to go tell the others what they had seen, Mary stooped and entered the tomb.

Two angels now sat on the slab where the body of Jesus had been.

One sat at the foot and the other at the head. "Why are you weeping?" they asked her.

Numb, Mary said, "I don't know where they put my Lord. I don't know who took him or where he is."

As she spoke, the angels seemed to look through her. She sensed they were not looking through to her heart but were in fact looking past her to someone standing behind her. Mary turned to see a silhouetted figure standing in the morning light of the grave's open mouth.

"Why are you weeping? Whom do you seek?" the man asked.

Initially Mary supposed this man was the tomb's gardener, so she asked, "Did you move my Lord? Where have you taken him? Tell me. I have come to tend to him."

Stepping out of the shadow, the man said, "Mary."

"Rabboni!" Mary said as she collapsed breathlessly at the feet of the man she now recognized as Jesus himself—her Lord, her hope, her deliverer.

Mary took hold of his feet because she needed to know that he was real. Jesus said, "Do not be afraid. You are safe. But do not cling to me now. I have not yet ascended to the Father. Go and do as the angel said. Tell the others you have seen me. Tell them I am going ahead of them into Galilee and I will meet them there."

But why? Why would Jesus and the angel give these instructions? Could it be that Jesus had a purpose for the lives of his disciples that lay beyond this grave even though they had fled in his greatest hour of need? Could it be that the glory of his resurrection wasn't just that he defeated death but that in that glorious defeat he meant to join his followers to his resurrection for the rest of eternity?

Mary ran to where the disciples were staying. The disciples had locked themselves in for fear of what might happen if the religious leaders found them. Mary pounded on the heavy door, demanding to be let inside. When they opened the door, she burst into the room and said, "I have seen the Lord himself! He told me to tell you that he is ascending to his Father, but before he does, he will meet you in Galilee. He wants us to go there to wait for him." Clearly Peter, John, and Mary had seen something that awakened in them a sense of hope and purpose, but it was hard to comprehend. Though some of the disciples received Peter, John, and Mary's testimonies with measured excitement, others simply could not believe what they were hearing.

Then suddenly Jesus appeared in the room with them. "Peace to you," he said.

The disciples were terrified, thinking they were seeing a ghost.

Jesus said, "Why are you so afraid of what you see? Why do you doubt your eyes?"

Then extending his hands to them, he said, "See my hands. Look at my feet. Touch me if that would turn your doubt to belief. No ghost has flesh and bone. But I do."

Still the disciples sat in dumbfounded silence, waging battles between the disbelief and joy in their hearts. They remembered that when Jesus had told them he would suffer and die—which he had done—he would also rise again on the third day. And here, three days after, he stood before them telling them that his death was not an aberration to his plan but part of it, just as he had said.

Jesus said, "Do you have any food?"

They offered him a piece of broiled fish, which he took and ate in front of them.

The absurdity of this last layer of evidence that he had risen from the grave broke through their disbelief and released the disciples' pent-up joy. They laughed at the sight of their risen Lord swallowing fish he had lifted to his mouth with his nail-scarred hand.

Jesus said, "Again I say to you, friends: Peace be with you."

He then moved around the room breathing his heavy breath on each of them, saying, "Receive the Holy Spirit. You will deliver my mercy to the broken and destitute. When you forgive people their sins, they will be forgiven. When you withhold forgiveness, it will be withheld. You will carry into the world this revolution I have begun."

And then he vanished from their sight.

Thomas, who had not been with the other disciples when Jesus appeared, returned to find a very different group of men from the one he had left.

"He was here, Thomas!" they said.

"What? Who?" Thomas said, confused.

"Jesus. He was here. We saw him. We saw his hands and feet. He ate a piece of fish right here in front of us, Thomas."

"Oh, he did?" Thomas said, not trying to hide his skepticism. Ever the pragmatist, Thomas knew that the best course for him and his friends in the wake of the tragedy they had all been through in recent days was to stay together, hold each other up, and keep their heads as they worked through their sorrow. Now in his absence, it seemed they had all crossed over into a world of delusion.

"Listen to me, men. I have not seen him. Dead men do not come back to life. Unless I see those nail marks with my own eyes, and unless I put these fingers," Thomas said raising up his right hand, "into the spear wound in his side, I will never believe. I will not do it."

Eight days later, while Thomas and the other disciples were back in their rented room, secure behind their heavy lock, Jesus came in again and stood among them.

"Peace be with you," Jesus said.

Thomas never saw the joy on his brothers' faces because when he saw Jesus, it was as though they were the only two people in the room—the only two people in the entire world. Jesus moved toward Thomas and they stood face to face. Jesus lifted his hands, palms up.

"Do you see my wounds, Thomas? Go ahead. Touch them. Take your hand and put it into my side. I know you have not believed the testimony of your brothers. But I am telling you now: believe. Put away your disbelief."

"My Lord and my God!" Thomas said. And he began to weep, as though a dammed-up river of hope had been released. This was the fight of faith. There were many things in Thomas's life that he wanted to believe, but he knew that it was a dangerous thing to put his faith in something for no other reason than that he wanted it to be true. Madness lay down that road. For a man belonging to a people who had taken the name of a God they had never seen, based on covenant promises that same God had made hundreds of years before, Thomas knew the dangers of blind faith. What good was the hope of freedom when he lived in a land ruled by godless tyrants? What good was faith in a God who was living and active when the best candidate for the Messiah he had ever seen was arrested and put to death by God's own people?

It wasn't that Thomas didn't want to believe. It was that he didn't want what he believed in to expose him as a fool.

"You believe because you see me, Thomas," Jesus said. "Blessed are those who have not seen me but believe anyway."

38

DO YOU LOVE ME?

John 21:1-23

A<small>FTER A FEW DAYS THE DISCIPLES</small> made their way from Jerusalem back to their home in Galilee. Early one morning Simon Peter sat under the moonlight beside the lake with his brother Andrew. Nathanael, Thomas the Twin, James, and John were with them. The morning breezes off the water felt good on their faces. The terrain, the sea air, and the familiarity of home gave the men a trace of comfort they had not known for some time. They stared out across the sea, lost in thought, still tracing their way through the things they had seen over the past few weeks.

Without breaking his gaze Peter said, "I am going out there. I'm going fishing."

Without looking up, the others said, "We will join you."

Peter wasn't sure what was supposed to happen next, and behind his uncertainty lay a few cold, hard, immovable details. Chief among them was the fact that only days earlier, during Jesus' greatest hour of need, Peter had denied knowing him. It wasn't just that Peter had denied knowing Jesus. It was that this was something Jesus had predicted he would do. And Peter had rebuked Jesus for making such an assertion.

And yet. When the rooster crowed early that Friday morning, something undeniably true welled up from the deepest recesses of this man: he had been tested and he had failed. This was no small failure either. He had no idea he was capable of such betrayal. It made him question the three years he had invested in following Jesus. Jesus had died with the words of Peter's denials still echoing down the limestone streets of Jerusalem, and it seemed that those echoes had found their way to the shores of his home. Where could he go to flee from God's presence? How could he flee from God's Spirit? If he made his bed in Jerusalem, the hound of heaven haunted his dreams. If he settled on the far side of the sea, even there the whispers of Jesus' prediction blew upon him from the still surface of the lake. Neither the holy city nor his home could quiet the voices. Maybe only hell could do that. But even if he made his bed in the grave, surely the Lord's hand would reach him there too.

Peter loved his Lord. And he knew Jesus loved him. But some collapses are so great that a man cannot help but ask himself how much is lost. Had he lost the love of Jesus? If he had, had he also then lost the call of Jesus? When Jesus appeared to them in that upper room a few days earlier and told them he was sending them out into the world, did this include Peter? How much was lost?

The brothers set out into the waters and let down their nets. The sea was still. Though the waters teemed with fish, they were no-where near the disciples. The men saw no life beneath the surface. Peter used the stillness to study the waters beneath the surface of his own heart. Those waters were alive with flashes of movement and glints of light.

Peter thought about how he and his brother Andrew had chosen this lake for their livelihood and how Jesus had called him from these waters to become a fisher of men. Peter was one of Jesus' closest friends—loyal to the core and brave. He had witnessed more miracles from Jesus' hands than he could count. He was a man of daring faith. It was on this very lake that he had seen Jesus walking on the water. While the others had stared in horror, Peter climbed out of the boat to meet Jesus and walked on the water too, if only for a few steps before his faith gave way to fear. Still, he alone had stepped out.

Peter was opinionated, which sometimes exposed him as a fool. But Jesus seemed to like Peter's tenacity. And sometimes Peter got things right. When Jesus had asked his disciples who they thought he was, it was Peter who said, "You are the Christ, the Son of the living God." When he had said this, Jesus had told him it was nothing short of a revelation from the Spirit of God himself and that on Peter's confession Jesus would establish his church on earth.

When Jesus had first called him, Peter left everything to follow. Those years had been filled with amazing encounters, narrow es-capes, and intimate proximity to the greatest teacher the world had ever known. Peter knew Jesus as God's promised and coming Messiah, but he also knew him as a friend who had stuck with him through his folly.

But now Jesus was gone, and Peter was back in his boat consid-ering whether he needed to return to his former trade.

As the dawn began to glow above the eastern hills, Peter and the others saw a man standing on the nearby shore. Peter threw him a wave. The man cupped his hands to his mouth and shouted, "Do you have any fish?"

In unison, the failed fishermen shouted back, "No."

The man on the shore said, "Try casting your nets on the other side of your boat. You'll find some there."

The disciples sighed at the man's suggestion, because when it came to fishing, it always seemed that everyone had an opinion. They hadn't caught anything yet, but they weren't ready to call it a day either. They decided to give it a try.

Immediately large fish filled their nets. When the men tried to haul the nets back into their boats, they couldn't. They had caught too many. But as the disciples strained and pulled at the nets, a wave of familiarity broke over Peter. This had happened before. It was a morning not unlike this one. Peter and his brother had been fishing without any luck when a man they did not know well asked to borrow their boat so he could put out a bit from the shore to teach the pressing crowds. The rabbi had told them to push out a little deeper and let their nets down for another try. When they did, their nets filled so quickly and so fully that when they tried to pull them into the boat, the nets broke under the strain.

On that day Peter had fallen on his knees before Jesus, the rabbi in his boat, and said, "Leave me alone, Lord. I am a sinful man."

On that day Jesus had told Peter, "Do not be afraid, Simon. Follow me, and I will make you a fisher of men."

The man on the shore was recreating that scene—that first day when Jesus called Peter to follow him. As if waking up, Peter recognized him.

"It is the Lord," Peter exclaimed as he leapt from the boat to swim to shore. What else could he do? Love had come to confront him.

The dripping disciple stood before his Lord, not sure what to say but desperate to get underway with whatever needed to happen in that moment.

Jesus spoke first. Motioning to a charcoal fire he had made, he said, "Bring me some of that fish."

Peter looked at the fire and saw some bread and fish already prepared. Jesus had made breakfast for his friends. Peter went to the boats and hauled the heavy, full nets ashore. He put a couple more fish on the fire.

Jesus said, "Come have breakfast with me."

The disciples all knew this was Jesus, but none of them had the courage to speak. They watched in bewildered fascination as Jesus took the bread from the fireside, blessed it, broke it, and handed it to them as he had done that Thursday in the upper room before his arrest.

Jesus looked at his friends as they ate. Turning to Peter, he said, "Do you love me, Simon, son of John?"

Peter swallowed and said, "Lord, you know that I love you. Yes."

Jesus asked him again, "Son of John, do you love me?"

Peter gave the same answer. "Yes, Lord. I love you."

With this confession came the burden of the riddle he had become—this man who truly did love his Lord wore the same skin as the man who swore an oath that he had never met him.

Jesus studied Peter for a while and asked him again, "Peter, do you love me?"

Tears pooled in the corners of Peter's eyes. Grieved that Jesus would not drop this line of questioning, Peter said, "Lord, you know everything. You know me. You know my failure. But you also know that as sure as I am sitting here, I love you. God help me. I do love you."

Jesus said, "I want you to feed my sheep, Peter. I want you to tend my lambs."

Peter broke into tears. For all Peter's boasting and nearsightedness, Jesus' call on his life had not been rendered obsolete by his personal failure.

Jesus said, "I want you to tend to my lambs, just as I said you would do when I first called you to follow me. I told you I would make you a fisher of men. Peter, listen to me. When you were young, you did what you wanted. You went where you wanted. But when you are old, your life will not be your own anymore. You will be led to places you do not want to go, for my name's sake. You are not simply called to bear my name. You are called to take that name out into the world."

Turning to John, Peter asked, "What about John? What will come of him?"

Jesus answered, "What is that to you? I am telling you your story, not his. I'm calling you, my friend, to follow me. That is enough for you."

Jesus did not make this breakfast and re-create the scene of the first time Peter left everything to follow Jesus just so Peter could return to his life as a fisherman with a clear conscience. He had come to reinstate him. He was saying to Peter, "I told you I was going to make you into something you were not—a fisher of men. I meant it. Regardless of your failures, my love for you stands and so does my call on your life."

Peter's heart changed. The reach of Jesus' resurrection was beginning to show. Jesus didn't go through all that suffering just for his own victory over the grave. He did this to rescue all those who would believe in him. Through the messy lives of those who could love him and fail him in the same breath, he would bring rivers of the grace of God to a thirsty world, and their stories would be eternally, inextricably joined to his, world without end.

39

BEHOLD
THE MAN OF
SORROWS

Isaiah 53; Luke 24:1-35

*T*HE ROAD WAS SEVEN MILES from Jerusalem to Emmaus. Cleopas and his wife could have made the journey in three hours if they'd hurried. But they were walking a little more slowly than normal so they could process what they had seen in Jerusalem during the Passover. They spoke of their sorrow, their disappointment, and their confusion, moving at the pace of two sorrowful people talking through their grief.

As they walked in the direction of the setting sun, a stranger caught up to them on the road and listened to their conversation for a while before asking them why they were sad.

"Are you the only person in Jerusalem who doesn't know what happened there these past few days?" Cleopas asked.

"What things?" the stranger replied.

Cleopas said, "Have you not heard of what happened to Jesus of Nazareth—a prophet of the Lord, mighty in word and deed? Did you not hear how our own chief priests and rulers delivered him over to Pontius Pilate to be beaten, condemned to death, and crucified?"

The stranger said nothing.

Cleopas looked at his weary wife and spoke for the both of them. "We had so much hope. We hoped he would be the one to redeem Israel. But now we don't know what to think. He died three days ago. He was a good man. A holy man. Does this world hold nothing sacred?"

Cleopas told the stranger that if death was the end of Jesus of Nazareth's story, how could he be the one they hoped for? Jesus had seemed prophetic and powerful, but what help could he offer from the grave? Popular teachers had come and gone—duping the gullible into trusting them for things no mere mortal could deliver. Some had even died as martyrs. But Cleopas and his family had hoped Jesus would be more than a martyr. They had hoped he would redeem them. Instead their own religious leaders had him killed. They were bitterly disappointed.

Cleopas went on to tell the stranger how some women had visited Jesus' tomb that very morning and claimed to have found it empty. They said they spoke with an angel who told them Jesus was alive.

It was a fantastic story, Cleopas said. Amazing, really. And if it were true, it would salvage their hope. If the tomb was empty, that would mean Jesus had defeated death itself. The rumor was that even a couple of Jesus' disciples had gone to the tomb and found it just as the women had described. Oh, that it were all true. But everyone knows such things do not happen.

Cleopas said, "That's the story anyway, but no one we know claims to have actually seen him in person."

The fact of the matter was that in their world, when a person died, he didn't come back to life. This was the case one hundred times out of one hundred, excluding the legendary Lazarus. Without evidence of Jesus' resurrection, it was foolish to hope. Besides, Cleopas reasoned, it was hard to reconcile how God's Redeemer would have to suffer so much. Jesus' suffering made his identity as God's chosen one suspect.

"That," the stranger said, "is the logic of a fool. What is so hard to understand about God's chosen one suffering? Do you not know the Scriptures? Can you not see the pattern of God's work in this world? Suffering always precedes glory. Was not Abraham childless, homeless, and embroiled in disputes through his sojourn in the Promised Land? Was not Sarah barren and faithless in her old age as she followed her husband into a land she did not know because of a promise it seemed he did not intend to keep? And what about Joseph? He was sold into slavery by his own brothers and left to rot in Pharaoh's prison before rising to a position where he could save his own family from starvation.

"Or Moses. Was not everything against him from the start? Was not David tormented by Saul before rising to power? What about Hosea and his unfaithful wife? Or Jonah and his stubborn heart, which landed him in the belly of the great fish who spit him out onto the shores of a people he did not want to love?"

Cleopas was presuming that God's faithfulness was most evident when he shielded his people from difficulty. This was a profound error common to believers of his day and ever since. Glory preceded by suffering was God's pattern throughout all of Scripture. The world would recognize the true Messiah by how he fit this pattern, not how he defied it.

The stranger said, "Was it not necessary that the Son of Man would suffer these many things and more before entering into his glory? You are slow of heart to believe what the prophets have said."

The stranger then took them through the words of the prophets. Isaiah had foretold that the Messiah would be wounded for the transgressions and iniquities of his people and that God would lay on him the punishment that would bring them peace.

Neither Cleopas nor the religious leaders in Jerusalem could recognize Jesus as the Christ because they were looking for someone other than what the prophets foretold, a pattern other than what Scripture laid out for them. They expected someone who would rise from a position of power and crush his enemies. Though the prophets spoke of the Messiah's certain travail, Jesus' own peers saw his agony as evidence against his claim to be the Christ. And by forsaking the story of God's redeeming work among them up to this point, a story whose pattern was that suffering preceded glory, they were blinded from knowing their Savior by way of his suffering.

The stranger took Cleopas and his wife through the Scriptures, from the books of Moses to the Prophets, showing them how suffering and humility were woven together in every story of God's redeeming grace. God did this because his call on the lives of his people was not to a life of freedom from him but to a life of dependence on him.

When they arrived at their home in Emmaus, the stranger bid farewell to continue on his journey. But Cleopas implored him to stay, share a meal, and get some rest. The stranger agreed and went into their home.

When they sat down to eat, the stranger reached for a loaf of bread on the table. He blessed the bread, broke it, and gave it to his disciples. And there in the intimacy of fellowship, Cleopas's eyes were opened, and he realized the stranger at their table was Jesus himself. Just as quickly as Cleopas and his wife realized what had happened, Jesus disappeared from their sight.

Cleopas and his wife sat in silence, stunned not only by Jesus' mysterious disappearance but by the generous gift of his presence. As a fog burns away in the morning sun, all the events of the past few hours became clear.

"I knew it," Cleopas whispered.

"Me too," his wife said.

"When he talked with us on the road, when he opened up the Scriptures, when he showed us the error in our thinking, my heart burned inside me," Cleopas said. "We need to go to Jerusalem to tell his disciples what happened here."

This was the story Cleopas told—the story the stranger on the road had told him. The arm of the Lord has been revealed. The Christ, Jesus of Nazareth, grew up in humility, like a tender shoot out of dry ground. He had no majesty that anyone would pay attention to, no beauty that we would desire him. His glory would be preceded by his suffering. He was despised and rejected by his own people, a man of sorrows and well-acquainted with grief. As one from whom men hide their faces, he was despised and without esteem. But he came to bear the sorrows of his own, to carry our grief, even though while he was in the midst of travail, we regarded him as afflicted and smitten by God.

But he was wounded for our transgressions. He was crushed for our iniquities and sins. God put on him the punishment that would bring us peace, because all of us, like sheep, have wandered away from the fold. We have chosen paths of our own, and the Maker has laid our rebellion on his Christ.

Before his accusers, he did not open his mouth to defend himself. Like a lamb to the slaughter, he did not resist the will of his father. Under the darkness of oppression and deceit, he was led away, cut off from among his own people. They humiliated him, killing him like a criminal, though he had committed no crime or spoken a word of deceit.

He did all of this because it was the Lord's will to crush him. His soul would become an offering for our guilt. But on the other side of all this suffering, he would find the satisfaction of being the righteous servant of the Lord who would make many to be accounted righteous.

He was numbered among the transgressors, but he bore our sins in his body on the cross, so that we might die to our sin and live in the freedom of his righteousness.

Though he was in the form of God, he came to us as a tiny baby, born in the likeness of man to a poor mother in a stable outside of David's town. He made himself nothing, taking on the nature of a servant, and humbled himself through his obedience to the will of his father, an obedience that led him to his horrific death on the cross.

We were like straying sheep, but by his grace we have been returned to the shepherd of our souls. Behold the Man of Sorrows. Through his agony and by his wounds we have been healed.

40

BEHOLD THE KING OF GLORY

Philippians 2:5-11; 1 Corinthians 15:3-49;
1 Peter 1:3-9; Romans 8; Revelation 21

*N*O FATHER SHOULD HAVE TO WATCH his own son die. But it was for this reason that Jesus came into the world. From the manger in Bethlehem to the cross on Golgotha to his reconciling breakfast with Peter on the shores of Galilee, Jesus bore in himself the supremacy of God, who was pleased to reconcile to himself all things on earth and in heaven, making peace by Jesus' blood shed on the cross.

Jesus was born into a fractured world. Every moment of the Romans' and the Hebrews' lives was marked with struggle, fear, anger, and pride. The blind, the paralyzed, and the outcast among them rose and fell on the waves of a creation caught in a storm. Jesus came treading upon their roughest seas, speaking peace into the gale. His triumph over the grave has called those who were perishing to be born again into a new and living hope. The peace he brought by his resurrection is neither myth nor fantasy. It is an inheritance that will never perish, kept for those who believe, world without end.

In terms of time and space, the scale of Jesus' earthly ministry was small—three years in a parcel of land where the corners of the world came together. The great Roman Empire—more powerful than anything the world had ever seen—has long since fallen. The religious leaders who presided over Jesus' crucifixion have faded into the night. But the impact of those three years in the Holy Land, culminating in the empty tomb, has shaken the world. Jesus wasn't just a teacher or a political leader or an activist or an example to emulate. He was the Son of God who stepped out of eternity and into time to take upon himself the full measure of the world's brokenness.

In life Jesus humbled himself to the point of death on the cross. And God has exalted him and given him the name that is above all other names, so that at the name of Jesus every knee would have no choice but to bow, in heaven, on earth, and under the earth, and every tongue acknowledge that Jesus Christ is the Lord to the glory of God the Father.

If Jesus has not risen, those who trust in him are to be pitied because their hope extends no further beyond their wishful thinking. Their faith is futile, and they remain in their sins. But if Jesus has risen, then his disciples are born into a new hope, because just as death entered the world through one man, Adam, now resurrection has done the same through the incarnate Son of God, who has prevailed over the power of the curse. The last enemy, death itself, has been destroyed.

Jesus' resurrection opened a door between the fallen, groaning world into which he was born and the renewal of all things. That door was a stone rolled back by the very finger of God from the mouth of a grave outside of Jerusalem. Jesus Christ, God's eternal Son, present at creation, came in the flesh to be the mediator between God and man. He lived the life of perfect righteousness that all men have failed to live. He died as a lamb led to the slaughter, offering himself up as the perfect sacrifice to atone for the sins of the world, once and for all. He rose from the grave defeating death itself. Bearing all authority in heaven and on earth, he lives as the appointed heir of all things. He rules over every corner of creation, putting every enemy under his feet while making alive by his grace through faith those who were dead in their sins.

The risen Jesus not only gave his people new life; he also gave them each other, putting them together into a community of faith where they would live, move, and have their being under the mercy of their gracious King who would call them his beloved bride—the one for whom he would return. He sent his Holy Spirit to live inside their hearts. His Spirit would cultivate in them a boldness, humility, and unity that would make them more into a single being than a collection of individuals. They would be members of one body made up of many parts, each needing the others. Together they would be the church—the radiant, beloved bride of Jesus Christ.

The church's mission would be shaped by her hope—the hope that every sad thing would come untrue and that every broken thing would be put right. The King of glory called his bride not only to know him and pine for his return but to live as his agents of renewal in this world even now.

For this reason Peter and the others lived the remainder of their days laying down their lives for the sake of making known the gospel of Jesus Christ. Many of them died as martyrs in their service to their Lord. But what came from them, through the power of the Holy Spirit, was a movement that spread like a fire around the world and continues even now.

Though the members of the bride of Jesus sin against each other and their Lord through their stubbornness and pride, they endeavor to live as citizens of another kingdom—not one built by human hands but one ushered in by the Maker of the universe himself.

It is not their own works or power or resolve that will preserve them. The power of the Spirit of Jesus Christ living in them will keep them to the end. All whom the Father gives to Jesus will come to him, and whoever comes to him he will never cast out.

So his people remain, waiting for him to return to consummate the redemption that his resurrection set in motion. They wait in eager anticipation for their adoption as God's children and the redemption of their bodies. But even though they wait, the King of glory will come for his bride, and with him will come a glorious kingdom.

Jesus' resurrection is the guarantee of the coming renewal of all things. On that day the world into which he was born will become like an old, old tale. The catastrophe of the fall of our first parents will be erased. The banner that lay for so long just inside the garden wall, cut off from humanity by the flaming swords of Eden, will fly above the city of God. The old order of things will pass away. A New Jerusalem will rise—a holy city prepared as a bride, adorned for the day of her visitation.

There will be no temple in the city because the citizens will worship in the presence of their reigning King. There will be no sun or moon to shine on them because the glory of the King will be all the light they need. His radiance will illuminate a path for nations and kings to approach the throne of glory so that they may, to their unspeakable joy, bow their knees in worship. The city's gates will be opened, never to be closed due to fear or weakness.

All of creation will know that this is the city of the King of glory because they will hear the voice from the throne saying, "Behold! The dwelling place of God is with men, and he will dwell with them and be with them as their God forever. He will wipe away every tear from their eyes, and death shall be no more."

The old order of things will pass away. Jesus, the King who lives, will empty the world of its pain, sorrow, disease, betrayal, and decay, and he will fill it anew with his love, mercy, grace, power, and glory.

If this story is true—if God did not spare his own Son but graciously gave him up for us all—what would he possibly withhold? What could conceivably separate us from that love? Could trial, suffering, tyranny, scarcity, nakedness, danger, or sword? No. Jesus has already conquered all these things, and all who put their faith in him share in his victory. Because Jesus has risen, paying the wage of sin itself, nothing—neither life nor death, nor angels nor demons, nor things present nor things to come, nor height, nor depth, nor anything else in all creation—will be able to separate us from the love of God in Jesus Christ.

And if nothing can separate us from the love of God, then who can condemn his children? Jesus himself—the beginning and the end of our story, the Son of God who died and was raised—sits even now at the right hand of God, interceding for us, mediating our case by the blood of a new covenant.

The Lord God told Jesus' disciples, "This is my beloved Son, in whom I am well pleased. Listen to him."

Listen to him. Hear the dying Jesus cry out from the cross, "It is finished."

Hear the risen Christ proclaim, "All authority in heaven and on earth has been given to me."

The kingdom of God is a kingdom that cannot be shaken. In the center of that kingdom stands a throne, and on that throne sits a King.

Behold the Lamb of God, the incarnate mediator who came to take away the sins of the world.

Behold the man of sorrows, the suffering servant on whom the Lord has laid the iniquity of us all.

Behold the King of glory, who declares from his eternal throne, "I am making all things new."

Now there are also many other things that Jesus did. Were every one of them to be written, I suppose that the world itself could not contain the books that would be written.

But these are written so that you may believe that Jesus is the Christ, the Son of God, and that by believing you may have life in his name.

JOHN 21:25; 20:31

ACKNOWLEDGMENTS

To the following I owe a debt of deep gratitude.

Lisa, Chris, Maggie, Kate, and Jane: Thank you for loving me so well and for sharing me with the various coffee shops and libraries of Nashville so I could write this book. Your support and affection are among the best gifts God has ever given me.

Andrew Peterson: Thank you for calling me to write and for then calling me to write well.

Pete Peterson: Thank you for your keen and wise editorial eye and your constant encouragement.

Jonathan Rogers: Thank you for being my true friend and gracious mentor.

Claire Gibson: Your investment and input into this book came at the perfect time. Thank you. Congratulations on finishing your novel.

Nancy Guthrie: Thank you for taking time to help me process the structure and flow of this book and for caring so much about fidelity to Scripture.

Winn and Mike Elliott and Edgehill Café: Thank you for providing space for me to write.

He is the image of the invisible God, the firstborn of all creation. For by him all things were created, in heaven and on earth, visible and invisible, whether thrones or dominions or rulers or authorities—all things were created through him and for him. And he is before all things, and in him all things hold together. And he is the head of the body, the church. He is the beginning, the firstborn from the dead, that in everything he might be preeminent. For in him all the fullness of God was pleased to dwell, and through him to reconcile to himself all things, whether on earth or in heaven, making peace by the blood of his cross.

COLOSSIANS 1:15-20

NOTES

16   *The tempter, sometimes*: Genesis 3:1; 1 Peter 5:8.
16   *He had come to offer*: Hebrews 10:1-18.
16   *Why are you hungry*: Matthew 4:3-4.
17   *I don't live on bread*: Deuteronomy 8:3; Matthew 4:4.
17   *You know that if you threw*: Matthew 4:6.
17   *It is written*: Matthew 4:7.
17   *Bow down and worship*: Luke 4:5-7.
17   *Leave me, Satan*: Deuteronomy 6:13; Matthew 4:10.
18   *Holding on to that flicker*: Luke 4:13.

3 BEHOLD THE LAMB OF GOD
19   *The same Spirit who came*: Matthew 4:11; John 1:32.
19   *An air of expectancy*: Luke 2:38.
20   *I am the voice*: John 1:19-23, 26.
21   *The scribes and teachers*: Isaiah 7:14.
21   *I've given myself*: John 1:29.
21   *All my life I've known*: John 1:31, 33.
21   *Look at him, everyone*: John 1:29, 33; Matthew 3:17.
21   *Jesus had come to offer*: 1 Corinthians 5:7; Ephesians 5:2.
22   *his offering would be sufficient*: Hebrews 10:10.
22   *Just as through one man*: Romans 5:12.
22   *But Jesus would set death*: Romans 5:15.
22   *He would seize the power*: Hebrews 2:14-15.
22   *His righteousness would reign*: Romans 5:17.
22   *So they gathered their things*: John 1:35-37.
23   *They were in no position*: John 1:38-39.
23   *You're Simon, the son of John*: John 1:40-42.
23   *Come with me, Philip*: John 1:44.
24   *Nathanael, we have found*: John 1:45.
24   *Can anything good come*: John 1:46; 21:2.
24   *I saw you under*: John 1:48.
24   *If you are the Son*: John 1:49.
24   *Nathanael, you believe*: John 1:51.

4 ONE HUNDRED AND FIFTY GALLONS
28   *What does this have to do*: John 2:3-4.
28   *My son can help*: John 2:5.
28   *My hour has not yet come*: John 2:4.
28   *This was an opportunity*: Genesis 1:11; Matthew 4:3; John 2:11.
29   *Filled with water*: Mark 7:3-4; John 2:6.

29   *Now draw some of that water:* John 2:7-8.
30   *Where did this wine come:* John 2:9.
30   *The answer only raised:* John 2:6.
30   *the disciples found their faith:* John 2:11.
30   *It was as though this marriage:* Isaiah 53:3; Revelation 19:6-9.

5 DESTROY THIS TEMPLE
32   *Passover was the festival:* Exodus 12.
32   *He would make the journey:* Luke 2:41; John 2:12-13.
33   *It was an ancient promise kept:* Deuteronomy 9:10.
33   *There he would feed them:* Exodus 16:4-36.
33   *And he would whisper:* Exodus 13:21; 17:6; 23:22-33; 25-27; Deuteronomy 34:9-12.
33   *From that desert:* Genesis 26:3.
33   *This kingdom would be strong:* 1 Samuel 16–17.
34   *With the occupying forces of Rome:* Lamentations 1; 2 Kings 18:13-37.
34   *be called a house of prayer:* Isaiah 56:7.
35   *He stooped to pick up:* John 2:15.
35   *Their bartering voices:* Isaiah 29:13.
35   *What have you done?:* John 2:15-16.
36   *What was meant to be:* Matthew 21:13.
36   *the far worse crime:* Exodus 3:10-22.
36   *Knowing their hearts:* John 2:18-20, 23-25.
37   *His zeal for God's house:* Psalm 69:9; John 2:17.

6 ZEUS AND THE PHARISEES
39   *He knew about how King Josiah:* 2 Kings 22:8-20; 23:1-3.
41   *Pigs were ceremonially unclean:* Leviticus 11:7.
43   *So one night under the cover:* John 3:1.
43   *Rabbi, we see you are a teacher:* John 3:2.
44   *Aren't you one of Israel's:* John 3:10-15.
44   *God loves this world:* John 3:16-18.
44   *People love their darkness:* John 3:19-21.

7 HEROD'S HALF BROTHER'S WIFE
45   *Jesus stopped for a while:* John 3:22-23; 4:1-2.
45   *Rabbi, this man:* John 3:26.
45   *Listen, when God gives:* John 1:20; 3:27-30; Isaiah 40:3; Matthew 3:3.
46   *They needed to believe:* Luke 3:9; John 3:36.
47   *But his marriage to Herodias:* Leviticus 18:16.

48   *And if pressed even further*: Mark 6:20.
48   *You know what I have to say*: Mark 6:18.
48   *But if Antipas killed John*: Mark 6:19; Matthew 14:5.
48   *he elected instead to seize John*: Matthew 14:3.
48   *So when Jesus heard that John*: Matthew 4:12.
49   *If you knew who it is*: John 4:9-10.
49   *Where can I get that water*: John 4:13-15.
50   *Your people and my people*: John 4:24.
50   *Listen. I am he*: John 4:25-26.

8 FAMOUS

55   *Jesus grew up there*: Mark 3:31; Luke 4:16.
55   *The Spirit of the Lord is resting*: Luke 4:18-19; Isaiah 61:1-2.
56   *Jesus then rolled up the scroll*: Luke 4:20.
56   *here in this room*: Luke 4:21.
56   *A prophet isn't welcome*: Luke 4:24-27.
57   *Let's take him to the cliffs*: Luke 4:29.
57   *Peter's hometown of Capernaum*: Luke 4:31.
57   *This was also the visit*: John 4:46-54.
57   *Stories about him spread*: Matthew 4:17, 23-25; Luke 4:31.
58   *Listen, Peter. Let's push out*: Luke 5:4.
58   *But since you're asking*: Luke 5:5.
58   *full to the point of sinking*: Luke 5:6-7.
59   *Leave me, O Lord*: Luke 5:8.
59   *Friends, do not be afraid*: Luke 5:10.
59   *During those months in Capernaum*: Mark 2:1-2.
60   *Can I get you anything?*: Matthew 8:14-15.
60   *your sins are forgiven*: Luke 5:17-20.
61   *Does he think he can forgive*: Luke 5:21.
61   *Just amazing*: Luke 5:22-26.

9 LORD OF THE SABBATH

62   *As the crowd dispersed*: Matthew 9:9.
63   *Follow me*: Luke 5:27.
63   *Why does your teacher eat*: Matthew 9:10-11.
63   *You act as though*: Luke 5:33; Philippians 2:5-7.
64   *I desire mercy*: Hosea 6:6.
64   *I'm not here to change*: Matthew 9:12-13.
64   *Wherever it took him*: Acts 1:13-14
65   *When the waters stirred*: John 5:7.

65   *Do you want to be healed?*: John 5:6.

65   *I come here every day*: John 5:7.

66   *Get up. Pick up your mat*: John 5:8.

66   *The man who healed me*: John 5:10-11.

66   *And the Pharisees had gone*: Exodus 20:8-11; Leviticus 23:3.

66   *I didn't catch his name*: John 5:12-13.

67   *As you walk, walk upright*: John 5:14.

67   *After this, the man went back*: John 5:15.

68   *Stretch out your hand*: Matthew 12:9, 11-3.

68   *Something greater than the temple*: Matthew 12:6-8.

10 ONLY SAY THE WORD

69   *Great crowds continued to follow*: Matthew 5–7.

69   *If there is a man among us*: Luke 7:4-5.

70   *The centurion's servants returned*: Luke 7:6-10.

70   *People from the procession said*: Luke 7:12.

70   *Do not weep*: Luke 7:13.

71   *The young man sat up*: Luke 7:14-15.

71   *God has visited his people*: Luke 7:16.

71   *Don't you care*: Mark 4:38.

72   *And the crowds had pressed*: Mark 1:29–2:12.

72   *Quiet. Be still*: Mark 4:39.

73   *Who is this man*: Mark 4:40-41.

73   *When Jesus and his disciples returned*: Matthew 9:1.

73   *He wept as he spoke*: Mark 5:23.

74   *Your faith has made you well*: Mark 5:31-34.

75   *Talitha, little one, wake up*: Mark 5:35-41.

75   *The community wouldn't know*: Mark 5:42-43.

75   *Who knew human contact*: Matthew 8:14-17; Luke 4:33-37; 5:12-16.

11 THE DEATH OF JOHN

76   *Though Herod had locked John*: Mark 6:20.

77   *So he kept John*: Mark 6:19-20.

77   *I was sent for this very purpose*: Mark 1:14-15; Luke 4:43.

77   *Their prophet Daniel had foretold*: Daniel 2:44.

78   *John's disciples would come to visit*: Luke 7:18.

78   *Are you the mighty one*: Luke 3:16; 7:19.

78   *Go and tell John*: Luke 4:18; 5:12-25; 7:11-17, 20-22; Isaiah 29:18

78   *You who went out*: Luke 7:24-27; Malachi 3:1.

78   *To whom did John come?*: Luke 7:31-34.

79   *After John's disciples returned*: Matthew 14:14; Luke 6:19.

79   *A prophet has no honor*: Mark 6:1-4.

80   *He had come to his own*: Mark 6:5; John 1:11.

80   *I want you to heal*: Matthew 10:5-15.

80   *Friends, you will be hated*: Matthew 10:16-42.

80   *So twelve men*: Matthew 10:1-4.

81   *Are you sure?*: Mark 6:24.

81   *I want the head of John*: Mark 6:25.

81   *He liked John*: Mark 6:20.

82   *I will not be scorned*: Mark 6:27-28.

12 THE STORM TREADER

85   *So when he heard*: Matthew 14:13.

85   *The crowds watched them*: Matthew 14:13-14.

85   *Jesus' disciples took their boat*: Luke 9:10.

86   *He stayed and healed all*: Mark 6:34.

86   *Let's not send them away*: Matthew 14:16; John 1:44; 6:5-7.

86   *What do we have with us*: Mark 6:37-38.

86   *There is a boy here*: John 6:8-9.

86   *Take this, all of you*: Matthew 14:18-19.

87   *Go gather up what's left*: John 6:12.

87   *Behold the King of glory*: John 6:14.

87   *Their murmurs of wonder*: John 6:15.

87   *They had grown up on the stories*: Exodus 16; 1 Kings 17:1-5; 2 Kings 4:42-44.

87   *He would be the kind of King*: Philippians 2:5-9.

88   *And Jesus knew the tempter*: Matthew 4:1-11.

88   *If they didn't remove themselves*: Mark 6:54; Matthew 14:22.

88   *Jesus began to pick his way*: Matthew 14:23.

89   *They strained to cut through*: Matthew 14:24.

89   *He made his way*: Mark 6:8.

89   *Do not be afraid*: Matthew 14:27.

89   *Lord, if it is you*: Matthew 14:28.

89   *Lord, save me*: Matthew 14:30.

90   *When they got back to the boat*: Matthew 8:23-27.

90   *But they did not know*: Matthew 14:33.

13 BREAD OF LIFE

91   *Jesus obliged the crowds*: Matthew 14:34-36.

91   *How did you get here?*: John 6:22-25, 59.

92   *What is that to you?*: John 6:26.
92   *Do you think we don't?*: John 6:26-31.
92   *I am the bread of life*: John 6:32-35.
92   *Did he think he was fooling*: John 6:41-42.
93   *I know you can't see*: John 6:47-51.
93   *How can this man dare*: John 6:52.
93   *Whoever feeds on my flesh*: John 6:54-58.
93   *But Jesus claimed to be*: John 6:32-35.
94   *You think I speak*: John 6:62-65.
94   *What about you men?*: John 6:67.
94   *Lord, where would we go?*: John 6:68-69.
94   *They resented the way*: John 5:18.
95   *So Jesus stayed away*: John 7:1.
95   *The Gentiles praised*: Matthew 15:24, 31.
95   *Jesus took his time*: Mark 7:31.
95   *You are an adulterous generation*: Matthew 16:1-4.
96   *If they wanted to spin*: Matthew 16:5-12.

14 YOU ARE THE CHRIST

97   *near the village of Caesarea Philippi*: Luke 9:18.
98   *Some said he was John*: Luke 9:19.
98   *You are the Christ*: Matthew 16:16.
98   *Simon, son of Jonah*: Matthew 16:17-18.
98   *As the Lord had done with Abraham*: Genesis 17:5.
98   *Peter, listen to me*: Matthew 16:19.
98   *People would not understand*: Matthew 16:2.
99   *All this he told them*: Mark 8:31-32.
99   *Lord, you need to stop*: Matthew 16:22.
99   *Get behind me, Satan*: Matthew 16:23.
99   *he did not recognize*: Matthew 4:8.
100   *If you want to follow me*: Luke 9:23-24.
100   *What good does it do*: Matthew 16:26.
101   *Peter saw that Jesus was glowing*: Luke 9:28-29, 32; Matthew 17:2.
101   *Jesus wore the glory*: John 1:14; Revelation 1:16.
101   *Elijah had been taken up*: Deuteronomy 34:5-6; 2 Kings 2:10-12; Luke 9:31.
101   *This is my Son*: Matthew 17:5.
101   *Get up. Do not be afraid*: Matthew 17:7-8.
102   *Friends, Elijah has already come*: Matthew 17:9-13.

15 BEFORE ABRAHAM WAS BORN

103   *Soon I will be delivered*: Luke 9:44.

103   *if trouble lay anywhere*: Luke 9:45.

104   *Show yourself to the world*: John 7:3-4.

104   *You go on without me*: John 7:6-8.

104   *He set his face*: Luke 9:51.

104   *Meanwhile in Jerusalem*: Mark 11:27.

105   *My teaching is not*: John 7:16-19.

105   *Jesus wanted to pick up*: John 5:1-17.

105   *Jesus told them he knew*: John 5:45-47.

105   *The last time I was with you*: John 7:20-24.

106   *Is this not the man*: John 7:25-27.

106   *You think you know me*: John 7:28-29.

106   *So they sent temple officers*: John 7:32.

106   *When the officers returned*: John 7:44.

107   *He remembered how Jesus said*: Matthew 11:25.

107   *Our law says*: Exodus 14:15; John 7:50.

107   *Are you from Galilee too*: John 7:51-52.

108   *The temple authorities accused*: John 8:42-48.

108   *Now we know you are of the devil*: John 8:52-53.

108   *They picked up stones*: John 8:54-59.

16 BORN BLIND

111   *Teacher, was it this man's sin*: John 9:2.

111   *This is neither his fault*: John 9:3-5.

112   *The act was an echo*: Genesis 2:7.

112   *The man who claimed*: John 9:7.

113   *No. I am the man*: John 9:9.

113   *The man from Nazareth*: John 9:11.

113   *I don't know*: John 9:12.

114   *The man is a prophet*: John 9:16-17.

114   *He is our son*: John 9:20-23.

115   *Why do you keep asking*: John 9:27.

115   *You may be this man's disciple*: John 9:28-29.

115   *Really? This is amazing*: John 9:30-33.

115   *Then they ordered their officials*: John 9:34.

115   *Do you believe*: John 9:35.

116   *If you were blind*: John 9:36-41.

117   *This only angered them*: John 10:24-40.

17 THE GOOD SAMARITAN

118   *They would have to set aside:* Luke 10:2-4.
119   *even demons fled:* Luke 10:17.
119   *I saw Satan fall:* Luke 10:18-20.
119   *I thank you, Father:* Luke 10:21-22.
119   *Blessed are your eyes:* Luke 10:23-24.
120   *Under the guise of dinners:* Luke 11:53-54.
120   *What is written:* Luke 10:25-26.
120   *That's right. Do that:* Luke 10:27-28.
121   *And who is my neighbor?:* Luke 10:29.
123   *You go and do the same:* Luke 10:30-37.
123   *Theological knowledge without love:* 1 Corinthians 13.

18 THE LEAVEN OF THE PHARISEES

126   *As long as Jesus wished to stay:* Psalm 16:3; Luke 10:38-42; 11:29.
126   *This generation is wicked:* Luke 11:29-32.
126   *A light is shining:* Luke 11:33-36.
126   *Do you take offense:* Luke 11:38-44.
127   *Teacher, you insult us:* Luke 11:45.
127   *You load people down:* Luke 11:46-52.
127   *Beware of their hypocrisy:* Luke 12:1-7.
128   *They began to press Jesus:* Luke 11:53-54.
128   *He continued teaching:* Luke 12:8–13:21.
128   *Is it true that only:* Luke 13:23.
128   *Why are you concerned:* Luke 13:24-27.
129   *The day you stand:* Genesis 12:1-3; Luke 13:28-30.
130   *O Jerusalem:* Luke 13:31-35.

19 LOST THINGS FOUND

131   *They were suspicious:* Luke 14:1.
132   *Is it lawful to heal:* Luke 14:3.
132   *He had performed healings:* John 5:1-18.
132   *Listen to me:* Luke 14:4-5.
132   *When you come to a feast:* Luke 14:8-11.
133   *When you give a feast:* Luke 14:12-14.
134   *Blessed is the one:* Luke 14:15.
134   *And because they regarded:* Luke 14:15-24.
134   *If you are not willing:* Luke 14:26-27.
134   *In a world where people worked:* John 16:33.
135   *They were incredulous:* Luke 15:1.

135   *The return of that sheep*: Luke 15:3-7.

135   *This joy, Jesus told them*: Luke 15:8-10.

137   *Everything I have*: Luke 15:11-32.

20 LAZARUS OF BETHANY

139   *The one you love*: John 11:3.

140   *This illness is for the glory*: John 11:4.

141   *No. Lazarus is dead*: John 11:11-15.

142   *If you had been here*: John 11:21.

142   *Even now I know*: John 11:22.

142   *No, listen to me, Martha*: John 11:23, 26.

142   *this wage of sin*: Romans 6:23.

143   *Why didn't he spare*: John 11:32, 36-37.

143   *Martha, trust me*: John 11:39-40.

143   *Father, you are always listening*: John 11:41.

143   *Unbind that man*: John 11:44.

21 A WORLD UPSIDE DOWN

145   *And they had never seen*: 1 Corinthians 2:9.

145   *After this, people put their faith*: John 11:45.

146   *If we let this Jesus*: John 11:47-50.

146   *Caiaphas set in motion*: John 11:53.

146   *He and his disciples sought refuge*: John 11:54.

146   *Listen to me*: Luke 17:22-37.

147   *Two men went up*: Luke 18:9-14

147   *No, let the children come*: Matthew 19:1-2, 13-15.

148   *We are going to go*: Matthew 20:17-19.

148   *Though at first they did not understand*: Matthew 17:22-23; Luke 18:9-22, 43-45; 18:34.

149   *Grant to one of us the seat*: Mark 10:35-37.

149   *they had been named the Sons of Thunder*: Luke 8:51-56; 9:28-36, 54; Mark 3:17.

149   *Lord, we can*: Mark 10:38-39.

149   *You men will drink the cup*: Mark 10:39-40.

150   *When the other disciples heard*: Mark 10:41.

150   *Greatness will not come*: Mark 10:43-44.

22 THE LIVING LEGEND

153   *As they left Jericho, a blind man*: Luke 18:35.

154   *Son of David, have mercy*: Mark 10:47.

154   *Bartimaeus believed the Spirit*: Luke 4:18.

154   *Though they had never met*: Isaiah 61:2; Joel 2:32; Luke 18:39.

154   *Take heart, beggar*: Mark 10:49.

155   *Springing to his feet*: Mark 10:50.

155   *I want to see*: Mark 10:51.

155   *Who else could deliver him*: Romans 7:24.

155   *You want to see? Then see*: Luke 18:42.

156   *My way is wherever you go*: Mark 10:52; Luke 18:43.

156   *Yes, but it is on account*: John 12:11.

157   *Be assured: the influence*: John 12:10-11.

157   *They would tell the old stories*: Exodus 12:13.

157   *in that place the Lord*: Deuteronomy 12:11.

158   *shatter insurmountable suffering*: Matthew 8:28-34; 15:30-31; Mark 8:22-26; Luke 5:17-26; 7:1-10.

158   *But now, they concluded*: John 12:10.

158   *What do you think?*: John 12:2.

158   *This was Martha's strong suit*: Luke 10:38-42.

23 THE KING'S CORONATION

160   *The sooner they could arrest*: John 11:55-57.

161   *In the village ahead*: Mark 11:3.

161   *Before long the two*: Luke 19:32.

162   *Though David had several heirs*: 2 Samuel 7:16; 13; Psalm 89:41; 1 Chronicles 22:9-10.

162   *I will be king*: 1 Kings 1:1, 5.

162   *And he didn't invite his father*: 2 Samuel 12:1-15; 1 Kings 1:9-10.

162   *Your sons, your generals*: 1 Kings 1:17-19.

163   *As I swore to you*: 1 Kings 1:20-21, 25, 30.

163   *Round up your men*: 1 Kings 1:33-35.

163   *Long live King Solomon*: 1 Kings 1:41-48.

163   *So as quickly as they had gathered*: 1 Kings 1:44, 49-50.

164   *God alone had the right*: 1 Samuel 24:6.

164   *Rejoice, daughter of Jerusalem*: Zechariah 9:9.

164   *The people came*: John 12:17-18.

165   *Blessed is the coming kingdom*: Matthew 21:9; Mark 11:9-10; Luke 19:38.

24 HOSANNA

168   *My time has not yet come*: Mark 1:21-28; John 7:8; 9:27-31.

168   *But he warned even*: Luke 9:18-21; John 8:34-38.

168   *Look, the whole world*: John 12:19.
168   *If these people fall silent*: Luke 19:40.
169   *Rejoice, daughter of Jerusalem*: Isaiah 53:5; Zechariah 9:9.
169   *In his ears echoed*: Luke 19:38.
169   *If only you had known*: Luke 19:42-44.
169   *The punishment that would bring*: Isaiah 53:5.
170   *As the hour grew late*: Mark 11:11.

25 THE VINEDRESSER'S TREE
172   *Sir, let me tend to it*: Luke 13:6-9.
174   *May no one ever eat fruit*: Mark 11:14.
175   *If you have faith*: Matthew 21:21-22.
175   *Jesus had stressed this point*: Mark 11:23; Luke 17:6; Matthew 17:20.
175   *The city was older*: 1 Kings 8:1-11; 10:1-13.

26 INDIGNATION
176   *Would he incriminate himself*: Luke 19:47.
177   *The men who sold pigeons*: Mark 11:15-16.
177   *Get out of here*: Matthew 21:13.
177   *Jesus had cleared the temple*: John 2.
178   *Hosanna to the Son of David*: Matthew 21:15.
178   *To their great comfort*: Matthew 21:14-15.
179   *They were embarrassed and angry*: Matthew 21:15.
179   *The chief priests and the scribes*: Luke 19:47.
179   *Jesus' reply was as strong*: Matthew 21:16.
179   *Have you never read*: Matthew 21:16; Psalm 8:2.
180   *As the day gave way*: Matthew 21:17; Mark 11:19.
181   *Caiaphas, the high priest*: Mark 11:27.
181   *What troubled the Sanhedrin most*: John 12:19; 14:6; 1 Timothy 2:5;
       Hebrews 4:14-16.

27 JOHN'S BAPTISM
182   *Who gave you the authority*: Mark 11:28.
183   *I will ask you*: Mark 11:29-30.
183   *the Lord suddenly come*: Malachi 3:1-2.
183   *Give us a minute*: Mark 11:31.
183   *He was a martyred Jew*: Mark 6:14-29.
184   *We don't know*: Mark 11:33.
184   *Since you won't answer*: Mark 11:33.
185   *The tenants killed*: Mark 12:1-8.

186 *That owner will surely come:* Mark 12:9-11; Psalm 118:22-23.
187 *Though no one noticed:* Mark 12:13-17, 35-40.
187 *This woman has given more:* Luke 21:1-4.
187 *This would have to happen:* Luke 22:1-6.
188 *Look at that city, teacher:* Mark 13:1.
188 *We don't understand:* Mark 13:2-4.
188 *Jesus had spoken like this:* Luke 9:44; John 2:19.
188 *I know you're afraid:* Mark 13:5.

28 THE SCENT OF OPULENCE
189 *Earthquakes were coming:* Mark 13:5-8, 12.
189 *They would stand:* Mark 13:9-10.
190 *You will be hated by all:* Mark 13:11.
190 *If they were going to find:* Philippians 2:1-2.
191 *People could choose his company:* Matthew 26:6.
191 *At first his statements:* Matthew 17:22-23; Mark 4:40.
191 *While they reclined around:* John 12:3.
192 *Gripping the bottle:* Mark 14:3.
193 *She anointed her King's head:* Psalm 23:5; Isaiah 52:7; Romans 10:15; John 11:25-44.
193 *Think of the poor people:* Matthew 26:8-9.
193 *As the scent electrified:* Psalm 19:1.
194 *She has given me this gift:* Matthew 26:10-13.
194 *For three years Judas Iscariot:* John 12:6.
194 *He had seen miracles, signs:* Mark 6:7-13.
194 *At the time, no one:* Proverbs 20:27.
194 *How much will you give me:* Matthew 26:14-15.
195 *But even before he took:* Matthew 27:3-4.
195 *With every blow:* 2 Corinthians 2:14.

29 THIRTEEN MEN
196 *Andrew had been a disciple:* John 1:35-40.
197 *Beside Andrew sat James:* Mark 3:17.
197 *James the Younger:* Mark 2:14; 3:18.
197 *Though James's place:* Matthew 10:2-4.
197 *Philip from Bethsaida:* John 1:43-45.
197 *When Philip told Nathanael:* John 1:46.
198 *He was one of the men:* Matthew 10:5-10; Luke 6:16.
198 *Let us go with him:* John 11:16; 14:5.
198 *In one moment he refused:* Matthew 4:19; 16:23; 26:35; Luke 5:11.

198   *Peter was insightful yet dense*: Matthew 16:16, 21–23; 26:75; John 18:10.
199   *Then by all means*: John 13:6-9.
199   *Do you understand*: John 13:12-15.
199   *Sorrow cut the disciples' hearts*: John 13:21; Matthew 26:22.
200   *What you are going to do*: John 13:23-27.
200   *Their first question wasn't*: Mark 14:19.
200   *But Judas was also greedy*: John 12:6.
200   *He seemed to belong*: Mark 14:19; John 6:70; 13:2, 27.
201   *He went out*: John 1:9; 3:19; 8:12; 9:5; 11:9; 12:46; 13:30.

30 THE LAST CUP

202   *I am the Lord*: Exodus 6:6.
203   *I am the way*: John 14:1-7.
203   *Do you not know me*: John 14:18-17.
203   *I will not leave you*: John 14:18-27.
203   *I will deliver you*: Exodus 6:6-7.
204   *This bread is my body*: Mark 14:22.
204   *I will redeem you*: Exodus 6:6-7.
204   *This is my blood*: Mark 14:23.
204   *I will not drink*: Mark 14:25.
204   *Though Jesus' voice*: Psalm 118:22-29; John 13:21.
205   *You will all fall away*: Matthew 26:31.
205   *Zechariah was talking*: Zechariah 13:7; Matthew 26:31.
205   *Listen. After I am raised up*: Matthew 26:32.
206   *As they reached the garden*: Mark 14:32-33.
206   *Now, after all that had unfolded*: Luke 22:44; John 13:21.
206   *If there is a way*: Matthew 26:39.
206   *An angel appeared*: Luke 22:43.
206   *They slept for sorrow*: Luke 22:45.
207   *Wake up. Stay alert*: Mark 14:38.
207   *Enough sleeping*: Mark 14:39-41.

31 TRIAL AT NIGHT

208   *The one I kiss*: Matthew 26:48.
209   *Judas wrapped Jesus*: Matthew 26:49-50.
210   *I told you, I am*: John 18:4-8.
210   *I haven't lost a single one*: John 17:12.
210   *Jesus reached out*: Luke 22:51-53.
210   *This calmed the soldiers enough*: Matthew 26:56.
211   *In many ways he facilitated*: John 18:2.

211   *Annas, the former high priest*: John 18:12-24.
211   *The arresting party brought Jesus*: Matthew 26:57; Mark 14:55.
211   *So serious was this law*: Deuteronomy 17:6; 19:16-19.
212   *I have lived my life*: John 18:20-21.
212   *If what I said was untrue*: John 18:22-23.
212   *He pressed for it*: John 18:14.
212   *Have you nothing to say?*: Mark 14:60.
213   *But Jesus, as a sheep*: Isaiah 53:7.
213   *Tell us all. Are you the Christ*: Mark 14:61.
213   *He spoke with an authority*: Matthew 7:29; Mark 1:22; Luke 4:32.
213   *I am, and you will see*: Mark 14:62.
213   *Before me stood one*: Daniel 7:13-14.
214   *Blasphemy was a capital offense*: Leviticus 24:16.
214   *They spun him over*: Mark 14:65.
214   *In the face of injustice*: Isaiah 50:6; 1 Peter 2:23.

32 THE RECKONING

216   *Sell all that you have*: Mark 10:17-21.
216   *It is difficult for the wealthy*: Mark 10:22-23.
217   *It is impossible for man*: Mark 10:27.
217   *Those who leave everything*: Mark 10:28.
218   *Even if the others fall*: Matthew 26:33.
218   *Peter, hear my words*: Matthew 26:34; Mark 14:72.
218   *No, I will not*: Matthew 26:35.
218   *Peter had followed*: Luke 22:54.
218   *I don't know*: Mark 14:68.
219   *No, sir, you did not*: John 18:26-27.
219   *May I be cursed if I'm lying*: Matthew 26:74.
220   *Satan has demanded*: Luke 22:31-32.
220   *Pontius Pilate, the governor of Judea*: Matthew 27:1-2.

33 WHAT IS TRUTH?

222   *What does this have to do*: John 18:28-31.
222   *It isn't just our law*: Luke 23:2; John 18:31.
222   *Early in his rule*: Luke 13:1.
223   *Are you asking this*: John 18:34.
223   *If I were after their throne*: John 18:35-36.
224   *Pilate was frustrated*: John 19:12.
224   *He had heard much*: Luke 23:8.

224   *Have nothing to do with*: Matthew 27:19.
224   *His fascination turned to scorn*: Luke 23:11.
224   *What is truth*: John 18:37-38.
225   *I find no basis*: Luke 23:16.
225   *Jewish law taught*: Proverbs 17:15.
225   *Hail, King of the Jews*: John 19:2-3.
225   *Crucify him! Crucify him*: John 19:5-6.
226   *Speak. Defend yourself*: John 19:10.
226   *The most important law*: Mark 13:28-33.
226   *Render unto Caesar*: Mark 12:15-17.
227   *Fine! I wash my hands*: Matthew 27:24.
227   *He is not our king*: Matthew 27:25.
227   *We have no king*: John 19:10-15.

34 CRUCIFIXION
229   *Hail, King of the Jews*: Matthew 27:26-30; Mark 15:15-20; John 19:2-3.
230   *After this they put his clothes*: Matthew 27:31; Mark 15:20.
230   *He looked so despised*: Isaiah 53:3-4.
230   *Take up that cross*: Mark 15:21-22; Luke 9:23.
230   *What I have written*: John 19:19-22.
231   *Father, forgive them*: Luke 23:34.
231   *They didn't want to tear it*: John 19:23-24.
232   *And a sword will pierce*: Luke 2:34-35.
232   *John, she is your mother*: John 19:26-27.
232   *If you are the Son of God*: Matthew 27:40-42.
232   *You must be thirsty*: Mark 15:23.
232   *Are you not the Christ?*: Luke 23:39.
233   *Today you will be with me*: Luke 23:40-43.
234   *Listen. He's calling for Elijah*: Matthew 27:46-47.
234   *I thirst*: John 19:28.
234   *It is finished*: John 19:30.
234   *Father, into your hands*: Luke 23:46.

35 THE FORGOTTEN DAY
235   *The quaking darkness*: Romans 8:22-23.
236   *Between the Lord and his people*: Genesis 3:24.
236   *They were struck with terror*: Exodus 33:20; Luke 23:45.
236   *Surely this man was innocent*: Luke 23:47-48; Matthew 27:54.
236   *This would defile*: Deuteronomy 21:22-23.
237   *They took his lifeless body*: John 19:33-37.

237   *While this was happening*: Mark 15:43.
237   *Would you please turn over*: John 19:38.
237   *They also both believed*: Mark 15:43; John 3:2.
238   *They believed Jesus was*: Luke 23:51; John 7:51.
238   *Nicodemus had sought Jesus*: John 3:1-2.
238   *The two men picked up*: John 19:39-42.
238   *Mary Magdalene and James*: Mark 15:47.
239   *When this imposter*: Matthew 27:64.
239   *They had heard Jesus*: John 2:19.
240   *I'll give you a guard*: Matthew 27:65.
240   *The chief priests went*: Matthew 27:66.

36 HE IS NOT HERE

241   *From the day Jesus set her free*: Luke 8:1-3.
241   *Mary Magdalene and Mary*: Mark 16:1.
242   *That Friday, when he let out*: Matthew 27:51.
242   *The women were stunned*: Matthew 28:2.
243   *Do not be afraid*: Matthew 28:5-6.
243   *He has risen*: Matthew 28:6.
243   *I must go up to Jerusalem*: Matthew 16:21; 20:19.
243   *These very predictions*: Matthew 27:63-64.
244   *He had lain it down*: John 10:18.
245   *They have taken my Lord*: John 20:2.
245   *He saw the linen grave clothes*: Luke 24:11; John 20:3-5.
245   *And they saw the linen cloth*: John 20:6-7.
245   *They did not know what to do*: John 20:8-9.
245   *Someone tell me*: John 20:11.

37 FLESH AND BONE

247   *The chief priests handed*: Matthew 28:12-15.
247   *One sat at the foot*: John 20:11-12.
248   *"Rabboni!" Mary said*: John 20:13-16.
248   *Do not be afraid*: Matthew 28:10; John 20:17.
248   *I have seen the Lord*: John 20:18.
248   *Peace to you*: John 20:19.
249   *Still the disciples sat*: Luke 24:39-41.
249   *They offered him a piece*: Luke 24:42-43.
249   *They laughed at the sight*: John 20:20.
249   *Receive the Holy Spirit*: John 20:22-23.
250   *Listen to me, men*: John 20:25.

250   *Do you see my wounds:* John 20:27.

251   *You believe because you see:* John 20:29.

38 DO YOU LOVE ME?

252   *Nathanael, Thomas the Twin:* John 21:1-2.

252   *We will join you:* John 21:3.

253   *It was that this was something:* Matthew 26:34.

253   *But even if he made:* Psalm 139.

254   *Still, he alone:* Matthew 14:19, 22-23.

254   *You are the Christ:* Luke 8:27-30.

254   *Peter knew Jesus:* Matthew 16:13-23; 17:1-8; Mark 1:21-28; John 10:22-39.

255   *On that day Peter had fallen:* Luke 5:1-11.

255   *Do not be afraid, Simon:* Matthew 4:19.

256   *Peter looked at the fire:* John 21:9-10.

256   *They watched in bewildered fascination:* John 21:12-13.

257   *I want you to feed:* John 21:17.

257   *I want you to tend:* John 21:18-19.

257   *What is that to you?:* John 21:22.

39 BEHOLD THE MAN OF SORROWS

259   *They spoke of their sorrow:* Luke 24:17-24.

260   *We had so much hope:* Luke 24:19-21.

260   *That's the story anyway:* Luke 24:22-24.

261   *What is so hard to understand:* Genesis 12:1-20; 18:1-15; 45:1-28.

261   *Or Moses. Was not everything:* Exodus 2; 1 Samuel 18; Hosea 3; Jonah 1–4.

262   *Was it not necessary:* Luke 24:25-26.

262   *Isaiah had foretold:* Isaiah 53:3-6.

263   *Just as quickly as Cleopas:* Luke 24:31.

264   *He was numbered among:* Isaiah 53.

264   *He made himself nothing:* Philippians 2:5-8.

264   *Through his agony:* Isaiah 53; 1 Peter 2:24-25.

40 BEHOLD THE KING OF GLORY

265   *Jesus bore in himself:* Colossians 1:15-20.

266   *It is an inheritance:* 1 Peter 1:3.

266   *And God has exalted him:* Philippians 2:8-11.

266   *The last enemy:* 1 Corinthians 15:17-25.

266   *Jesus' resurrection opened:* Ephesians 1:18-23.

267 Jesus Christ, God's eternal Son: John 1:1-5; Hebrews 1:1-2; 2:5-9.

267 He rose from the grave: Matthew 28:18; Hebrews 1:2-3.

267 He rules over every corner: 1 Corinthians 15:20-26.

267 making alive by his grace: Ephesians 2:5.

267 Together they would be the church: John 17:21; Ephesians 4:1-16.

267 Many of them died as martyrs: Acts 12:2.

268 All whom the Father gives: John 6:37.

268 They wait in eager anticipation: Romans 8:23.

268 A New Jerusalem will rise: Revelation 21:1-2.

268 The city's gates will be opened: Revelation 21:22-25.

269 Jesus, the King who lives: Revelation 12:3-4.

269 neither life nor death: Romans 8:31-39.

269 sits even now at the right hand: Hebrews 12:23-24.

269 This is my beloved Son: Mark 9:7.

269 All authority in heaven: Matthew 28:18; John 19:30.

270 The kingdom of God is a kingdom: Hebrews 12:28.

270 Behold the Lamb of God: John 1:29.

270 Behold the man of sorrows: Isaiah 53:12.

270 I am making all things new: Revelation 21:5.

RETELLING THE STORY SERIES

The Retelling the Story series explores the narrative arc of the Bible in compelling language that is faithful to the text of Scripture. The stories are told to help readers hide God's Word in their hearts by way of their imaginations.

Also by Russ Ramsey

CPSIA information can be obtained
at www.ICGtesting.com
Printed in the USA
LVHW052153170221
679356LV00005B/1047